Myths and Legends of the World

Volume 2

John M. Wickersham
Editor in Chief

Macmillan Reference USA/An Imprint of The Gale Group
New York

Developed for Macmillan Reference USA by
Visual Education Corporation, Princeton, NJ.

For Macmillan

Publisher: Elly Dickason

Editor in Chief: Hélène G. Potter

Cover Design: Irina Lubenskaya

For Visual Education

Project Director: Darryl Kestler

Writers: John Haley, Charles Roebuck, Rebecca Stefoff

Editors: Cindy George, Eleanor Hero, Linda Perrin, Charles Roebuck

Copyediting Supervisor: Helen A. Castro

Indexer: Sallie Steele

Production Supervisor: Marcel Chouteau

Photo Research: Susan Buschhorn, Sara Matthews

Interior Design: Maxson Crandall

Electronic Preparation: Fiona Torphy

Electronic Production: Rob Ehlers, Lisa Evans-Skopas, Laura Millan, Isabelle Ulsh

Macmillan Reference USA
1633 Broadway
New York, NY 10019

Printed in the United States of America
1 2 3 4 5 6 7 8 9 10

Library of Congress Cataloging-in-Publication Data

Myths and legends of the world / John M. Wickersham, editor in chief.
p. cm.
Includes bibliographical references and index.
Contents: v. 1. Abel-Coriolanus — v. 2. Corn-Io — v. 3. Iphigenia-Quetzalcoatl — v. 4. Ra-Zoroastrian mythology.
ISBN 0-02-865439-0 (set : alk. paper)
1. Mythology—Juvenile literature. 2. Legends. [1. Mythology—Encyclopedias. 2. Folklore—Encyclopedias.] I. Wickersham, John M. (John Moore), 1943-
BL311 .M97 2000
398.2—dc21 00-030528

Corn

deity god or goddess

First grown in Mexico about 5,000 years ago, corn soon became the most important food crop in Central and North America. Throughout the region, Native Americans, Maya, Aztecs, and other Indians worshiped corn gods and developed a variety of myths about the origin, planting, growing, and harvesting of corn (also known as maize).

Corn Gods and Goddesses. The majority of corn **deities** are female and associated with fertility. They include the Cherokee goddess Selu; Yellow Woman and the Corn Mother goddess Iyatiku of the Keresan people of the American Southwest; and Chicomecoatl, the goddess of maize who was worshiped by the Aztecs of Mexico. The Maya believed that humans had been fashioned out of corn, and they based their calendar on the planting of the cornfield.

Male corn gods do appear in some legends. The Aztecs had a male counterpart to Chicomecoatl, called Centeotl, to whom they offered their blood each year, as well as some minor corn gods known as the Centzon Totochtin, or "the 400 rabbits." The Seminole figure Fas-ta-chee, a dwarf whose hair and body were made of corn, was another male corn god. He carried a bag of corn and taught the Seminoles how to grow, grind, and store corn for food. The Hurons of northeastern North America worshiped Iouskeha, who made corn, gave fire to the Hurons, and brought good weather.

The Zuni people of the southwestern United States have a myth about eight corn maidens. The young women are invisible, but their beautiful dancing movements can be seen when they dance with the growing corn as it waves in the wind. One day the young god Paiyatemu fell in love with the maidens, and they fled from him. While they were gone, a terrible famine spread across the land. Paiyatemu begged the maidens to turn back, and they returned to the Zuni and resumed their dance. As a result, the corn started to grow again.

Origins of Corn. A large number of Indian myths deal with the origin of corn and how it came to be grown by humans. Many of the tales center on a "Corn Mother" or other female figure who introduces corn to the people.

In one myth, told by the Creeks and other tribes of the southeastern United States, the Corn Woman is an old woman living with a family that does not know who she is. Every day she feeds the family corn dishes, but the members of the family cannot figure out where she gets the food.

One day, wanting to discover where the old woman gets the corn, the sons spy on her. Depending on the version of the story, the corn is either scabs or sores that she rubs off her body, washings from her feet, nail clippings, or even her feces. In all versions, the origin of the corn is disgusting, and once the family members know its origin, they refuse to eat it.

The Corn Woman solves the problem in one of several ways. In one version, she tells the sons to clear a large piece of ground, kill her, and drag her body around the clearing seven times. However, the sons clear only seven small spaces, cut off her head, and drag it around the seven spots. Wherever her blood fell, corn grew. According to the story, this is why corn only grows in some places and not all over the world.

In another account, the Corn Woman tells the boys to build a corn crib and lock her inside it for four days. At the end of that time, they open the crib and find it filled with corn. The Corn Woman then shows them how to use the corn.

Other stories of the origin of corn involve goddesses who choose men to teach the uses of corn and to spread the knowledge to their people. The Seneca Indians of the Northeast tell of a beautiful woman who lived on a cliff and sang to the village below. Her song told an old man to climb to the top and be her husband. At first, he refused because the climb was so steep, but the villagers persuaded him to go.

When the old man reached the top, the woman asked him to make love to her. She also taught him how to care for a young plant that would grow on the spot where they made love. The old man fainted as he embraced the woman, and when he awoke, the woman was gone. Five days later, he returned to the spot to find a corn plant. He husked the corn and gave some grains to each member of the tribe. The Seneca then shared their knowledge with other tribes, spreading corn around the world.

Mayan stories give the ant—or some other small creature—credit for the discovery of corn. The ant hid the corn away in a hole in a mountain, but eventually the other animals found out about the corn and arranged for a bolt of lightning to split open the mountain so that they could have some corn too. The fox, coyote, parrot, and crow gave corn to the gods, who used it to create the first people. Although the gods' earlier attempts to create human beings out of

Green Corn Dance

Native Americans of the Southeast hold a Green Corn Dance to celebrate the New Year. This important ceremony, thanking the spirits for the harvest, takes place in July or August. None of the new corn can be eaten before the ceremony, which involves rituals of purification and forgiveness and a variety of dances. Finally, the new corn can be offered to a ceremonial fire, and a great feast follows.

This painting by George Caltin shows the Hidatsa people of the North American Plains celebrating the corn harvest with the Green Corn Dance. The ceremony, held in the middle of the summer, marks the beginning of the New Year.

† *See **Names and Places** at the end of this volume for further information.*

mud or wood had failed, the corn people were perfect. However, the gods decided that their new creations were able to see too clearly, so they clouded the people's sight to prevent them from competing with their makers.

The Lakota Plains Indians say that a white she-buffalo brought their first corn. A beautiful woman appeared on the plain one day. When hunters approached her, she told them to prepare to welcome her. They built a lodge for the woman and waited for her to reappear. When she came, she gave four drops of her milk and told them to plant them, explaining that they would grow into corn. The woman then changed into a buffalo and disappeared.

Corn Mother. According to the Penobscot Indians, the Corn Mother was also the first mother of the people. Their creation myth says that after people began to fill the earth, they became so good at hunting that they killed most of the animals. The first mother of all the people cried because she had nothing to feed her children. When her husband asked what he could do, she told him to kill her and have her sons drag her body by its silky hair until her flesh was scraped from her bones. After burying her bones, they should return in seven months, when there would be food for the people. When the sons returned, they found corn plants with tassels like silken hair. Their mother's flesh had become the tender fruit of the corn.

Another Corn Mother goddess is Iyatiku, who appears in legends of the Keresan people, a Pueblo† group of the American Southwest. In the Keresan emergence story, Iyatiku leads human beings on a journey from underground up to the earth's surface. To provide food for them, she plants bits of her heart in fields to the north, west, south, and east. Later the pieces of Iyatiku's heart grow into fields of corn. ***See also*** **Aztec Mythology; Mayan Mythology; Native American Mythology.**

Creation Stories

People have long wondered how the world came into being. They have answered the question with stories that describe the origin of the universe or the world and usually of human life as well. Creation myths, known as cosmogonies, express people's understanding of the world and their place in it.

The world's mythologies and religions offer an immense variety of creation stories. Yet scholars have discovered that the cosmogonies of different cultures fall into broad categories and contain many shared themes.

Forms and Themes of Creation

Some creation stories, such as those of Africa and Polynesia, existed for years in spoken form but were not written down until recently. Other cultures preserved their cosmogonies in written texts, and some of these have survived from ancient times. The Babylonian **epic** *Enuma Elish,* written thousands of years ago,

epic long poem about legendary or historical heroes, written in a grand style

cosmic large or universal in scale; having to do with the universe

primal earliest; existing before other things

underworld land of the dead

abyss very deep gulf or hole

tells how people in Mesopotamia† explained the beginning of the world. A Mayan text called the *Popol Vuh* describes the creation of the ancestors of the Maya.

Types of Creation. Some methods of creation appear again and again in cosmogonies from different parts of the world. One of the most common images is a description of the beginning of the world as a birth, a kind of creation familiar to everyone. The birth may result from the mating of a pair of **cosmic** parents. The Maori of New Zealand, for example, say that the union of Rangi and Papa (Father Sky and Mother Earth) produced all things.

The hatching of an egg is another familiar kind of birth. Some creation myths tell of a cosmic egg containing the seeds or possibilities of everything. The hatching of the egg lets the possibilities take form. The Hindu texts known as the *Upanishads* describe the creation of the world as the breaking of a cosmic egg.

Another type of cosmogony says that the actions, thoughts, or desires of a supreme being or creator god brought the world into existence. The book of Genesis in the Old Testament of the Bible tells how God created the world and everything in it. Other accounts of creation by a supreme being can be found in many regions, from the island of Hokkaido in northern Japan to the island of Tierra del Fuego in southern South America.

Sometimes the created order simply emerges from a **primal** chaos—a state of disorder. In Norse† mythology, the scene of creation is an emptiness of wind and mist until clouds form and harden into the frost giant Ymir, from whose body the world is made. Many Native American myths tell how animals and people appeared on earth by climbing out of a chaotic or primitive **underworld.**

The primal chaos is often a flood or a vast expanse of water. The people of ancient Egypt—who relied on the yearly floods of the Nile River to support their agriculture—said that before creation there existed only Nun, a watery **abyss.** In some flood myths, creation takes place as the waters recede or as land rises. In others, an earth diver, a bird or an animal, plunges to the bottom of the water and brings up mud that becomes the earth. Such myths, which are common among Native Americans, seldom explain where the mud or the earth-diving creature came from. Many cosmogonies concern the shaping or ordering of the world rather than its creation from nothingness. They often begin with some substance, being, or active force already in existence.

In some mythologies, the creation of people occurs through emergence from the earth. Native American groups such as the Hopi, Zuni, and Navajo say that the first people traveled though a series of lower worlds to reach their permanent home. In some stories, a flood forces the occupants of the lower worlds to climb upward until they arrive on the surface.

Themes in Creation Myths. In explaining how creation led to the world as it now exists, cosmogonies explore several basic themes. Most creation myths illustrate one or more of these themes.

†*See **Names and Places** at the end of this volume for further information.*

differentiation process of becoming different and separate from another thing

The theme of separation or **differentiation** deals with the forming of distinct things out of what was once a formless unity. Separation may be a physical act. In Polynesian myth, for example, the children of Mother Earth and Father Sky force their parents apart so that the world can exist between them. Cosmogonies may describe creation as taking place in stages that mark the process of differentiation. The Old Testament says that God took six days to create light and darkness, the heavens, the earth and plants, the sun and moon, the sea creatures and animals, and the first people.

A second theme is imperfection. According to many cosmogonies, the creator planned to make a perfect world, but something went wrong. As a result, flaws such as evil, illness, and death entered the creation. The Dogon of West Africa say that the world is imperfect because one of a pair of twins broke out early from the cosmic egg. The Hawaiians relate that the earth goddess Papa cursed humans with death after she discovered an incestuous affair between her husband and daughter.

Dualism, or tension between opposing forces, is an underlying theme of many creation stories, especially those that revolve around conflict. Greek myths about the war between the Titans† and the gods are just one example of conflict between cosmic parents and their offspring. Sometimes the conflict involves twins or brothers. Some Native Americans of the northeast woodlands explain that the world is the way it is because two gods played a role in its creation. Gluskap, good and wise, created plants, animals, and people. His evil, selfish brother Malsum made poisonous snakes and plants.

The theme of sacrifice reflects the idea that life is born out of death. Someone must die, or at least shed blood, before the world and life can begin. The *Enuma Elish* tells how the god Marduk killed the primeval goddess Tiamat and cut her body into two parts that became the heavens and the earth. Sometimes the first people are made from a god's blood, perhaps mixed with dust or clay. Creation may also involve the slaying of a primal beast or monster.

A few cosmogonies describe cycles in which the world is created and destroyed a number of times. Hindu scriptures say that Brahma† has remade the world many times. Four ages, or *yugas,* make a *kalpa,* or eon. When a *kalpa* ends, creation dissolves into chaos.

The Aztecs of Mexico believed that the present world was the fifth that the gods had created. It was fated to end in universal destruction by earthquakes. The four previous worlds had been destroyed by a great flood, the falling of the sky, a fire storm, and a wind storm. The Maya believed that the gods made three unsuccessful attempts to create human beings before achieving a satisfactory result. Their first creations—animals, people made of mud, and wooden people—disappointed them in various ways, and they abandoned or destroyed them. Finally, the gods made people of maize (corn) who were perfect, so perfect that their creators clouded their vision to prevent them from seeing too far.

The Omaha Big Bang

Modern scientists think that the universe began billions of years ago with an explosion of matter and energy called the Big Bang. The Native American Omaha people have their own "big bang" account of creation. At first all living things were spirits floating through space, looking for a place to exist in bodily form. The sun was too hot. The moon was too cold. The earth was covered with water. Then a huge boulder rose out of the water and exploded with a roar and a burst of flame that dried the water. Land appeared. The spirits of plants settled on earth. Animal spirits followed. Finally the spirits of people took bodily form on earth.

dualistic consisting of two equal and opposing forces

Stories of the Great Beginning

Every region of the world has produced numerous creation stories, and some cultures and religions have more than one. A sampling of myths from various sources shows both the endless variety of cosmogonies and the similarities in their structures and themes.

Africa. Some African creation myths feature a huge snake, often identified with the rainbow, whose coils make up the universe. In West and Central Africa the idea of creation from a cosmic egg is common.

Twins or paired, **dualistic** powers appear in many African creation stories. The Fon of West Africa tell of the first mother, Nana Buluku, who gave birth to the twins Mawu (moon) and Lisa (sun), the parents of all the other gods, who were also born in sets of twins. Some African cosmogonies, however, are less concerned with the creation of the physical universe and the gods than with the appearance of the first man and first woman and the ordering of human society.

The notion of a supreme creator god appears throughout Africa. The Bushongo people of the Congo region called the creator Bumba. He was the sole inhabitant of a watery universe until he vomited up the sun, which dried the water. Then he vomited up the first animals and people.

The Americas. The Incas of South America claimed that darkness covered the earth until the god Con Tiqui Viracocha rose out of a lake, bringing with him the first people. He made more people out of rocks, then sent them out to populate the whole world. When these inhabitants rebelled against Con Tiqui Viracocha, he punished them by stopping the rainfall. A god named Pachachamac overthrew Con Tiqui Viracocha and created a new race of people, the ancestors of humans.

Creation myths of Native Americans generally explain how the world took its present form, including the origins of human culture. Some tales feature a creator god or pair of gods, such as the Sun Father and Moonlight-giving Mother of the Zuni people. Many groups, including the Cheyenne, have stories of an earth diver.

Indians of the Southwest may have developed myths of emergence because their agricultural way of life led them to think of growth as a movement upward from below the earth's surface. The Hopi of Arizona say that creation brought four worlds into existence. Life began in the bottom level or cave, which eventually grew dirty and crowded. A pair of twin brothers carried plants from heaven, and the people climbed up the cane plant into the second cave. When that place became too crowded, they climbed up again into the third cave. Finally, the brother gods led the people out into this world, the fourth level of creation.

Near East. The ancient Egyptians believed that before the world existed there was only Nun, the watery nothingness. Then

† *See **Names and Places** at the end of this volume for further information.*

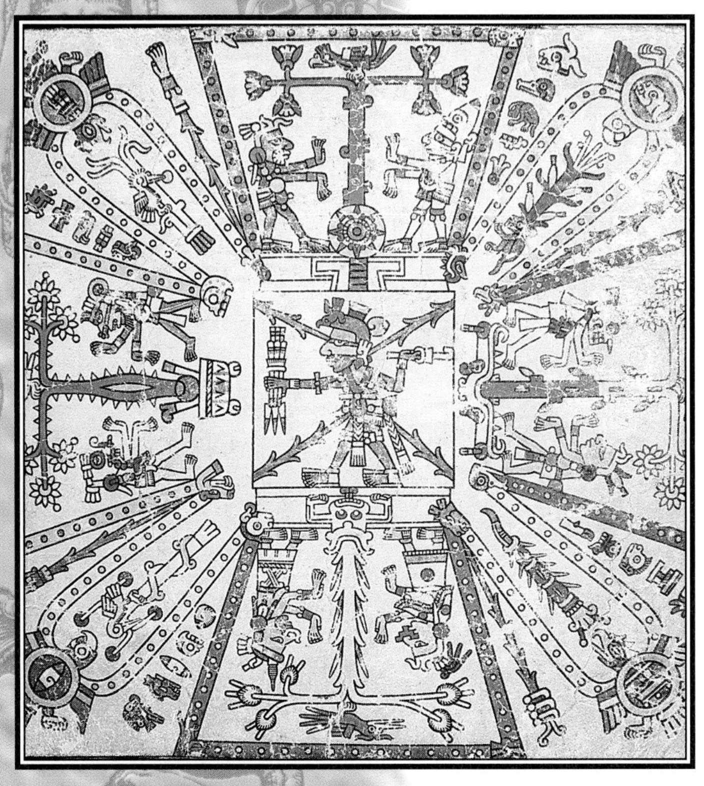

Aztec mythology tells of four creator gods, each associated with a direction and a color—Tezcatlipoca, the north and black; Quetzalcoatl, the west and white; Huitzilopochtli, the south and blue; and Xipe Totec, the east and red. This drawing shows Hueheuteotl, the god of fire, surrounded by the four directions.

a mound of land rose, giving the first **deity** a place to live. In some accounts, the first deity took the form of a bird. Others said that a lotus flower containing a god rose from the water. **Cults** developed around several Egyptian creator gods: Amun and Atum, the sun gods; Khnum, who made men and women from clay and breathed life into them; and Ptah, who created the other gods by saying their names.

Among the Semitic† creation myths of western Asia is the story of how God formed the world, the Garden of Eden, and Adam and Eve, the first parents. It is the cosmogony of the Christian, Jewish, and Islamic faiths.

In the dualistic Persian or Iranian cosmogony, the good and wise lord Ahura Mazda began creation by sending beams of light into an abyss where Ahriman, lord of evil and sin, lived. Ahura Mazda cast Ahriman into hell for 3,000 years. This gave Ahura Mazda time to create spirits of virtue, angels, and the creatures of earth, including Gayomart, the first man. When Ahriman's time in hell ended, he created flies, germs, pests, and other evils. One of his wicked followers brought disease and death to Gayomart, but a plant that grew from Gayomart's remains bore fruit that became the human race.

deity god or goddess
cult group bound together by devotion to a particular person, belief, or god

Asia. Japanese tradition, preserved in a volume of mythological history called the *Kojiki,* says that before creation there was an oily sea. Gods came into being in the High Plains of Heaven. After seven generations of deities came the first human ancestors, whose task was to make solid land. They stirred the sea with a jeweled spear. Drops that fell from the spear formed the islands of Japan.

A Chinese creation myth tells how Pan Gu hatched from a cosmic egg. One part of the eggshell formed the heavens; the other part became the earth. For 18,000 years, Pan Gu stood between them, keeping them apart by growing ever taller. Finally he became weary, lay down, and died. From his eyes came the sun and moon, from his hair the stars, from his breath the wind, and from his body the earth.

Indian mythology, linked to both the Hindu and the Buddhist religions, contains many creation stories. Hindus often speak of Brahma as the creator god who brought the universe into being through his thoughts. Sometimes creation involves the sacrifice of a primal being such as Purusha, from whose body all the gods were made. Other myths describe the breaking of a cosmic egg or the union of heaven and earth as cosmic parents.

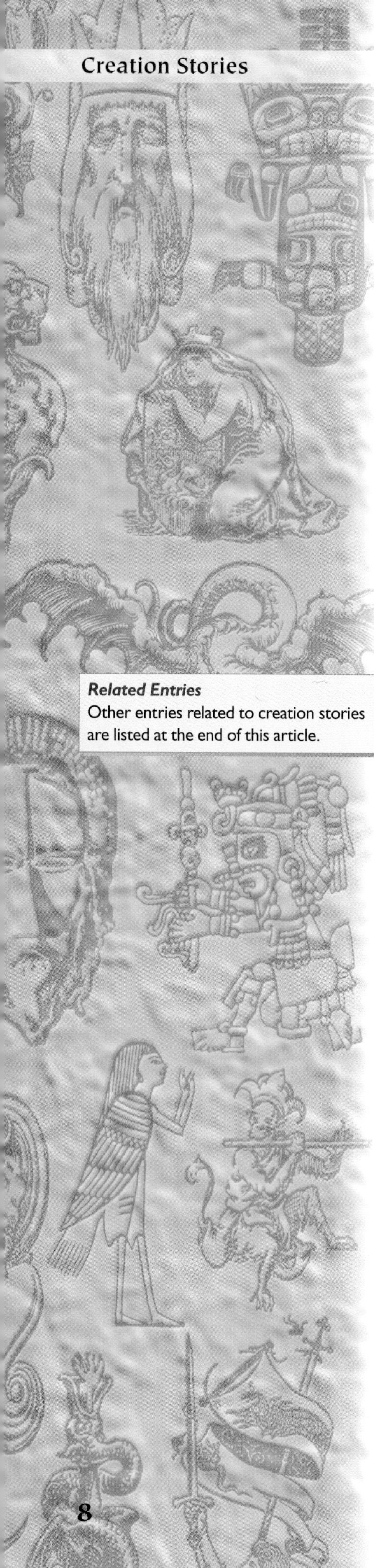

This scene from a sarcophagus in Thebes illustrates part of an Egyptian creation myth. According to this myth, the world was produced from the union of the earth god Geb and the sky goddess Nut.

Related Entries
Other entries related to creation stories are listed at the end of this article.

Australia and the Pacific. In the mythology of Australia's native peoples, the period of creation was called Dreamtime, or The Dreaming. During this time, ancestral beings created the landscape, made the first people, and taught them how to survive. Some Aboriginal myths tell of a great flood that destroyed the previous landscape and the former society. According to many accounts, a great serpent caused the flood when he became angry with the ancestral people.

The vast Pacific Ocean contains the Polynesian, Melanesian, and Micronesian island groups, which produced a variety of cosmogonies. Not surprisingly, many of these myths involve water.

According to some Polynesians, a creator god named Tangaloa sent a bird messenger over an endless primal sea. At last Tangaloa threw a rock into the sea so the tired bird would have a place to land. Then the god created all the islands in the same way. The bird made the first people by giving arms, legs, hearts, and souls to maggots. Other Polynesian stories describe creation as the union of two opposing qualities: Po (darkness) and Ao (light). Polynesian and Micronesian cosmogonies often include the act of separating the earth from the sky. Melanesian creation myths generally involve ancestral heroes who wander from place to place, forming the landscape and creating the rules of society.

Europe. Norse creation myths tell how the giant Ymir took shape in the huge icy emptiness called Ginnungagap. Ymir's great cow licked the ice, creating the first gods, including Odin†. The gods killed Ymir and divided his body into a series of worlds on three levels: Asgard, the realm of gods; Midgard, the realm of people, giants, dwarfs, and elves; and Niflheim, the realm of the dead. The gods created the first man and woman from an ash tree and an elm tree.

†*See **Names and Places** at the end of this volume for further information.*

(The creation of people from trees has a parallel in Native American stories about Gluskap making man from an ash trunk.)

Greek cosmogonies, echoed by the Romans, begin with birth and end with struggle. Gaia, the earth mother, emerged from chaos and gave birth to Uranus, the sky. The union of Uranus and Gaia produced plants, animals, and children, the Titans. Imprisoned by their father, the Titans overthrew Uranus, only to be overthrown by their own children, the gods. Another Greek creation myth, possibly borrowed from the ancient Near East, combines many images and themes. It tells how a primal goddess emerged from the waters of chaos. Her union with a serpent produced a cosmic egg that split to become the heaven and the earth. ***See also*** **African Mythology; Australian Mythology; Aztec Mythology; Buddhism and Mythology; Celtic Mythology; Chinese Mythology; Dreamtime; Egyptian Mythology; Enuma Elish; Finnish Mythology; Floods; Gluskap; Greek Mythology; Hinduism and Mythology; Inca Mythology; Japanese Mythology; Mayan Mythology; Melanesian Mythology; Micronesian Mythology; Native American Mythology; Norse Mythology; Persian Mythology; Polynesian Mythology; Roman Mythology; Semitic Mythology; Upanishads.**

Crispin, St.

Crispin and his brother Crispinian are saints in the Roman Catholic Church. They are said to have died around A.D. 285 as **martyrs** to their faith.

martyr person who suffers or is put to death for a belief

According to legend, the brothers were Romans who traveled to Gaul (present-day France) and earned their keep as shoemakers, while teaching about Christianity. At that time, the religion was illegal in Gaul and the rest of the Roman empire. When questioned by the authorities, the brothers admitted they were Christians. Their punishment was torture and execution.

Over the years, Catholics have honored the brothers with processions and festivities on October 25, which came to be called St. Crispin's Day. One modern theory claims that St. Crispin originated as the **pagan** Roman god of shoemakers and that a Christian myth later transformed him into a saint. Shakespeare includes the two brothers as a single character, Crispin Crispian, in his play *Henry V.*

pagan term used by early Christians to describe non-Christians and non-Christian beliefs

Crockett, Davy

Davy Crockett was a frontiersman, Indian scout, and politician who became one of America's first folk heroes. His backwoods philosophy, homespun humor, and image as a rough-edged hunter and Indian fighter made him an extremely popular figure during his lifetime. Crockett's reputation—and the tall tales about him—grew to legendary proportions after his death.

Born in Tennessee in 1786, Crockett had no formal schooling and worked on farms as a child. From 1813 to 1815, he served as a scout under Andrew Jackson (who later became the country's president), fighting the Creek Indians. His wartime record and plainspoken humor made him popular with voters. He was elected to the Tennessee legislature in 1821 and to the U.S. Congress in

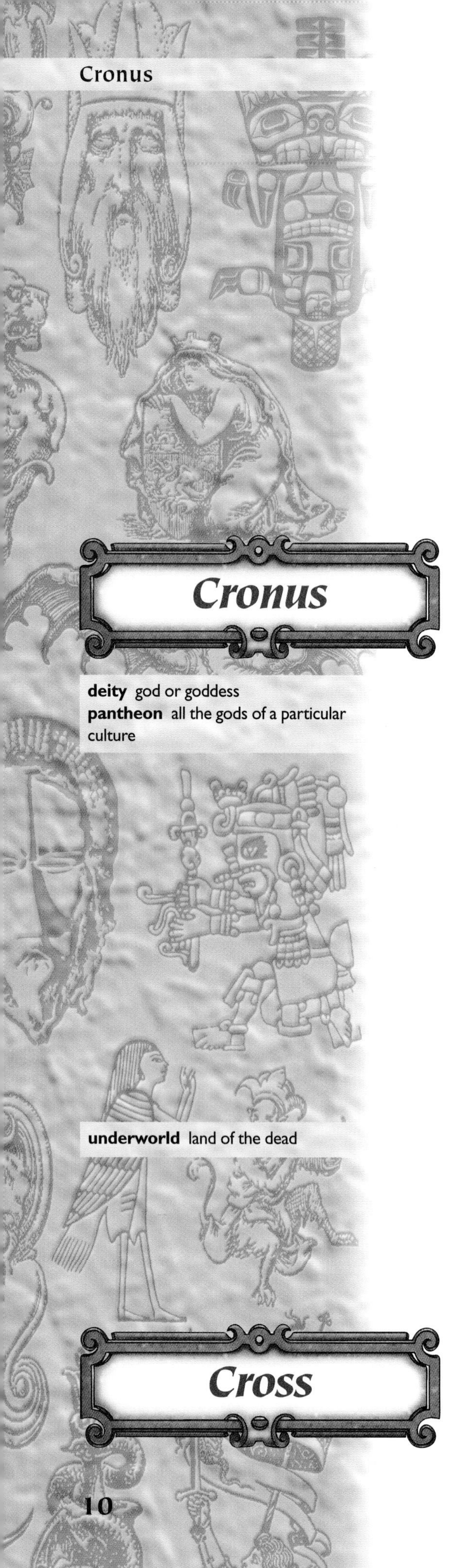

1827. He went to Texas to help settlers there overthrow Mexican rule but died defending the Alamo on March 6, 1836.

Crockett was known as the "coonskin congressman" because of his many stories about hunting raccoons and bears. He loved to tell tall tales that showed him as stronger, smarter, braver, and a better shot than anyone else in the land. The stories grew more fantastic after his death, thanks largely to a series of adventure books featuring Crockett as the hero. In these tales, he climbed Niagara Falls on an alligator's back, drank the entire Gulf of Mexico, twisted the tail off a comet, and outsmarted a businessman. He also traveled the world performing marvelous feats of daring and skill. In many ways, Davy Crockett is America's own celebrated hero, whose deeds and adventures compare to those of legendary ancient warriors such as Achilles† and Beowulf†.

Cronus

deity god or goddess

pantheon all the gods of a particular culture

Cronus was the youngest of the Titans, the Greek **deities** who ruled the world before the arrival of Zeus† and the other Olympian gods and goddesses. Cronus seized power from his father, the sky god Uranus, and was later ousted by his own children. The Romans adopted Cronus as a member of their **pantheon,** renamed him Saturn, and worshiped him as a god of agriculture.

According to legend, Uranus had imprisoned several of his children in the body of his wife, the earth goddess Gaia. To punish him, Gaia asked her son Cronus to cut off Uranus's sex organs during the night. After carrying out his mother's wishes, Cronus replaced his father as ruler. He married his sister, Rhea, another Titan, and they began to have children. Learning that one of his offspring was fated to overcome him just as he had overcome his father, Cronus swallowed each baby as it was born. Rhea, however, managed to save their youngest child, Zeus, by feeding Cronus a stone wrapped in infants' clothing. She then arranged for the baby to be raised in secret.

underworld land of the dead

When Zeus was grown, he forced Cronus to vomit up the swallowed children: the deities Hestia, Demeter†, Hera†, Hades†, and Poseidon†. Zeus also freed the giants and the Cyclopes† who had been imprisoned. Together they went to war against Cronus and the Titans and, after a violent struggle, emerged victorious. Zeus then banished the Titans to Tartarus, a place deep in the **underworld.**

In another version of the myth, Cronus's rise to power ushered in a peaceful golden age, which ended when the Titans were defeated. Following the battle, Cronus was sent to rule a distant paradise known as the Islands of the Blessed. ***See also* Cyclopes; Gaia; Giants; Greek Mythology; Saturn; Uranus; Zeus.**

Cross

One of the oldest and most widespread symbols in history, the cross is best known as a sign of the Christian faith. However, the cross has played a significant role in many other cultures as well. Peoples as different as the ancient Egyptians and modern peace marchers have adopted it to represent an idea they considered important.

*†See **Names and Places** at the end of this volume for further information.*

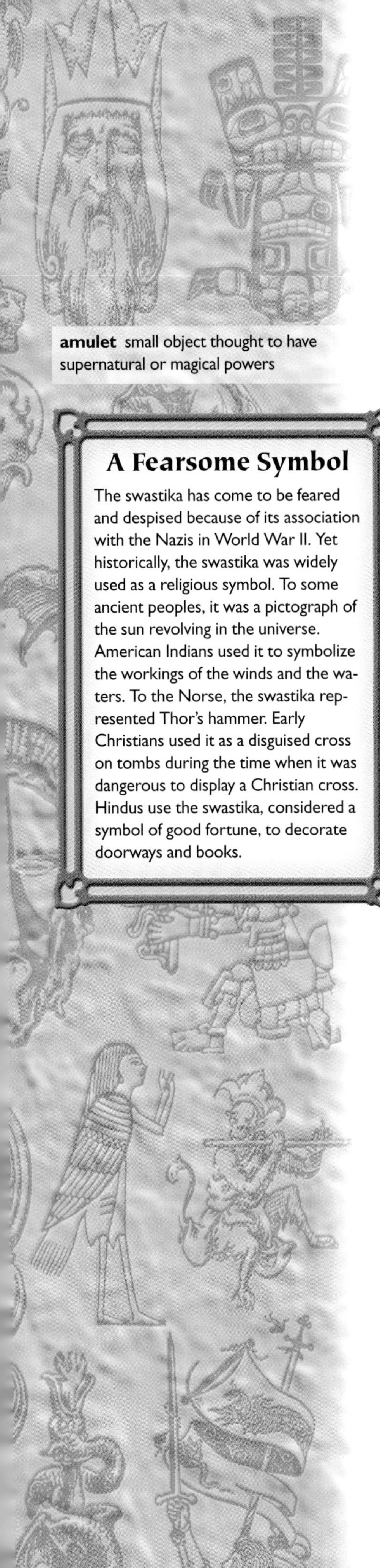

amulet small object thought to have supernatural or magical powers

A Fearsome Symbol

The swastika has come to be feared and despised because of its association with the Nazis in World War II. Yet historically, the swastika was widely used as a religious symbol. To some ancient peoples, it was a pictograph of the sun revolving in the universe. American Indians used it to symbolize the workings of the winds and the waters. To the Norse, the swastika represented Thor's hammer. Early Christians used it as a disguised cross on tombs during the time when it was dangerous to display a Christian cross. Hindus use the swastika, considered a symbol of good fortune, to decorate doorways and books.

Shapes and Uses of the Cross

Throughout the world and through the ages, people have used the shape of the cross to decorate religious articles, to protect against illness, to bring good luck, and for countless other purposes. Many different versions of the cross exist, including the X-shaped St. Andrews cross and the T-shaped tau cross (named after the Greek letter). In addition, a wide variety of items have been made in the shape of the cross, including small **amulets** and jewelry, church altars and gravestones, and decorations on flags and shields.

Among the ancient civilizations who used the cross as a religious symbol were the Egyptians. The ankh, or Egyptian cross, was a tau cross with a circle or oval on top. The T part of the cross represented life or wisdom, and the circle or oval stood for eternity. Under the pharaoh Akhenaten, the ankh became the symbol of the Egyptian sun god, and gods and pharaohs were often shown holding the cross. Early Egyptian Christians adopted it as a symbol of eternal life through Christ's sacrifice.

Other ancient peoples, such as the Phoenicians† of the eastern Mediterranean and the Aztecs of central Mexico, also used the ankh. For the Aztecs, it was a symbol of secret knowledge available to only a few.

The Greek cross, with two equal bars that intersect in the middle, was adopted by many peoples. The ancient Assyrians, Babylonians, and Persians all used it to represent the basic elements—earth, water, wind, and fire—from which they believed all living things were created. They also marked religious articles with the sign of the cross. Ancient Buddhists and Hindus followed a similar practice. In addition, the Greek cross has been found on items used by the Druids of Celtic† Britain and by the Aztecs. But its meaning for these peoples has not been established.

The ankh, or Egyptian cross, features a T-shaped cross with a circle on top. The T part represents life or wisdom, and the circle stands for eternity.

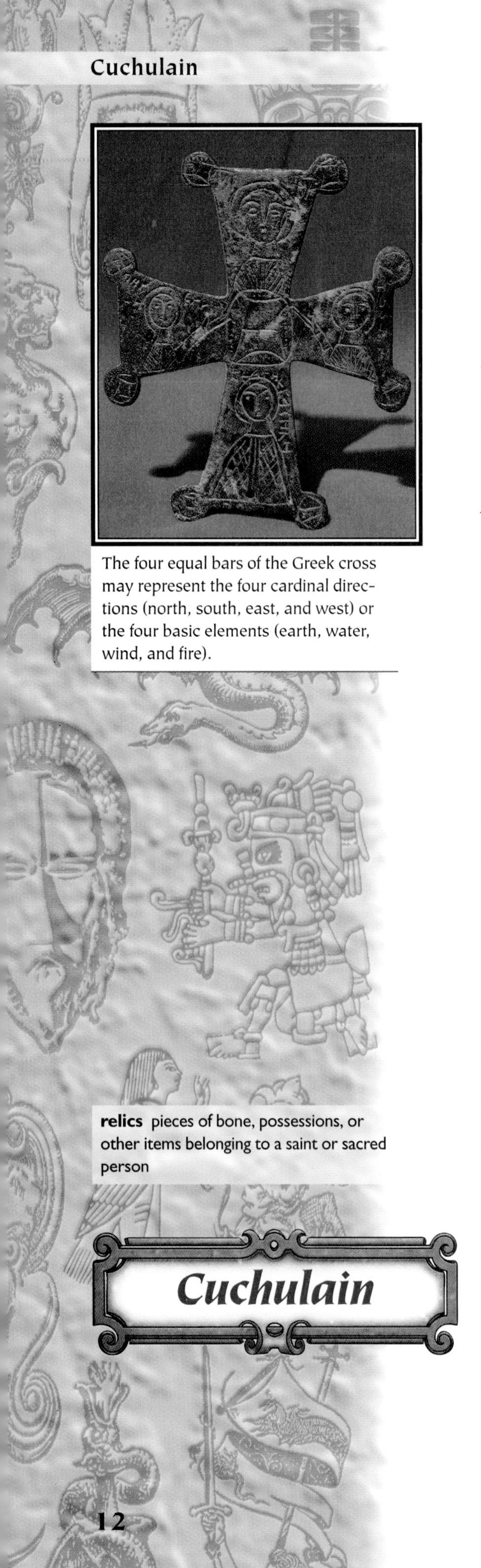
The four equal bars of the Greek cross may represent the four cardinal directions (north, south, east, and west) or the four basic elements (earth, water, wind, and fire).

In other cultures, the Greek cross represented the four principal directions (north, south, east, and west). The Plains Indians place the cross within a circle to signify the four main directions of the heavens. In the Bible, paradise is said to be divided by four rivers that form a cross. In parts of Africa, people believe that crossroads are places where the worlds of the living and the dead meet.

The Christian Cross

The cross is the most important symbol of Christianity. It stands for the cross on which Jesus was crucified and represents the greatness of God's sacrifice and the spiritual salvation that humans gained as a result.

A Changing Symbol. In the ancient Near East and Mediterranean world, crucifixion was used mainly as a method of execution for political and religious opponents, pirates, and slaves. The condemned were tied or nailed to a cross and died of exhaustion or heart failure.

Early Christians were hesitant to adopt the cross as their symbol. Many could not accept an instrument of death as the symbol of their devotion. Moreover, until the A.D. 300s, when Christianity became the official religion of the Roman empire and crucifixion was banned, open use of the cross could lead to persecution.

The earliest crosses were empty, emphasizing Christ's triumph over death and the eternal life available to humankind. By the 300s, the figure of a lamb was added over it, symbolizing Christ. Later the human figure of Christ was portrayed on the cross, emphasizing at first his divine nature but later his human suffering.

The True Cross. According to legend, the cross on which Jesus had been crucified was found by St. Helena, the mother of the Roman emperor Constantine, during a pilgrimage to the Holy Land. The story relates that she found three crosses (Jesus had been crucified along with two thieves). To determine which of them belonged to Christ, Helena ordered that a corpse be brought and placed on each cross in turn. When the corpse was laid on one of the crosses, it came to life, thus showing that that was the cross of Christ. Fragments of the cross were later sold as **relics** and honored in churches throughout Europe.

relics pieces of bone, possessions, or other items belonging to a saint or sacred person

Cuchulain

Cuchulain, one of the greatest heroes of Irish mythology and legend, was a warrior in the service of Conchobhar, king of Ulster. Best known for his single-handed defense of Ulster, Cuchulain is said to have lived in the first century B.C., and tales about him and other heroes began to be written down in the A.D. 700s. Cuchulain's adventures were recorded in a series of tales known as the Ulster Cycle.

Early Life. Like many Irish heroes, Cuchulain had a short, adventurous, and tragic life. He was the son of Dechtire, sister of

King Conchobhar. She and some of her handmaidens were kidnapped on her wedding night by Lug, the sun god, who appeared to her as a fly. Dechtire swallowed the fly and later gave birth to a son whose original name was Setanta.

From the beginning, the child possessed extraordinary powers. He could swim like a fish at birth. He had seven fingers on each hand, seven toes on each foot, and seven pupils in each eye. At the age of 7, he fought off 150 boy warriors to gain entrance to his uncle's court. When he was 12, Setanta accidentally killed the watchdog of the smith Cullan and offered to guard Cullan's property until another dog could be trained. It was at that time that he changed his name to Cuchulain, which means "hound of Cullan." He grew up to be a handsome, well-spoken man who was very popular with women.

Trials and Achievements. Cuchulain fell in love with Emer and asked her to marry him. Emer insisted that Cuchulain must first prove his valor by undergoing a series of trials and sent him to the war goddess Scatha to be trained in warfare. On his journey to Scatha, Cuchulain had to pass through the plain of Ill Luck, where sharp grasses cut travelers' feet, and through the Perilous Glen, where dangerous animals roamed. Then Cuchulain had to cross the Bridge of the Cliff, which raised itself vertically when someone tried to cross it. Cuchulain jumped to the center and slid to the opposite side.

To repay Scatha for his training, Cuchulain fought her enemy Aife, the strongest woman in the world. After defeating Aife, he made peace with her, and she bore him a son, Connla. While returning home to claim his bride, Cuchulain rescued a princess and visited the **underworld.**

underworld land of the dead

Back home, Cuchulain achieved his greatest victory. When Queen Medb of Connacht sent a great army to steal the Brown Bull of Ulster, Cuchulain stopped them single-handedly. He alone, of all the Ulster warriors, was unaffected by a curse that had weakened the strength of the fighting force. Unfortunately, during one of the battles, he was forced to fight his good friend Ferdiad, whom he killed. On numerous other occasions, Cuchulain defended Ulster against the rest of Ireland and won numerous contests of bravery and trustworthiness.

But misfortune followed him. Cuchulain killed his own son, Connla, learning his identity too late. In addition, Cuchulain died as a result of trickery. After offending Morrigan, the goddess of death and battles, he was summoned to fight at a time when he was ill. On the way to battle, he saw a vision of a woman washing the body and weapons of a dead warrior, and he recognized the warrior as himself. Knowing then that his own death was **imminent,** he fought bravely. When he was too weak to stand, Cuchulain tied himself to a pillar so that he could die fighting on his feet. He was 27 years old.

imminent about to take place; threatening

The Warrior. Cuchulain had several magical weapons: his sword, his visor, and his barbed spear, Gae Bulga, which inflicted wounds

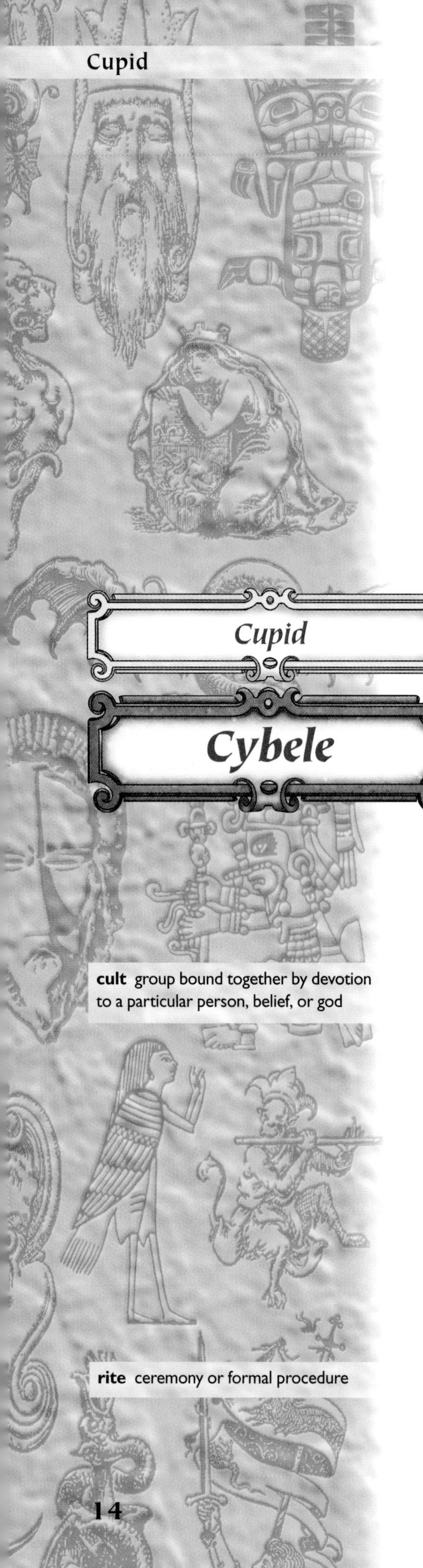

from which nobody ever recovered. When Cuchulain went into battle, he would go into a frenzy. His cry alone would kill a hundred warriors from fright. His physical appearance—namely, that of a handsome man—changed completely. Cuchulain's hair stood on end, one of his eyes bulged out while the other disappeared in his head, his legs and feet turned to face backward, his muscles swelled, and a column of blood spurted up from his head. His body became so hot that it could melt snow.

When swept away in a war frenzy, Cuchulain could not distinguish between friends and enemies. On one occasion, he was so full of the lust for battle that he needed to be stopped. A group of Ulster women marched out naked carrying vats of cold water to bring him to his senses. When Cuchulain stopped his chariot in embarrassment, he was grabbed by warriors who threw him into three vats of cold water to calm him down. The first vat burst apart, the second boiled over, but the third merely got hot. ***See also*** **CELTIC MYTHOLOGY; LUG.**

Cupid

See *Eros.*

Cybele

Cybele was the fertility goddess of Phrygia, an ancient country of Asia Minor†. In Greek and Roman mythology, Cybele personified Mother Earth and was worshiped as the Great Mother of the Gods. She was also associated with forests, mountains, and nature. Although usually shown wearing a crown in the form of a city wall or carrying a drum, the goddess may also appear on a throne or in a chariot, accompanied by lions and sometimes bees.

From Asia Minor, Cybele's following spread to Greece, where she was associated with Demeter, the Greek goddess of fruitfulness, and was regarded as the mother of all the gods. Around 200 B.C., the **cult** of Cybele reached Rome, and she became well known throughout the Roman world.

cult group bound together by devotion to a particular person, belief, or god

According to myth, Cybele discovered that her youthful lover Attis was unfaithful. In a jealous rage, she made him go mad and mutilate himself under a pine tree, where he bled to death. Regretting what she had done, Cybele mourned her loss. Zeus† promised her that the pine tree would remain sacred forever.

During the Roman empire, followers of Cybele held an annual spring festival dedicated to the goddess. The ceremonies involved cutting down a pine tree that represented the dead Attis. After wrapping the tree in bandages, the followers took it to Cybele's shrine. There they honored the tree and decorated it with violets, which they considered to have sprung from Attis's blood. As part of this religious ceremony, priests cut their arms so that their blood fell on Cybele's altar and the sacred pine tree. They also danced to the music of cymbals, drums, and flutes. During these wild **rites,** some followers even mutilated themselves, as Attis had. Cybele was usually portrayed by artists in a chariot drawn by lions. ***See also*** **ATTIS.**

rite ceremony or formal procedure

*†See **Names and Places** at the end of this volume for further information.*

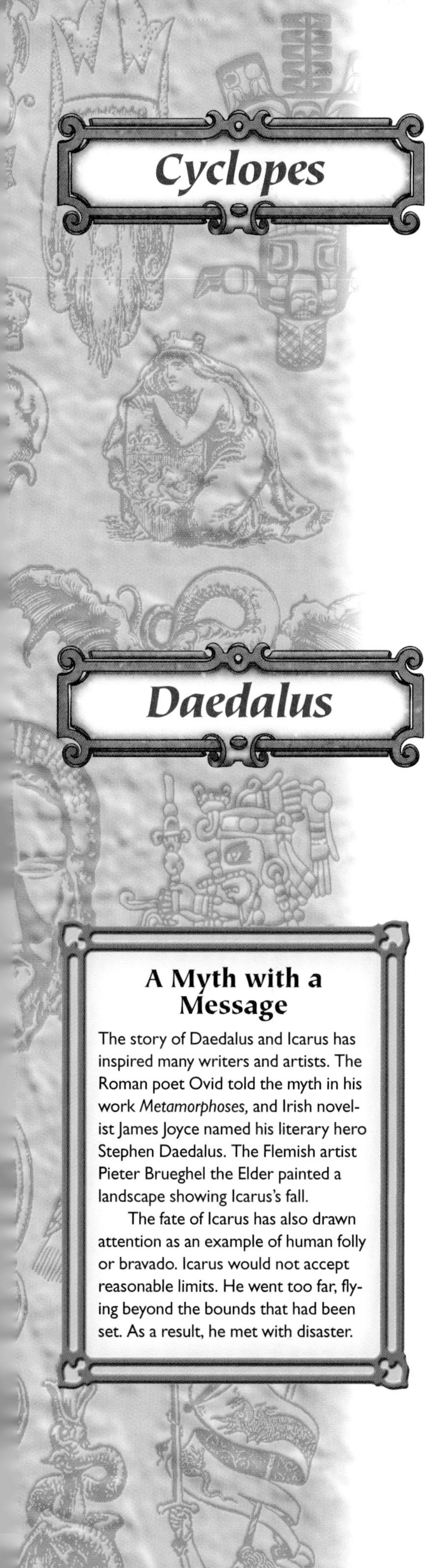

Cyclopes

In Greek mythology, the Cyclopes were a group of giants who possessed only one eye set in the middle of their forehead. They were said to be skilled workers, and the Greeks credited them with building the walls of several ancient cities. The Romans believed that the Cyclopes worked at Mount Etna with Vulcan, the god of fire and metalworking.

The Greek poet Hesiod wrote about three of the Cyclopes: Brontes (thunder), Steropes (lightning), and Arges (brightness). The sons of Uranus (sky) and Gaia (earth), these Cyclopes gave Zeus† the gifts of thunder and lightning with which he defeated the Titans† and became ruler of the universe. Later authors related that Zeus killed Apollo's† son Asclepius, causing Apollo to kill the Cyclopes in revenge.

In the *Odyssey*†, Homer† described how Odysseus† was captured by the cruel and barbaric Cyclops Polyphemus, the son of Poseidon†. Polyphemus ate six of Odysseus's crew members. However, Odysseus and the rest of his crew managed to escape by blinding the single eye of Polyphemus. ***See also*** **ASCLEPIUS; ODYSSEUS; VULCAN.**

Daedalus

In Greek mythology, Daedalus was a skilled craftsman and inventor who designed and built the Labyrinth on Crete, where the Minotaur was kept. Daedalus also made the wings that he and his son Icarus used to escape from Crete. The name *Daedalus* means "ingenious" or "clever."

The Master Craftsperson. Daedalus lived in Athens, where he was known for his skills as an inventor, artist, and sculptor. Indeed, it was said that the statues Daedalus made were so realistic that they had to be chained to keep them from running away.

Daedalus's nephew Talus (also called Perdix) came to serve as an apprentice to his uncle. The boy soon showed remarkable talent, inventing the saw by copying either the jawbone of a snake or the spine of a fish. Before long, Daedalus grew jealous of Talus, believing that the boy might become as great a craftsman as he was. This idea was more than Daedalus could bear. He killed Talus by pushing him off a cliff into the sea.

The Labyrinth. Because of his crime, Daedalus was forced to leave Athens. He went to Crete, an island in the Mediterranean Sea, and began working for King Minos, the Cretan ruler.

Minos had asked the sea god Poseidon (Neptune) for a sacrificial bull, and a beautiful white bull had emerged from the sea. Indeed, the bull was so magnificent that Minos decided to keep it rather than sacrifice it to Poseidon. The angry sea god punished the king by causing his wife, Pasiphae, to fall helplessly in love with the bull. At the request of the queen, Daedalus built a lifelike model of a cow in which she could conceal herself and spend time with her beloved bull. As a result of these visits, Pasiphae gave birth to the Minotaur, a monstrous creature with the body of a man and the head of a bull.

A Myth with a Message

The story of Daedalus and Icarus has inspired many writers and artists. The Roman poet Ovid told the myth in his work *Metamorphoses,* and Irish novelist James Joyce named his literary hero Stephen Daedalus. The Flemish artist Pieter Brueghel the Elder painted a landscape showing Icarus's fall.

The fate of Icarus has also drawn attention as an example of human folly or bravado. Icarus would not accept reasonable limits. He went too far, flying beyond the bounds that had been set. As a result, he met with disaster.

According to Greek myth, Daedalus and his son Icarus take flight on wax wings made by Daedalus. When Icarus ignores his father's warning not to fly too high, the sun melts the wax, and Icarus falls into the water and drowns.

King Minos wanted to hide the Minotaur. He ordered Daedalus to construct a prison from which the monster could never escape. Daedalus designed the Labyrinth, a mazelike network of winding passages that had only one entrance. Its layout was so complex that no one who entered it could ever find a way out. King Minos kept the Minotaur imprisoned in the Labyrinth.

The Minotaur was given humans to eat. Some were provided by the city of Athens. After suffering defeat in battle with Crete, Athens had to send King Minos a yearly tribute of seven boys and seven girls. These unfortunate Athenians were sent into the Labyrinth one by one as food for the Minotaur.

One year the Greek hero Theseus† came to Crete as one of the youths. He was determined to put an end to the human sacrifice. Ariadne, the king's daughter, fell in love with Theseus and asked Daedalus to help her find a way of saving him. When Theseus went into the Labyrinth to slay the Minotaur, Ariadne gave him a ball of string that she had obtained from Daedalus. Theseus tied the string to the entrance of the Labyrinth and unwound it as he made his way toward the Minotaur. He killed the beast and then used the string to find his way out of the Labyrinth.

Daedalus and Icarus. When King Minos discovered what had happened, he was furious. To punish Daedalus for his role in the escape, the king imprisoned him and his young son Icarus in the Labyrinth.

Daedalus put his talents to work. Day after day, he collected the feathers of birds. He also gathered wax from a beehive. When he had enough feathers and wax, Daedalus set to work making two pairs of enormous wings, one pair for himself and the other for Icarus.

Daedalus carefully instructed his son how to use the wings to fly. He warned Icarus not to fly too high or too low. If he flew too high, the sun's heat could melt the wax that held the wings together. If he flew too low, he risked being swept up by the sea.

With that, father and son took off from Crete. The wings worked well, and Daedalus and Icarus began to fly across the sea. However, Icarus did not pay attention to his father's warning. He flew higher and higher until the sun's heat melted the wax in his wings. Icarus fell into the ocean and drowned. Daedalus managed to fly safely to Sicily. ***See also*** **ARIADNE; MINOS; MINOTAUR; THESEUS.**

*†See **Names and Places** at the end of this volume for further information.*

Dagda

cauldron large kettle

In Celtic† mythology, Dagda was an Irish god who was head of a group of Irish gods called the Tuatha Dé Danaan. He was considered the father of the gods and the lord of fertility, plenty, and knowledge. The word *Dagda* means "the good god."

According to legend, Dagda had several possessions associated with power and position. One was a huge **cauldron** that was never empty and from which no one went away hungry. The ladle was so big that two people could lie in it. Dagda also owned an orchard of fruit trees where the fruit was always ripe and two pigs that were cooked and ready to eat. In addition, he had a club with two ends—one for killing living people and the other for bringing the dead back to life. Dagda used his magic harp to order the seasons to change. In spite of his great power, Dagda was pictured as a fat man, plainly dressed and pulling his club on wheels. His favorite food was porridge. As the god of knowledge, he was the patron of the Druids, the priests of the Celtic religious order.

When the Tuatha Dé Danaan were forced to go underground, Dagda divided the land among the gods. His son Aonghus, the god of love, was absent during the division, and Dagda did not give his son a section because he wanted to keep Aonghus's palace for himself. When Aonghus returned, he tricked his father to get his palace back, leaving Dagda without land or power. ***See also*** **Celtic Mythology; Druids.**

Dagon

deity god or goddess

In the mythology of the ancient Near East, Dagon (or Dagan) was a major **deity** associated with fertility, vegetation, and military strength. Followers in Mesopotamia† built many temples dedicated to him. Some people believe that Dagon was worshiped as a fish god or a god of the sea, while others identify him as a god of grain and agriculture.

A temple dedicated to Dagon at Ashdod (in present-day Israel) is mentioned in the books of Judges and I Samuel in the Bible. In one story, the hero Samson destroys the temple and kills the worshipers inside by pulling down two pillars supporting the building's roof. ***See also*** **Samson; Semitic Mythology.**

Damocles, Sword of

imminent about to take place; threatening

Damocles was a member of the court of Dionysius, ruler of the Sicilian city of Syracuse during the 300s B.C. According to a legend passed on by the Roman writer Cicero, Damocles told Dionysius how much he envied his kingly wealth, power, and happiness. In response, Dionysius invited Damocles to come to a magnificent banquet.

Damocles was seated before a marvelous feast, when he happened to glance up in horror. Above his head hung a sharp sword, suspended by nothing more than a single thread. In this way, Dionysius showed Damocles that a ruler's life may appear grand, but it is filled with uncertainty and danger. The "sword of Damocles" has thus come to symbolize **imminent** danger.

Danaë

In Greek mythology, Danaë was the daughter of Acrisius, the king of Argos. An **oracle** told Acrisius that Danaë's son would someday kill him. To prevent the **prophecy** from coming true, Acrisius had his daughter imprisoned in a bronze tower. There the god Zeus† went to her in a shower of gold, and she became pregnant with a son, the hero Perseus. When Acrisius learned of the baby's birth, he ordered Danaë and her son locked inside a chest and set adrift at sea.

oracle priest or priestess or other creature through whom a god is believed to speak; also the location (such as a shrine) where such words are spoken

prophecy foretelling of what is to come; also something that is predicted

The chest reached the island of Seriphos, where it was discovered by a fisherman named Dictys, whose brother Polydectes was king. Dictys helped Danaë raise her son on the island. When Perseus was grown, Polydectes fell in love with Danaë, but she did not love him in return. Believing that he could pressure Danaë into marrying him if her son were absent, Polydectes sent Perseus on a quest for the head of Medusa†. Some sources say that Danaë went into hiding during Perseus's absence, others that Polydectes locked her away. In any event, Danaë resisted Polydectes' advances.

When Perseus returned, he saved Danaë by turning Polydectes to stone with the head of Medusa. Dictys became king, and Danaë and Perseus returned to Argos. According to some writers, she went on to found the city of Ardea in Italy. The original prophecy was fulfilled, however, when Perseus accidentally killed Acrisius with a stray **discus** during some athletic games.

discus heavy, circular plate hurled over distance as a sport

Ovid refers to this myth in his *Metamorphoses*†. Many artists, including Titian and Rembrandt, capture the story of Danaë in their paintings. ***See also*** **GREEK MYTHOLOGY; MEDUSA; PERSEUS.**

Danu

In Celtic† mythology, Danu (also known as Dana, Anu, and Don) is a fertility goddess and mother of the Tuatha Dé Danaan, a group of Irish gods. The worship of Danu originated in eastern Europe, and because she was associated with rivers, many European rivers carry versions of her name, including the Danube, the Don, and the Dnieper.

Some scholars believe that the Tuatha Dé Danaan were gods of the people who inhabited Ireland before the Celts. When these **deities** were defeated by another group, the Sons of Mil, they went to live underground. Each god received a personal domain, and the group eventually became known as "the little people" of Irish fairy stories. ***See also*** **CELTIC MYTHOLOGY.**

deity god or goddess

Daoist Mythology

See *Chinese Mythology.*

Daphnis and Chloe

The romantic tale of Daphnis and Chloe, told by the Greek author Longus, deals with the simple and peaceful lives of shepherds in the country. A young boy named Daphnis and a girl named Chloe are abandoned by their parents and raised by shepherds on the Greek island of Lesbos. The two meet and gradually fall in love as they grow up. After various trials, including Daphnis's capture by pirates, Daphnis and Chloe are reunited with their families and married to each other.

*†See **Names and Places** at the end of this volume for further information.*

The popular story spread to Europe in the 1500s. It was the main source for *The Winter's Tale* by Shakespeare and inspired various musical compositions, including the 1910 ballet *Daphnis et Chloé* by the French composer Maurice Ravel.

Dekanawida

Dekanawida, a semilegendary Native American leader, is credited with helping unite the five Iroquois tribes of northern New York in the late 1500s. According to legend, Dekanawida (whose name means "two rivers flowing together") was born to a virgin mother of the Huron people in Canada. Because of warnings that he would bring ruin to his people, his mother tried to drown him several times. However, on each occasion, he miraculously survived and reappeared the next morning lying next to her.

As an adult, Dekanawida left the Hurons and went south, where he met another legendary Indian figure, Hiawatha. Together the two men developed a plan for uniting the five Iroquois nations into a single confederacy. According to legend, Dekanawida came up with the idea but was a poor speaker, so Hiawatha became the spokesperson. The Iroquois Confederacy later served as a model for founders of the government of the United States. ***See also* HIAWATHA; NATIVE AMERICAN MYTHOLOGY.**

Delilah

In the Old Testament of the Bible, Delilah was a woman, probably a Philistine†, who received a large amount of silver for telling the enemies of Samson, the Israelite hero, the source of his great strength. After seducing Samson to win his confidence, she got him to reveal what made him strong—his long, thick hair. She then lured him to sleep and had his hair cut. As a result, Samson became weak, and the Philistines were able to seize him. The name *Delilah* has taken on the meaning of temptress or betrayer. The story of Samson and Delilah is the subject of a painting by Rembrandt and an opera by Saint-Saëns. ***See also* SAMSON.**

Delphi

Delphi, a town on the slopes of Mount Parnassus in Greece, was the site of the main temple of Apollo† and of the Delphic **oracle,** the most famous oracle of ancient times. Before making important decisions, Greeks and other peoples traveled to this sacred place to consult the oracle and learn the gods' wishes.

oracle priest or priestess or other creature through whom a god is believed to speak; also the location (such as a shrine) where such words are spoken

The Oracle at Delphi

According to Greek mythology, Zeus† wanted to locate the exact center of the world. To do this, he released two eagles from opposite ends of the earth. The eagles met at Delphi. Zeus marked the spot with a large, egg-shaped stone called the omphalos, meaning "navel."

Originally, Delphi was the site of an oracle of the earth goddess Gaia. The site was guarded by a monstrous serpent (or dragon, in

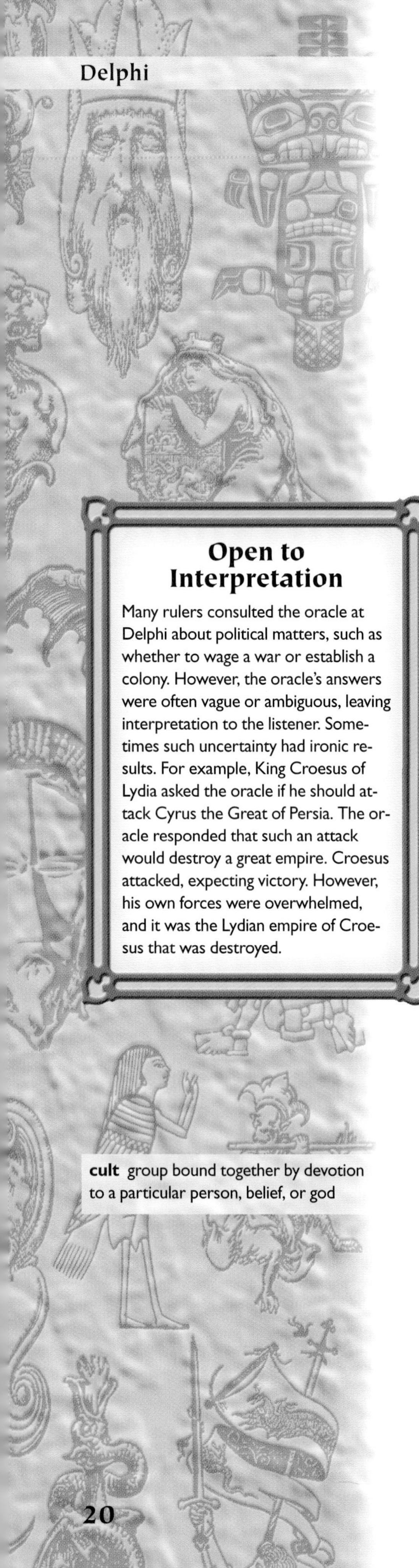

some accounts) called Pytho. Apollo killed Pytho and forced Gaia to leave Delphi. Thereafter, the temple at Delphi belonged to Apollo's oracle.

Consulting the Oracle. No one knows for certain how the process of consulting the Delphic oracle worked. However, over the years, a traditional account has been widely accepted. According to this description, a visitor who wanted to submit a question to the oracle would first make an appropriate offering and sacrifice a goat. Then a priestess known as the Pythia would take the visitor's question into the inner part of Apollo's temple, which contained the omphalos and a golden statue of Apollo. Seated on a three-legged stool, the priestess would fall into a trance.

After some time, the priestess would start to writhe around and foam at the mouth. In a frenzy, she would begin to voice strange words and sounds. Priests and interpreters would listen carefully and record her words in verse or in prose. The message was then passed on to the visitor who had posed the question. Some modern scholars believe that the priestess did not become delirious but rather sat quietly as she delivered her divine message.

Anyone could approach the oracle, whether king, public official, or private citizen. At first, a person could consult the oracle only once a year, but this restriction was later changed to once a month.

Open to Interpretation

Many rulers consulted the oracle at Delphi about political matters, such as whether to wage a war or establish a colony. However, the oracle's answers were often vague or ambiguous, leaving interpretation to the listener. Sometimes such uncertainty had ironic results. For example, King Croesus of Lydia asked the oracle if he should attack Cyrus the Great of Persia. The oracle responded that such an attack would destroy a great empire. Croesus attacked, expecting victory. However, his own forces were overwhelmed, and it was the Lydian empire of Croesus that was destroyed.

Influence of the Oracle. The ancient Greeks had complete faith in the oracle's words, even though the meaning of the message was often unclear. As the oracle's fame spread, people came from all over the Mediterranean region seeking advice. Numerous well-known figures of history and mythology visited Delphi, including Socrates and Oedipus.

Visitors would ask not only about private matters but also about affairs of state. As a result, the oracle at Delphi had great influence on political, economic, and religious events. Moreover, Delphi itself became rich from the gifts sent by many believers.

History of Delphi

The **cult** of Apollo at Delphi probably dates back to the 700s B.C., although the fame of the oracle did not reach its peak until the 500s B.C. In about 590 B.C., war broke out between Delphi and the nearby town of Crisa because Crisa had been demanding that visitors to the Delphic oracle pay taxes. The war destroyed Crisa and opened free access to Delphi. To celebrate the victory, Delphi introduced the Pythian Games, an athletic festival that took place every four years.

cult group bound together by devotion to a particular person, belief, or god

In early Roman times, Delphi was often plundered. For example, the Roman dictator Sulla took many of Delphi's treasures, and the emperor Nero is said to have carried off some 500 bronze statues. With Rome's conquest of Greece and the spread of Christianity,

†*See **Names and Places** at the end of this volume for further information.*

The temple of Apollo on Mount Parnassus in Greece was the site of the Delphic oracle. People from many lands went there to ask the oracle for advice.

Delphi's importance declined. The oracle was finally silenced in A.D. 390 to discourage the spread of **pagan** beliefs.

pagan term used by early Christians to describe non-Christians and non-Christian beliefs

The modern village of Kastri stood on the site of ancient Delphi until 1890. Then the Greek government moved the village to a nearby location, making the site of the ancient town available for excavation. Archaeologists have been working on the site since that time and have made many important discoveries relating to the temple of Apollo. ***See also*** **APOLLO; GAIA.**

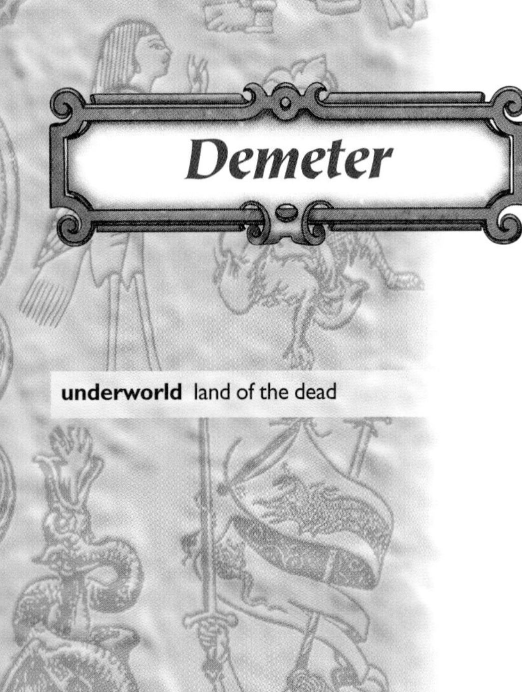

Demeter

Demeter, the Greek goddess of vegetation and fruitfulness, was known to the Romans as Ceres. She was the daughter of Cronus (Saturn)† and Rhea and the sister of Zeus†. Although Demeter was not one of the 12 gods of Olympus†, her origins can be traced back to very ancient times, perhaps to the Egyptian goddess Isis. Her name means "mother goddess" or "barley mother."

Demeter had a daughter by Zeus called Persephone†. The figures of Demeter and Persephone are closely related, and certain aspects of Persephone—for example, as a goddess of the **underworld**—are also associated with Demeter in different versions of the same myth.

underworld land of the dead

In one tale, Hades, the ruler of the underworld, fell in love with Persephone and kidnapped her to make her his queen. Demeter spent nine days and nights searching for her daughter, bearing a torch. When she failed to find Persephone, she took on the form

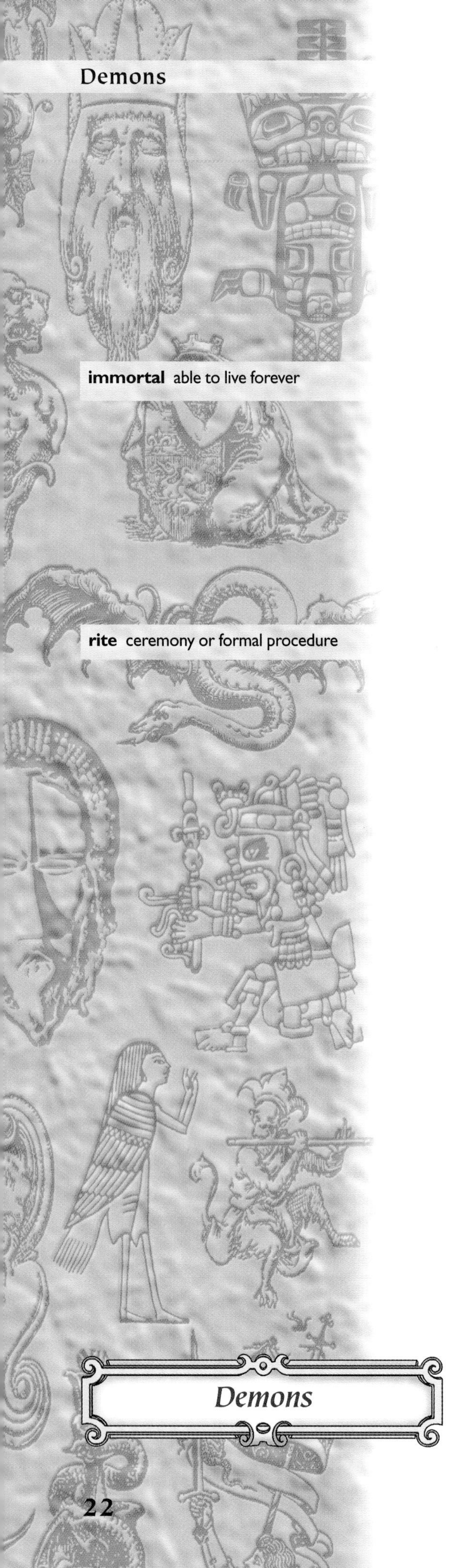

of an old woman and sat down by a well in the town of Eleusis, which was ruled by King Celeus. The king's daughters soon came along to draw water from the well and saw the old woman, who appeared to be crying. Taking pity on her, they asked her to return home with them to rest under their roof and take refreshment. At the palace, the queen, Metanira, and her servants showed so much hospitality that Demeter agreed to stay and care for the king's son Demophon.

immortal able to live forever

Demeter secretly planned to reward the king and queen by making their son **immortal.** During the day, she fed the boy with ambrosia, the food of the gods. At night, she laid him in the ashes of the fire to burn off his mortality. However, one night one of the queen's maids saw Demeter lay the boy in the fire and told the queen. Metanira surprised Demeter and cried out for her to stop. Demeter then revealed her true identity and proclaimed that the child would not be immortal but would grow up to do great things. According to legend, Celeus's son Triptolemus (perhaps another name for Demophon) later traveled around the earth introducing agriculture to all the peoples of the world. Demeter commanded the king to build a temple to her and taught him secret **rites** that the people should perform in her honor.

rite ceremony or formal procedure

Still grieving for Persephone, Demeter neglected the earth. As a result, all the crops withered and died, and famine spread over the world. Zeus was alarmed because he feared that all the humans would die, leaving no one to perform sacrifices to the gods. But Demeter would not restore life to the earth unless Persephone was returned to her. Zeus persuaded Hades to release Persephone, but during her stay in the underworld, she had eaten some pomegranate seeds. Because of this, Persephone was forever tied to Hades and required to spend part of the year with him in the underworld and only part on earth with her mother. This story was used to explain the cycle of the seasons. When Demeter was without her daughter, then the earth was barren. When Persephone rejoined her mother, plants could grow.

The rites held in Demeter's honor became the Eleusinian Mysteries, some of the most important ceremonies in ancient Greece. Scholars still do not know everything that took place during the secret rites. However, it is thought that the mysteries involved fasting, a procession from Athens to Eleusis, sacred dances, and a reenactment of the story of Persephone. Those who participated were promised a special future in the underworld after death.

Demeter's Roman name, Ceres, lives on in the word *cereal,* used to refer to all types of grain. The Spanish word for beer, *cerveza,* also comes from the name of the Roman goddess, because beer is made from barley. ***See also*** **Cybele; Hades; Isis; Persephone; Underworld.**

Demons

See *Devils and Demons.*

Devi

pantheon all the gods of a particular culture

Devi is the major goddess in the Hindu **pantheon.** Known both as Devi (goddess) and Mahadevi (great goddess), she takes many different forms and is worshiped both as a kind goddess and as a fierce one. In all of her forms, she is the wife of the Shiva, the god of destruction.

In the form of Durga, Devi is a warrior goddess charged with protecting the gods and the world from powerful demons. The gods used their combined strength to create Durga when they were unable to overpower a terrible buffalo demon named Mahisha. They gave Durga ten arms—so she could hold many weapons—and a tiger to carry her into battle. Durga and Mahisha fought a long, terrible, and bloody battle in which the two opponents changed

Devi, a major Hindu goddess, appears in many different forms. This color print shows a man worshiping Devi as Parvati, the beautiful and loving wife of Shiva.

trident three-pronged spear, similar to a pitchfork

shape many times. Durga finally managed to kill the demon by piercing his heart with her **trident** and cutting off his head.

Devi also takes gentler forms. As Sati, a loyal wife to Shiva, she burned herself alive to defend his honor and prove her love. When Shiva refused to let go of Sati's burning body, the god Vishnu† had to cut her body out of his arms. Her remains were then cut into 50 pieces and scattered to different places that became shrines. As Parvati, Devi is a gentle and loving wife who went through great sacrifice to win Shiva's love. Parvati has a softening influence on the harsh god and is often portrayed as an idealized beauty or pictured with Shiva in domestic scenes.

Another, and quite different, form of Devi is the fierce Kali. Like Durga, Kali defends the world from demons, but she can go into a rage and lose control. When she blindly begins to kill innocent people, the gods have to intervene. On one occasion, Shiva threw himself among the bodies she was trampling to bring her out of her madness. Images of Kali show her with black skin, three eyes, fangs, and four arms. She wears a necklace of skulls and carries weapons and a severed head. She is usually portrayed with her tongue hanging out in recognition of her victory over the demon Raktavira. To make sure that Raktavira was truly dead, Kali had to suck the blood out of his body because any drop that fell to the ground would produce a duplicate of him.

There are numerous other forms of Devi. As Uma, she appears as the golden goddess, personifying light and beauty. As Hariti, she is the goddess of childbirth. As Gauri, she represents the harvest or fertility, and as Manasa, she is the goddess of snakes. When she takes the role of mother of the world, Devi is known as Jaganmata. ***See also*** **Hinduism and Mythology; Shiva; Vishnu.**

Devils and Demons

supernatural related to forces beyond the normal world; magical or miraculous
adversary enemy; opponent
cosmic large or universal in scale; having to do with the universe

In myths, legends, and various religions, devils and demons are evil or harmful **supernatural** beings. Devils are generally regarded as the **adversaries** of the gods, while the image of demons ranges from mischief makers to powerful destructive forces. In many religions, devils and demons stand on the opposite side of the **cosmic** balance from gods and angels. Although devils and demons have been pictured in many different ways, they are usually associated with darkness, danger, violence, and death.

Supernatural Beings and the Force of Evil

Some people, including many Christian writers, have used the terms *devil* and *demon* almost interchangeably. But although devils and demons sometimes seem to be closely related or even identical, they also appear in myth and religion as two quite different creatures.

Devils. In most mythologies and religions, a devil is a leader or ruler among evil spirits, a being who acts in direct opposition to the gods. The general view is that devils are trying to destroy humans,

monotheistic believing in only one god

sorcerer magician or wizard

deity god or goddess

pantheon all the gods of a particular culture

chaos great disorder or confusion

to tempt them into sinning, or to turn them against their gods. **Monotheistic** religions often speak of one Devil, just as they recognize one God.

Devils and gods may be opposites, but they are also usually linked in some way. Many religious and mythological explanations say that devils are related to the gods or that they are gods of evil.

Demons. A demon (sometimes spelled *daemon*) is generally thought to be a harmful or evil spirit or supernatural being, sometimes a god or the offspring of a god. Demons may be the messengers, attendants, or servants of the Devil. They are often monstrous in appearance, combining the features of different animals or of animals and humans.

Demons were not always regarded as evil. The ancient Greeks spoke of a person's *daimon* as his or her personal spirit, guardian angel, or soul. In many cultures, demons were merely inhuman supernatural powers that could be evil or good at various times, depending on whether their actions harmed or helped people. Human witches, wizards, and **sorcerers** were thought to gain some of their abilities by summoning and controlling demons through magical practices.

The spread of religions has had an interesting effect on demons in world mythology. When one religion replaces another, the gods of the former religion may become demons in the new faith. For example, as Islam spread through West Africa, Central Asia, and Indonesia, some local **deities** did not disappear but were transformed into demons within a universe governed by the God of Islam.

Dark Powers in Culture and Religion

Devilish and demonic forces have taken many shapes and forms around the world. Frightening and dramatic stories and images of them have always had considerable appeal.

Egyptian Mythology. The devil could be seen in the evil god Set in ancient Egyptian mythology. Once a helpful god who ruled the kingdom of the blessed dead, Set's place in the Egyptian **pantheon** changed after he murdered his brother. Followers of the supreme god Horus conquered Set's followers, and the priests of Horus made Set the enemy of the other gods and the source of evil.

The Egyptians believed in the existence of demons. One such demon was Nehebkau, who appeared at times as a powerful earth spirit, a source of strength for the other gods. At other times, though, he was a menacing monster, a serpent with human arms and legs who threatened the souls of the dead. Like many demons, Nehebkau had more than one role.

Persian Mythology. In the mythology of Persia, now known as Iran, two opposing powers struggled for control of the universe. Ahura Mazda was the god of goodness and order, while his twin brother, Ahriman, was the god of evil and **chaos.** The Zoroastrian

religion that developed in Persia pictured the world in terms of tension between opposites: God (Ahura Mazda) and the Devil (Ahriman), light and darkness, health and illness, life and death. Ahriman ruled **malevolent** demons called *daevas* that represented death, violence, and other negative forces.

malevolent doing or wishing harm or ill toward others

Judaism and Christianity. Hebrew or Jewish tradition, later adopted by Christians, calls the Devil Satan, which means "adversary." Satan took on qualities of Ahriman, becoming the prince of evil, lies, and darkness. Jewish tradition also includes a female demon known as Lilith. Said to be the first wife of Adam, Lilith was cast out when she refused to obey her husband and was replaced by Eve.

In Christian belief, the Devil came to be seen as a fallen angel who chose to become evil rather than worship God. Satan rules the demons in Hell, the place of punishment and despair. In the Middle Ages, some Christians believed that a separate devil—or a separate aspect of the Devil—existed for each of the seven deadly sins. In their view, Lucifer represented pride, Mammon greed, Asmodeus lust, Satan anger, Beelzebub gluttony, Leviathan envy, and Belphegor sloth.

The common image of the Devil in Western culture is drawn from many sources. The Devil's pointed ears, wings, and sharp protruding teeth resemble those of Charu, the **underworld** demon of the Etruscans of ancient Italy. The Devil's tail, horns, and

underworld land of the dead

A group of Hindu demons, known as the Rakshasas, served the demon king Ravana. This painting shows a battle between the evil king and the hero Rama.

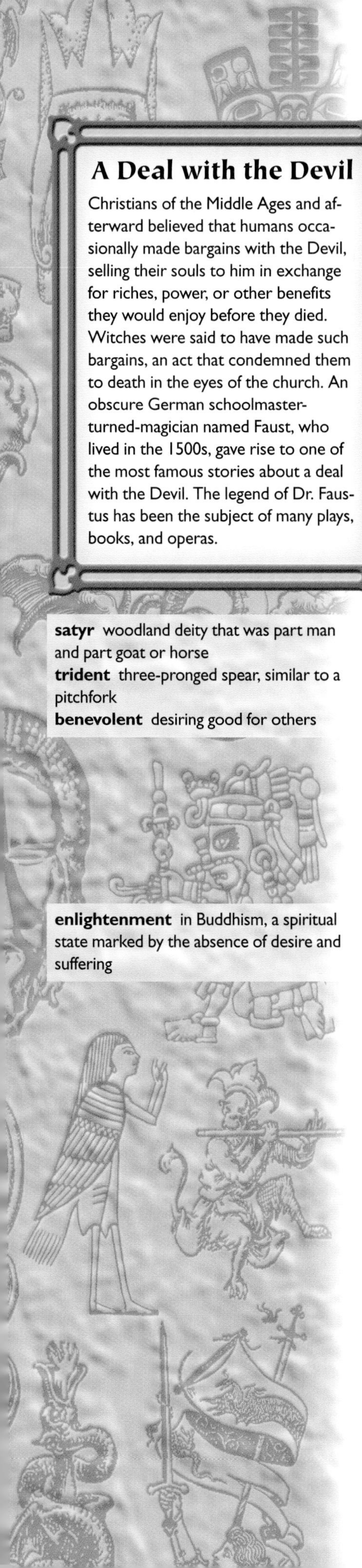

A Deal with the Devil

Christians of the Middle Ages and afterward believed that humans occasionally made bargains with the Devil, selling their souls to him in exchange for riches, power, or other benefits they would enjoy before they died. Witches were said to have made such bargains, an act that condemned them to death in the eyes of the church. An obscure German schoolmaster-turned-magician named Faust, who lived in the 1500s, gave rise to one of the most famous stories about a deal with the Devil. The legend of Dr. Faustus has been the subject of many plays, books, and operas.

satyr woodland deity that was part man and part goat or horse
trident three-pronged spear, similar to a pitchfork
benevolent desiring good for others

enlightenment in Buddhism, a spiritual state marked by the absence of desire and suffering

hooves are like those of **satyrs** and other animal gods of ancient Greece. The **trident** he is often shown brandishing is similar to those carried by the Greek gods Poseidon (Neptune), god of the sea, and Hades, lord of the underworld. The Hindu god Shiva, who represents the powers of destruction, also carries a trident. The Devil sometimes appears in other forms, such as a winged snake or dragon.

Islam. In the Muslim religion of Islam, which shares many elements of Jewish and Christian tradition, the Devil is called Iblis or Shaitan. Like Satan, he is a fallen angel. He commands an army of ugly demons called shaitans, who tempt humans to sin. The shaitans belong to a class of supernatural beings called djinni or jinni (genies). Some djinni are **benevolent** or neutral toward the human world, but those who do not believe in God are evil.

Hinduism and Buddhism. In the earliest form of Hinduism in India, the gods were sometimes called Asuras. But as the religion developed the Asuras came to be seen as demons who battled the gods. Another group of demons, the Rakshasas, served the demon king Ravana. Some were beautiful, but others were monstrous or hideously deformed. One demon, Hayagriva (meaning "horse-necked"), was a huge and powerful enemy of the gods whose troublemaking constantly threatened to overturn the cosmic order.

The Buddhist religion incorporated many elements of Hinduism, including the demon Hayagriva. It turned the Hindu demon Namuchi into Mara, the Evil One who tempts people with desires and deceives them with illusions. Mara tried to tempt the Buddha. He failed—but he still tries to keep others from reaching **enlightenment.**

Chinese and Japanese Mythology. Although traditional Chinese and Japanese religions did not recognize a single powerful devil, they had demons. In Chinese legends, the souls of the dead become either *shen,* good spirits who join the gods, or *gui,* malevolent ghosts or demons who wander the earth, usually because their descendants do not offer them the proper funeral ceremonies.

Japanese mythology includes stories about demons called Oni, generally portrayed with square, horned heads, sharp teeth and claws, and sometimes three eyes. Oni may have the size and strength of giants. Although these demons are cruel and mischievous, some tales tell of Oni who change their ways and become Buddhist monks.

African Mythology. The Bushpeople of southern Africa say that Gauna, the ruler of the underworld, is the enemy of Cagn, the god who created the world. Gauna visits the earth to cause trouble in human society and to seize people to take to the realm of the dead. He also sends the souls of the dead to haunt their living family members.

See also **African Mythology; Ahriman; Angels; Buddhism and Mythology; Chinese Mythology; Faust†; Gauna; Genies; Hell; Hinduism and Mythology; Japanese Mythology; Lilith; Monsters; Persian Mythology; Satan; Set; Witches and Wizards.**

Diana

In Roman mythology, Diana was the goddess of the woodlands, of wild animals, and of hunting. She also acted as a fertility goddess, who helped women conceive and give birth to children. As Rome's contact with Greece grew in ancient times, Diana became increasingly identified with the Greek goddess Artemis. In time, Diana and Artemis became essentially identical. Most literary references to the goddess use her Roman name, Diana.

Diana's Various Roles

The Romans viewed Diana as a many-sided goddess associated with forests and hunting. Artists usually portrayed her as a virgin hunter, often with a bow and quiver, accompanied by maidens, hunting dogs, or deer.

As goddess of childbirth, nursing, and healing—also called Lucina—Diana held an honored place among women. As goddess of light, she represented the moon. However, Diana was also identified with Hecate, the Greek goddess of darkness and witchcraft, and served as goddess of the kingdom of the dead.

Diana's nature was as varied as her many associations. As goddess of forests and hunting, she was considered to be pure and virginal. Yet she could also be arrogant and vengeful. As goddess of the moon, she had a changeable, unpredictable nature. As goddess of the dark world of the dead, she was unforgiving and bloodthirsty.

Because of her connections with creatures of the wild, with the hunt, and with the moon, Diana earned the title of "the triple goddess." Sculptors sometimes created statues of her with three heads: those of a horse, a dog, and a boar. Such statues were displayed at places where three roads met.

Goddess of Ephesus

The ancient Greek city of Ephesus was another center for the worship of Diana. The goddess had a magnificent temple there that took 220 years to construct and was regarded as one of the seven wonders of the ancient world. Within the temple was a famous ebony statue of Diana. The upper body of the statue was entirely covered with breasts, symbolizing Diana's role as goddess of fertility.

Diana's High Priest. The most celebrated place of worship for Diana was a sacred grove beside Lake Nemi, at Aricia near Rome. Associated with Diana at this shrine was the Roman hero Virbius. According to myth, he was Diana's first high priest at Aricia. All the priests who followed had to obtain the position by winning a fight to the death with the current high priest. The new high priest would keep his position until he in turn was conquered in combat. To win the right to fight the high priest, a challenger had to break off a large branch of a sacred oak tree in the grove at Lake Nemi.

It was said that the high priest had to be a runaway slave. In Rome, Diana was regarded as protector of the lower classes, particularly of slaves. In fact, the day of Diana's annual festival in Rome and Aricia was a holiday for slaves.

†*See* ***Names and Places*** *at the end of this volume for further information.*

pagan term used by early Christians to describe non-Christians and non-Christian beliefs

cult group bound together by devotion to a particular person, belief, or god

The Cult of Diana. The worship of Diana was widespread in the ancient world. Indeed, early Christians considered the **pagan** goddess their main rival. Diana's **cult** continued to attract followers for centuries, despite Christian opposition.

In the Middle Ages, Diana was denounced as "queen of the witches" or "goddess of the heathen." Religious leaders viewed her as a leader of witches and even referred to her as the devil. Nevertheless, the cult of Diana still had some followers in England as late as the 1700s. ***See also*** **ARTEMIS; HECATE; ROMAN MYTHOLOGY.**

Dido

In Greek mythology, Dido was the founder and queen of Carthage, a city on the northern coast of Africa. She was the daughter of Belus (or Mutto), a king of Tyre in Phoenicia†, and the sister of Pygmalion. Dido is best known for her love affair with the Trojan hero Aeneas†.

King Belus had wanted his son and daughter to share royal power equally after his death, but Pygmalion seized the throne and murdered Dido's husband. Dido and her followers fled from Tyre, landing on the shores of North Africa. There a local ruler named Iarbas agreed to sell Dido as much land as the hide of a bull could cover. Dido cut a bull's hide into thin strips and used it to outline a large area of land. On that site, Dido built Carthage and became its queen.

pyre pile of wood on which a dead body is burned in a funeral ceremony

epic long poem about legendary or historical heroes, written in a grand style

destiny future or fate of an individual or thing

Carthage became a prosperous city. Iarbas pursued Dido, hoping to marry her, but Dido refused. After her husband's death, she had sworn never to marry again. Iarbas would not take no for an answer and even threatened Carthage with war unless Dido agreed to be his wife. Seeing no other alternative, Dido killed herself by throwing herself into the flames of a funeral **pyre.** In another version of the story, she mounted the pyre and stabbed herself, surrounded by her people.

The Roman poet Virgil used part of the story of Dido in his **epic** the *Aeneid*†. In Virgil's account, the Trojan leader Aeneas was shipwrecked on the shore near Carthage at the time when Dido was building the new city. After welcoming Aeneas and his men, the queen fell deeply in love with him. In time, the two lived together as wife and husband, and Aeneas began to act as though he were king of Carthage. Then Jupiter† sent a messenger to tell Aeneas that he could not remain in Carthage. Rather, his **destiny** was to found a new city for the Trojans in Italy.

Dido was devastated when she heard that Aeneas planned to leave. She had believed that the two of them would eventually marry. Aeneas insisted that he had no choice but to obey the gods, and shortly afterward, he and his men set sail for Italy. When Dido saw the ships sail out to sea, she ordered a funeral pyre to be built. She climbed onto to it, cursed Aeneas, and using a sword he had given her, stabbed herself to death. In 1689, the English composer Henry Purcell wrote an opera, *Dido and Aeneas,* that was based on the story and characters from Greek mythology. ***See also*** **AENEAS; AENEID, THE; PYGMALION.**

Dionysus

deity god or goddess

cult group bound together by devotion to a particular person, belief, or god
city-state independent state consisting of a city and its surrounding territory
ritual ceremony that follows a set pattern

satyr woodland deity that was part man and part goat or horse

oracle priest or priestess or other creature through whom a god is believed to speak; also the location (such as a shrine) where such words are spoken
resurrection coming to life again; rising from the dead

Dionysus, the Greek god of fertility, wine, and ecstasy, was popular throughout much of the ancient world. In Rome he was known as Bacchus. A complex **deity,** Dionysus played two very different roles in Greek mythology. As the god of fertility, he was closely linked with crops, the harvest, and the changing of the seasons. As the god of wine and ecstasy, he was associated with drunkenness, madness, and unrestrained sexuality. His nature included a productive, life-giving side and a bestial, destructive side.

Background and Origins. Dionysus did not start out as a Greek god. His **cult** had its roots in Thrace (north of Greece), in Phrygia (in modern Turkey), or possibly on the island of Crete. Many Greek **city-states** at first rejected the cult of Dionysus because of its foreign origins and its wild, drunken **rituals.** When the cult first arrived in Rome, worshipers held their celebrations in secret. However, in both Greece and Rome, the cult of Dionysus overcame resistance and gained many followers.

The most common myth about the origins of Dionysus says that he was the son of Zeus† and of Semele, daughter of the founder of Thebes. Zeus's jealous wife, Hera, wanted to know the identity of the child's father. She disguised herself as Semele's old nurse and went to see Semele. When Semele told her that Zeus was the father, Hera challenged her to prove her claim by having Zeus appear in all his glory. Semele did so. However, because Zeus was the god of lightning, his power was too much for a human to bear. Semele was turned into ashes.

Before Semele died, Zeus pulled Dionysus out of her womb. Then cutting open his thigh, Zeus placed the unborn child inside. A few months later he opened up his thigh, and Dionysus was born. The infant was left with Semele's sister Ino, who disguised him as a girl to protect him from Hera. As punishment for helping Dionysus, Hera drove Ino and her husband insane.

Some legends say that Hera also drove Dionysus insane. Thereafter, Dionysus wandered the world accompanied by his teacher, Silenus, bands of **satyrs,** and his women followers, who were known as maenads. When Dionysus traveled to Egypt, he introduced the cultivation of grapes and the art of winemaking. When he went to Libya, he established an **oracle** in the desert. He also journeyed to India, conquering all who opposed him and bringing laws, cities, and wine to the country. On his way back to Greece, he met his grandmother, the earth goddess Cybele. She cured him of his madness and taught him the mysteries of life and **resurrection.**

This story contains three themes that run through the legend of Dionysus. One theme is the hostility that Dionysus and his cult face both from Hera and from the inhabitants of the places he visits. The second is the association of Dionysus with madness. The third is the idea of death and rebirth, an essential part of Dionysus's identity as god of the harvest and of fertility.

Fertility. Dionysus's influence over fertility extended beyond crops to animals and humans as well. This power made him the

† *See **Names and Places** at the end of this volume for further information.*

Dionysus, the Greek god of wine and fertility, was known to the Romans as Bacchus. This painting, completed by Caravaggio in the late 1590s, shows the youthful god crowned with grape leaves.

symbol of creative forces, the lifeblood of nature. Women flocked to his cult because of its association with the female responsibilities of childbearing and harvesting. According to tradition, these women would abandon their families and travel to the countryside to participate in Dionysia festivals, known in Rome as Bacchanalia. They wore animal skins and carried wands called thyrsi, made of fennel stalks bound together with grapevines and ivy. The thyrsi were symbols of fertility and reproduction and also of intoxication.

During the Dionysia festivals the maenads would enter a trance, dancing to the beat of drums and waving thyrsi. Sometimes they would go into a frenzy during which they gained **supernatural** powers. It was said that the maenads could tear apart animals—and even humans—with their bare hands.

In one myth, Dionysus visited Thebes disguised as a young man and caused the women there to fall under his power. He led them to a mountain outside the city, where they took part in his rituals. Pentheus, the king of Thebes, was furious and imprisoned Dionysus. Miraculously, the chains fell off and the jail cell opened by itself. Dionysus then told Pentheus of the wild celebrations he would see if he disguised himself as a woman and went to the mountain. The king, dressed as a woman, hid in a tree to watch the Dionysia. However, the women saw him and, in their madness, mistook him for a mountain lion. They killed him, tearing him limb from limb.

supernatural related to forces beyond the normal world; magical or miraculous

Wine and Madness. Drunkenness and madness are elements that appear in many of the stories about Dionysus. In one tale, Dionysus disguised himself as a young boy and got drunk on an island near Greece. Some pirates found him and promised to take him to Naxos, which Dionysus said was his home. However, the pirates decided to sell the boy into slavery. Only one of them, Acoetes, objected to the plan. When the pirates steered their ship away from Naxos, the wind died. Suddenly, a tangle of grapevines covered the ship. The oars turned into snakes, clusters of grapes grew on Dionysus's head, and wild animals appeared and played at his feet. Driven to madness, the pirates jumped overboard. Only Acoetes was spared. He sailed the ship to Naxos, where Dionysus made him a priest of the cult. It was on Naxos that Dionysus also met the princess Ariadne, who became his wife.

Dionysus and Apollo

In his discussion of the ancient Greeks, the German philosopher Friedrich Nietzsche used the terms *Dionysian* and *Apollonian* to describe the two sides of human nature. Dionysian urges—sensual and irrational impulses—are named for Dionysus. The term *Apollonian* refers to the rational side of human behavior associated with the god Apollo†. Interestingly, these two gods, with their very different natures, actually shared a shrine at Delphi. Dionysus was said to have the gift of prophecy, and the priests at Delphi honored him almost as much as they honored Apollo.

Titan one of a family of giants who ruled the earth until overthrown by the Greek gods of Olympus

One of the best-known tales about Dionysus concerns King Midas and the golden touch. Dionysus's teacher, Silenus, had a habit of getting drunk and forgetting where he was. One day after drinking, Silenus became lost while traveling in Midas's kingdom. He fell in a whirlpool and would have drowned had not Midas saved him. As a reward, Dionysus granted Midas anything he wished. Midas asked that everything he touched turn to gold. After the wish was granted, however, Midas discovered that all his food turned to gold and he was unable to eat. Then, when he hugged his daughter, she turned to gold too. Dionysus removed Midas's golden touch after the king had learned the price of his greed.

The Dying and Rising God. Because crops die in winter and return in spring, Dionysus was seen as a symbol of death and resurrection. In another story about his birth, Dionysus was the son of Zeus and Demeter, the goddess of crops and vegetation. Hera was jealous of the child and convinced the **Titans** to destroy him. Although Dionysus was disguised as a baby goat, the Titans found him, caught him, and tore him to pieces. They ate all of his body except his heart, which was rescued by Athena†. She gave the heart to Zeus, who gave it to Semele to eat. Semele later gave birth to Dionysus again. The story represents the earth (Demeter) and sky (Zeus) giving birth to the crops (Dionysus), which die each winter and are reborn again in the spring.

Literature and Art. Because of his popularity and the colorful stories about him and his followers, Dionysus has been a favorite subject of writers and artists. He appears in early Greek poetry such as Homer's *Iliad*†, where he is pictured as a young god. He is later mentioned in works of the Greek playwright Euripides† and the Roman poet Ovid†. Many poems and stories by English and American writers such as John Milton, John Keats, and Ralph Waldo Emerson include descriptions of Dionysus or his rituals. Famous sculptors such as Michelangelo have carved images of him, and artists throughout history have used him as the subject for paintings. He is sometimes portrayed as old and bearded and sometimes as youthful. Often he is shown surrounded by powerful animals, such as bulls and goats. ***See also*** **Apollo; Ariadne; Athena; Demeter; Hera; Iliad, The; Midas; Satyrs; Zeus.**

Djang'kawu

In Australian mythology, the Djang'kawu were three sacred beings—a brother and two sisters—who created all life on earth. The Aborigines of Arnhem Land in northern Australia tell the story of the three siblings in a series of 500 songs.

Arriving from heaven in a canoe with their companion Bralbral, the Djang'kawu set off to walk across the land carrying digging sticks called *rangga.* When the Djang'kawu sisters touched the ground with these sticks, they created the water, trees, animals, and all other features of the earth. The sisters were always pregnant, and their children populated the earth.

†*See* ***Names and Places*** *at the end of this volume for further information.*

Originally, the sisters controlled the magic objects that created life. However, one day while they were sleeping, their brother stole these objects. In the beginning, the sisters had both male and female sex organs, but their brother cut off the male parts so that the sisters appeared like other women. The story of the Djang'kawu is a story about fertility and the creation of the living world. It is also about how—according to myth—men control the power to perform sacred **rituals.** ***See also*** **AUSTRALIAN MYTHOLOGY; CREATION STORIES.**

ritual ceremony that follows a set pattern

Dracula

In the history and legend of eastern Europe, Dracula was the popular name of Vlad the Impaler, a merciless Romanian tyrant of the 1400s. Dracula means "heir of the Order of the Dragon," dedicated to fighting the Turks. However, in the worlds of fiction and film, the name *Dracula* has been associated with Count Dracula, the vampire. He was the main character in an 1897 novel by the British author Bram Stoker.

Vlad the Impaler. The historical Vlad the Impaler, or Vlad Tepeş, was prince of Walachia (near Transylvania) and lived from 1431 to 1476. The tales told about him were filled with horror and cruelty. Fond of dining outdoors, Vlad would have his enemies impaled on stakes around the dinner table so that he could listen to them scream as he ate. Once a group of Turkish envoys who came before him refused to remove their turbans. Vlad ordered that the turbans be nailed to their heads. In another story, Vlad told some guests that if they wished, he could put an end to their troubles. They said yes, whereupon he had them locked in a room and burned alive.

Bram Stoker's Dracula. The legends of Vlad the Impaler's inhuman behavior may have contributed to an association of Dracula with vampires, corpses that rise from the grave during the night to drink the blood of humans. However, it was Stoker's novel that forever linked the name *Dracula* with the "undead" bloodsucking creatures of the grave.

In Stoker's book, Count Dracula is a centuries-old vampire of Transylvania, a region in central Romania. During the day, he rests in his coffin, but at night, he rises to feast on human blood. The people he bites turn into vampires themselves. Dracula continues to claim victims until his pursuers succeed in driving a stake through his heart, finally ending his reign of terror.

Stoker's novel became the best-known vampire tale of all time. Produced as a play in 1927, the story was the basis of many movies, starting with the famous 1922 silent film *Nosferatu.* The classic motion picture version of Stoker's story, made in 1931, won international fame for the actor Bela Lugosi, who starred as the black-cloaked Count Dracula. This film established a pattern for vampire-based horror movies that continues to this day. ***See also*** **VAMPIRES.**

Dragons

In myths and legends of the world, dragons are often fire-breathing, reptilelike creatures with wings, huge claws, and a long tail. They are usually portrayed as frightening and destructive monsters. Gods and heroes must slay them in symbolic battles of good over evil. But a few cultures, notably those of China and Japan, view dragons in a positive light and use them as symbols of good fortune.

In ancient times, dragons often represented evil, destruction, and death. The dragon Apophis in Egyptian mythology was the enemy of Ra, the sun god. Babylonian creation myths describe the dragonlike monster Tiamat, who was associated with **chaos.** Dragons also play a role in the Bible, where they are frequently identified with Satan.

chaos great disorder or confusion

Dragons appeared in various Greek and Roman myths. For example, Apollo† fought the dragon Python, which guarded the **oracle** at Delphi. In Greece and Rome, dragons were thought to understand the secrets of the earth. They had both protective and fearsome qualities. As a result, the dragon came to be used as a military symbol. Roman soldiers of the first century A.D. inscribed dragons on the standards that they carried into battle. The ancient Celts† also used the dragon symbol on their battle gear, and to this day a red dragon appears on the flag of Wales.

oracle priest or priestess or other creature through whom a god is believed to speak; also the location (such as a shrine) where such words are spoken

In Norse† mythology, the best-known dragon is Fafnir, a giant who transformed himself into a dragon to guard treasure on which

In China, dragons symbolize power and happiness. They are also believed to bring good fortune and wealth.

†*See **Names and Places** at the end of this volume for further information.*

epic long poem about legendary or historical heroes, written in a grand style

patron special guardian, protector, or supporter

ritual ceremony that follows a set pattern

a curse had been placed. The young hero Sigurd slays Fafnir. The story was retold in the German **epic** the *Nibelungenlied.* In the story of Beowulf, the hero fights a dragon that has been terrorizing the people. He is mortally wounded in the struggle.

Christian legends generally blended the dragon's satanic image with elements of Greek and other mythologies. Many of the stories had symbolic meanings. In one famous legend, St. George, the **patron** saint of England, saved the daughter of a king from a dragon, symbolizing the triumph of the church over the devil. The dragon played a similar symbolic role in Christian art, representing sin overcome by saints and martyrs.

In contrast, the Chinese and Japanese hold the dragon in high regard. In their mythology and tradition, dragons symbolize power, happiness, and fertility and are believed to bring good fortune and wealth. Statues and carvings of dragons are common, and garments are often decorated with the dragon image. ***See also*** **BEOWULF; GEORGE, ST.; MONSTERS; NIBELUNGENLIED; TIAMAT.**

Dreamtime

In the mythology of the Australian Aborigines, Dreamtime, or The Dreaming, is the period of creation when the world took shape and all life began. During Dreamtime, ancestral beings created the landscape, made the first people, and taught the people how to live.

Spirits of Past, Present, and Future. The Aborigines believe that the spirits of ancestral beings that sleep beneath the ground emerged from the earth during Dreamtime. As they wandered across the land, the ancestral beings took on the forms of humans, animals, plants, stars, wind, or rain. During their epic journey, they created hills, plains, and other natural formations. Some of the beings brought forth rain. Some created the first people, and some established the laws by which people would live.

When the ancestral beings lay down upon the wet and still soft rocks, they often left impressions of themselves. The Aborigines believe that the ancestral beings continue to live in the places that bear their mark. There, deep down in the earth, they left various forces, including "child-spirits," which take on human form through a father and a mother on earth. One of the ways in which humans trace their origin to the ancestral beings of Dreamtime is through the child-spirits.

Dreamtime did not end at the time of creation because the ancestral beings and the child-spirits are eternal. When a life ends, the child-spirit returns to the earth and remains there until it comes back again in another human form. Moreover, by participating in certain **rituals,** individuals can reenact the journeys of their ancestors. Ancestral beings and human beings are thus closely and forever linked.

Dreamtime Stories. Different Aboriginal groups tell various Dreamtime stories about their ancestral beings. One group of

northern Australia describes how an ancestral being in the form of a snake sent bats for humans to eat during the Dreamtime. However, the bats flew so high that the people could not capture them. The snake gave up one of his ribs to create the boomerang. Using this weapon, the people could hunt and eat the bats.

The Arrernte people of central Australia speak of a great lizard ancestor. They describe how the lizard created the first people in Dreamtime and gave them tools for survival, such as stone knives and spears. The Arrernte, who consider the lizard sacred, believe that certain waterholes and rock formations mark the places where the great lizard did his work. ***See also*** **Australian Mythology.**

Druids

soothsayer one who foretells events

Druids were priests of an ancient Celtic† religious order. Powerful figures in the Celtic world, they served not only as religious leaders but also as teachers, judges, advisers, **soothsayers,** healers, and poets. The Druids held both religious and political power, leading to some blurring of the line between the spiritual and historical worlds.

Caesar's Account. The earliest records of the Druids date back to the 200s B.C. Various ancient Greek and Roman writers described the beliefs and practices of the Celtic priests, and Welsh and Gaelic poetry also provided some details. However, more complete information about the Druids comes from the writings of Julius Caesar (ca. 100–44 B.C.), the Roman general and statesman.

In his book *The Gallic Wars,* Caesar explained that there were two leading classes in Celtic society: the knights or warriors and the Druids. According to Caesar, the Druids did not have to perform manual labor, serve in the military, or pay taxes. Instead, the members of this learned class devoted their lives to leading religious worship and taking charge of human sacrifices.

Caesar reported that the Druids were highly respected and called on for advice and instruction. They also served as judges for most public and private disputes, from major and minor crimes to arguments about money and property. Every year, the Druids gathered at a sacred place in the territory of the Carnutes, regarded as the center of Gaul. There they settled legal matters and made decisions about awards and punishments. Disobeying the Druids' rulings led to excommunication—expulsion from the order—which was the most severe punishment.

By Caesar's account, training to become a Druid was a long and challenging process, taking up to 20 years. Those who wanted to join the order had to learn the religious laws and traditions and the philosophical principles of the Druids, memorize great numbers of ancient verses, and study the natural world and astronomy.

The Druids' Teachings. The Druids believed in a supreme god, whom they called Be' al, meaning "the source of all beings." The symbol of this supreme being was fire. But the Druids also worshiped many lesser gods.

†*See **Names and Places** at the end of this volume for further information.*

Druids, priests of an ancient Celtic order, served as both religious and political leaders.

The Druids taught that the human soul was **immortal** and that, upon death, it passed into the body of a newborn child. According to Caesar, such teaching was intended to make warriors less afraid of dying and thus increase their courage when they went into battle.

Rituals and Practices. The early Druids regarded the oak tree as sacred and carried out their religious **rituals** in oak forests. In fact, the name *Druid* means "knowing the oak tree" in Celtic. The mistletoe, a plant that often grows on oak trees, also had an important role in the religion. According to the ancient Roman writer Pliny, Druids worshiped the mistletoe because they believed it had dropped from heaven and offered a sign that the oak tree upon which it grew had been selected by their god. Furthermore, the Druids associated the mistletoe with healing powers.

Details of Druid ceremonies are few. However, Pliny did describe a fertility ritual in which a Druid clad in a white robe climbed an oak tree and used a golden sickle to slice off a mistletoe branch. The mistletoe fell onto a white cloak that had been placed below. Then the Druids sacrificed two white bulls, and a feast followed. The symbolism of this ceremony is not entirely understood, although the Druids seemed to associate white with purity.

immortal able to live forever
ritual ceremony that follows a set pattern

Reported in much greater detail was the practice of human sacrifice. The Druids believed that human sacrifices were necessary to win their god's favor. If illness, war, or some other crisis threatened, a number of people would be assembled, placed in wicker containers, and burned alive. Usually these individuals were criminals.

Druids in Myth and Legend. The Druids' powerful central role in religion and society helped earn them a place in mythology. It was believed that the Druids had strange and magical powers and could foretell the future. Some reports described how the Druids would stab some of their sacrificial victims and look for **omens** by observing the flow of blood or examining the victims' insides. It was also said that the Druids used human sacrifice and magic rituals as a means of controlling **supernatural** forces and ensuring prosperity and success.

omen sign of future events

supernatural related to forces beyond the normal world; magical or miraculous

In early Celtic literature, Druids were frequently represented as **prophets** and magicians as well as influential royal advisers. Some accounts told how Druids could read minds and predict

prophet one who claims to have received divine messages or insights

future events, while a few went even farther, characterizing Druids as "shape-shifters" who could take the form of birds or women. Some stories described the Druids as using their magic for evil, for example, turning people into animals.

Druids made frequent appearances in early Irish mythology, notably in the four groups of traditional tales. A Druid who lived in the household of King Conchobhar of Ulster sometimes had more power than the king himself because of his ability to predict the future. The Irish hero Finn was raised by a Druid. Throughout the myths, Druids used their powers of **prophecy** and magic both for good and for evil.

prophecy foretelling of what is to come; also something that is predicted

The image of the Druids changed over the centuries. By the 1700s, Druids as presented in literature had lost much of their connection with the ancient religious order. Some English writers even claimed that the Druids were descendants of the biblical Noah. Others said that the Druids were one of the ten lost tribes of Israel. ***See also*** **CELTIC MYTHOLOGY; FINN.**

Dryads

See *Nymphs.*

Durga

See *Devi.*

Dwarfs and Elves

In myths and tales, dwarfs and elves are small humanlike creatures, often endowed with magical powers. Dwarfs generally look like old men with long beards and are sometimes ugly or misshapen. Elves, known for their mischievous pranks, tend to be smaller in stature than dwarfs. Though usually associated with Scandinavian mythology, dwarfs and elves appear in the myths of many cultures, along with similar creatures such as fairies, gnomes, pixies, and leprechauns.

Dwarfs are sometimes represented as helpful creatures or wise advisers as, for example, in the fairy tale *Snow White and the Seven Dwarfs.* More commonly, though, they are unpleasant, stubborn, and distrustful with an air of mystery about them. They may act in deceitful ways, or they may be openly hostile. In some stories, dwarfs steal food or carry off children and beautiful maidens.

Elves take on a variety of forms. Different cultures have identified elves as nature spirits, minor gods, imaginary beings, dream creatures, and souls of the dead. Like dwarfs, elves have both positive and negative images. In the legend of Santa Claus, they work hard in Santa's toy shop. In other stories, they are mischievous beings who play pranks on humans and animals, such as leading travelers astray.

Scandinavian Dwarfs and Elves. In Norse† mythology, dwarfs and elves are usually male and often live in forests, in mountains, or in out-of-the-way places. There are two kinds of elves: the Dökkalfar, or dark elves, and the Ljosalfar, or light elves.

†*See **Names and Places** at the end of this volume for further information.*

artisan skilled crafts worker

supernatural related to forces beyond the normal world; magical or miraculous

seer one who can predict the future

The Dökkalfar dwell in caves or dark woods. The Ljosalfar live in bright places or in the sky.

Dwarfs and elves of the mountains are highly skilled metalworkers and **artisans** who have **supernatural** powers and make special gifts for the gods, such as a magic spear for Odin, the king of the gods; a ship for Freyja, the goddess of love and beauty; and a hammer for Thor, the god of thunder. But dwarfs and elves of the mines, who keep guard over underground stores of gold and precious stones, are unpredictable and spiteful. This association of dwarfs and elves with mining and precious metals exists in many legends and fairy tales.

Other Mythologies. In Germanic mythology, elves are tiny creatures who can bring disease to people and to cattle or can cause nightmares by sitting on a sleeper's chest. They also steal newborn babies and replace them with deformed elf children. In Central American myths, dwarfs are associated with caves, forests, and fertility. In one story, a Red Dwarf uses his ax to cause sparks that a **seer** interprets in telling someone's fortune. The Bushpeople of South Africa tell of the Cagn-Cagn, dwarfs who killed the god Cagn with the help of ants and later restored him to life.

In North America, dwarf people appear in various Native American myths. For instance, the Awakkule are strong mountain

Dwarfs and elves appear in the myths and legends of many different cultures. In this painting, Thor, the Norse god of thunder, chases a group of dwarfs across a mountain.

dwarfs who act as helpful spirits in Crow mythology. The Wanagemeswak are thin, river-dwelling dwarfs in the mythology of the Penobscot Indians. The Senecas have legends about the Djogeon, little people who live in caves, in deep ditches, or along streams. The Djogeon warn humans about dangers and sometimes bring good fortune. ***See also*** **Leprechauns; Norse Mythology; Santa Claus.**

Dybbuk

In Jewish folklore, a dybbuk (or dibbuk) is the spirit or soul of a dead person that enters a living body and takes possession of it. *Dybbuk* is a Hebrew word meaning "attachment." According to tradition, the dybbuk is a restless spirit that must wander about—because of its sinful behavior in its previous life—until it can "attach" itself to another person. The dybbuk remains within this person until driven away by a religious ceremony.

Belief in such spirits was common in eastern Europe during the 1500s and 1600s. Sometimes people who had nervous or mental disorders were assumed to be possessed by a dybbuk. Often a special rabbi was called to exorcise, or drive out, the evil spirit.

Shloime Ansky wrote a play in Yiddish called *The Dybbuk* in 1916. It concerns a rabbinical student named Khonnon who calls upon Satan to help him win Leye, the woman he loves. When Khonnon dies, he becomes a dybbuk and takes possession of Leye. After she is freed of the spirit, Leye dies, and her spirit joins that of Khonnon.

Echo

nymph minor goddess of nature, usually represented as young and beautiful

In Greek mythology, Echo was a mountain **nymph** who annoyed Hera, queen of the gods, by talking to her constantly. Echo's chatter distracted Hera and prevented her from discovering the love affairs of her husband, Zeus†. As punishment, Hera took away Echo's power of speech so that she could say nothing except the last words spoken by someone else.

Other myths tell of Echo's falling in love with Narcissus, the handsome son of a river god. However, Narcissus rejected Echo because she could only repeat his words. She was so upset that she faded away until only her voice was heard as an echo. Another myths states that Pan, god of the woods, pursued Echo but that she escaped him by running away. The angry Pan caused some shepherds to go mad and tear Echo apart, leaving nothing but her voice to echo through the mountains. Ovid's *Metamorphoses*† and Shakespeare's *Romeo and Juliet* both include passages about Echo. ***See also*** **Hera; Narcissus; Pan.**

Eden, Garden of

According to the book of Genesis in the Old Testament of the Bible, the Garden of Eden was an earthly paradise that was home to Adam and Eve, the first man and woman. The Bible says that God created the garden, planting in it "every tree that is pleasant to the sight, and good for food." Eden was a well-watered, fertile place from which four rivers flowed out into the world.

*†See **Names and Places** at the end of this volume for further information.*

After creating Adam, God placed him in the garden so that he could take care of it. God told Adam that he could eat the fruit from any tree except one: the tree of knowledge of good and evil. God then created animals and birds and gave Adam the task of naming them. Realizing that Adam needed a companion, God caused him to fall asleep, then took one of his ribs and created Eve from it.

Shortly afterward, the serpent—the most cunning of all the animals—approached Eve and asked if God had forbidden her to eat from any of the trees. Eve replied that she and Adam were not allowed to eat from the tree of knowledge of good and evil. The serpent told her that God knew that if they ate from the tree of knowledge they would become like gods. He persuaded Eve to eat the fruit of that tree, and Eve convinced Adam to take a bite as well. After they ate, their eyes were opened to the knowledge of good and evil. They realized they were naked and sewed together fig leaves to cover themselves.

Soon they heard God walking through the garden and, ashamed of their nakedness, they hid themselves. God called out to them and when Adam replied that he was hiding because he was naked, God knew that he had eaten the forbidden fruit. Adam admitted that Eve had given him the fruit to eat. When God asked Eve why she had done this, she told him that the serpent had tempted her. God then expelled them from the garden and punished them by causing women to bear children in pain and forcing men to work and sweat for the food they need to live.

allegory literary and artistic device in which characters represent an idea or a religious or moral principle

The story of the Garden of Eden is an **allegory.** It explains how humans fell from a state of innocence to one in which they must suffer during life and eventually die.

The peoples of ancient Mesopotamia† also believed in an earthly paradise named Eden, located somewhere in the east. According to some ancient sources, the four main rivers of the ancient Near East—the Tigris, Euphrates, Halys, and Araxes—flowed out of the garden. Scholars today debate the origin of the word *Eden.* Some believe it comes from a Sumerian† word meaning "plain." Others say it is from the Persian word *heden,* meaning "garden." ***See also*** **ADAM AND EVE; FIRST MAN AND FIRST WOMAN; SERPENTS AND SNAKES; TREES IN MYTHOLOGY.**

Egyptian Mythology

Bordered by deserts, Egypt's Nile River valley was relatively isolated from other centers of civilization in the ancient Near East for thousands of years. As a result, Egyptian religion remained almost untouched by the beliefs of foreign cultures. The religion included a large and diverse **pantheon** of gods and goddesses, and around these **deities** arose a rich mythology that helped explain the world.

pantheon all the gods of a particular culture
deity god or goddess

Conquest by the Macedonian ruler Alexander the Great in 332 B.C. and by the Romans about 300 years later weakened the Egyptian religion. By about A.D. 400, Christianity had become the dominant faith of the land.

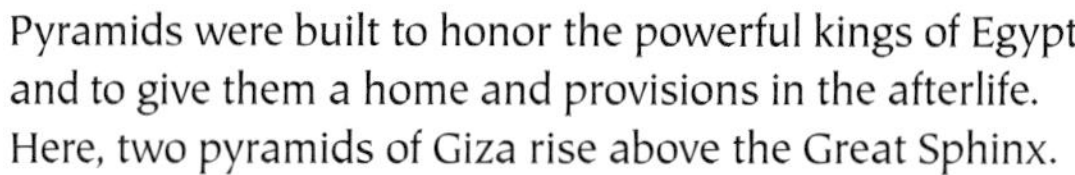

Pyramids were built to honor the powerful kings of Egypt and to give them a home and provisions in the afterlife. Here, two pyramids of Giza rise above the Great Sphinx.

Cults and Deities

cult group bound together by devotion to a particular person, belief, or god

Religion and religious **cults** played a central role in all aspects of ancient Egyptian society. The king, or pharaoh, was the most important figure in religion as well as in the state. His responsibilities included ensuring the prosperity and security of the state through his relationship with the gods.

Role of the King. The ancient Egyptians believed that the king was a divine link between humans and the gods. As a living god, he was responsible for supporting religious cults and for building and maintaining temples to the gods. Through such activities, he helped maintain order and harmony.

chaos great disorder or confusion

The idea of order, or *ma'at,* was a basic concept in Egyptian belief, reflecting such notions as truth, cooperation, and justice. Egyptians imagined their world as being surrounded by **chaos** that constantly threatened to overwhelm *ma'at.* By pleasing the gods through his religious obligations, the king could maintain order and protect society from disorder.

Because of his critical role in promoting the welfare of Egyptian society, the pharaoh was in some ways more important than any

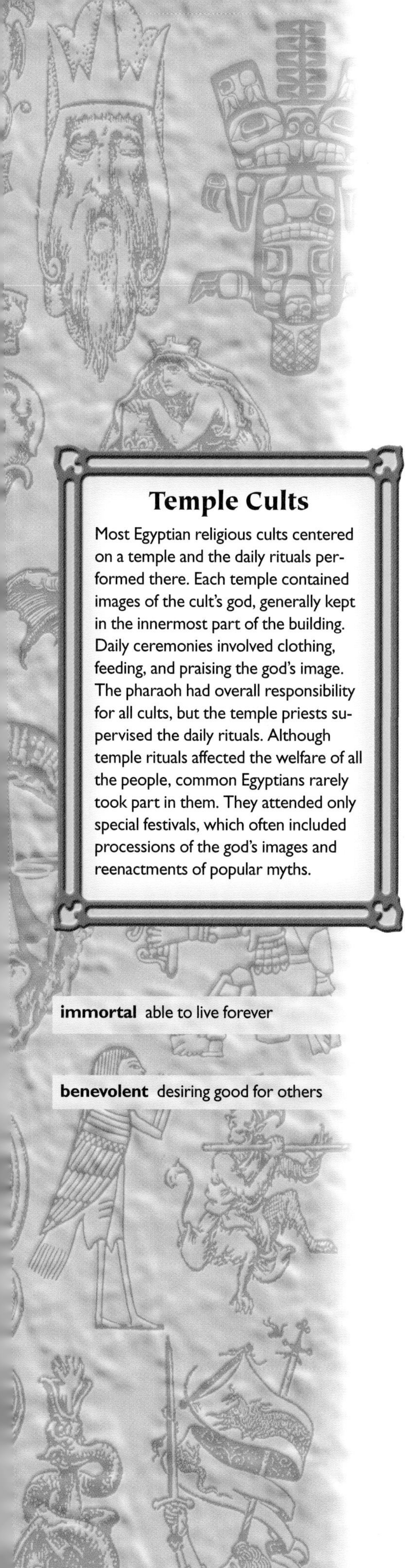

individual god. His official names and titles reflected his special relationship to the gods, particularly to the sun god Ra and the sky god Horus. Some kings sought to gain full status as gods during their lifetimes. Others achieved that position after their deaths.

The Egyptian Pantheon. Ancient Egypt had a remarkably large and diverse pantheon of deities, with many national, regional, and local gods and goddesses. Unlike the gods of some cultures, who lived in a special place in the heavens, Egyptian deities were thought to inhabit the temples of their cults. Daily temple rituals involved caring for the gods and providing them with food, clothing, and other necessities.

Egyptian gods tended to have shifting identities. Many did not have clearly defined characters, and their personalities might vary from one myth to another. Although most deities were known by certain basic associations—such as the connection of the god Ra with the sun—these associations often overlapped with those of other gods. Some deities possessed a collection of names to go with the different sides of their personality. For example, the goddess Hathor, who helped the sun god, was also called the Eye of Ra. Sometimes the names and characters of two or more gods were combined to form one deity, such as the combination of the sky god Amun and Ra (Re) into Amun-Ra. The creator god Atum merged with Ra to become Ra-Atum. Nevertheless, such deities might continue to exist separately as well as in their combined forms.

Temple Cults

Most Egyptian religious cults centered on a temple and the daily rituals performed there. Each temple contained images of the cult's god, generally kept in the innermost part of the building. Daily ceremonies involved clothing, feeding, and praising the god's image. The pharaoh had overall responsibility for all cults, but the temple priests supervised the daily rituals. Although temple rituals affected the welfare of all the people, common Egyptians rarely took part in them. They attended only special festivals, which often included processions of the god's images and reenactments of popular myths.

Egyptian gods also could assume different forms, often combining both human and animal features. If a deity was closely associated with a particular animal or bird, he or she might be shown in art with a human body and the head of that animal or entirely in animal form. Thus, Horus appears with the head of a falcon, Sekhmet with the head of a cat, and Set is portrayed as a donkey or huge dog. Sometimes a god was linked to several animals, each reflecting a different side of his character.

immortal able to live forever

benevolent desiring good for others

The gods were powerful and for the most part **immortal,** but their influence and knowledge had limits. Still, they had the ability to be in several places at the same time and could affect humans in many ways. Although generally **benevolent,** gods could bring misfortune and harm if humans failed to please them or care for them properly.

Egyptian deities were often grouped together in various ways. The earliest grouping was the ennead, which consisted of nine gods and goddesses. The most important of these, the Great Ennead of the city of Heliopolis in northern Egypt, contained the deities associated with creation, death, and rebirth. Another major grouping was the *ogdoad*—four pairs of male and female deities. Triads, found mainly in local centers, generally consisted of a god, a goddess, and a young deity (often male).

Major Deities. Although Egypt had thousands of gods and goddesses, only a few were regarded as major deities. The sun god Ra (Re) was a deity of immense power, considered to be one of the

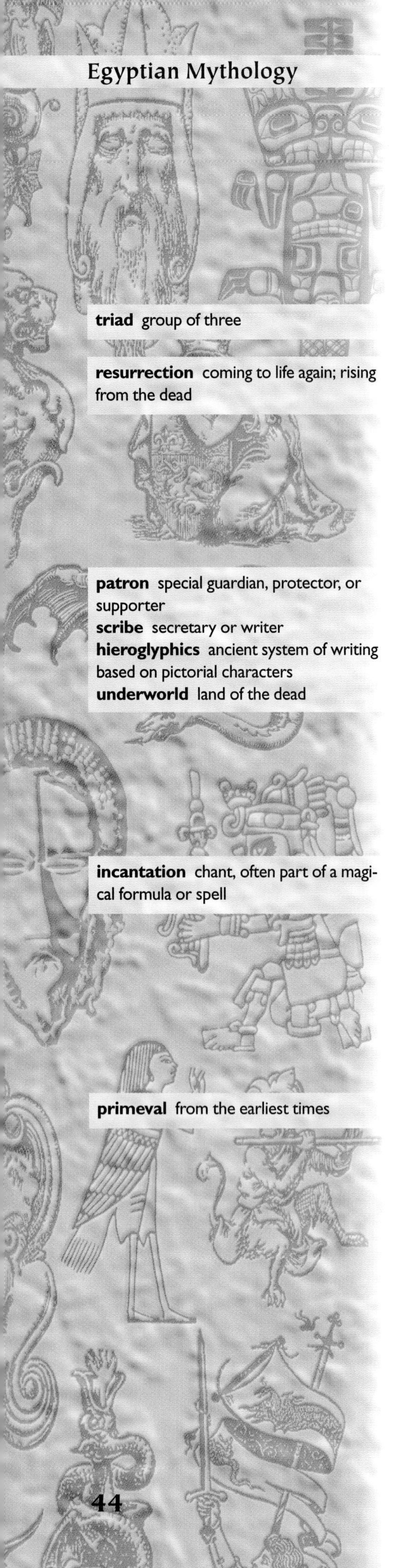

creators of the universe. The combined god Amun-Ra, a mysterious creator spirit, was the source of all life. Ra-Atum represented the evening sun that disappeared each night below the horizon and rose again at dawn. Another sun god, Aten, became the focus of religious reform in the 1300s B.C., when the pharaoh Akhenaten tried to make him the principal god of Egypt.

triad group of three

resurrection coming to life again; rising from the dead

Osiris, Isis, and Horus, who made up the best-known Egyptian **triad** of deities, played leading roles in some of the major Egyptian myths. Osiris, the lord of the underworld and god of death and **resurrection,** was the brother and husband of Isis, a mother goddess of Egypt. Horus was their son. Osiris and Isis were the children of the earth god Geb and the sky goddess Nut. Set, another child of Geb and Nut, changed from a benevolent god to an evil one and murdered his brother Osiris.

patron special guardian, protector, or supporter
scribe secretary or writer
hieroglyphics ancient system of writing based on pictorial characters
underworld land of the dead

One of the oldest goddesses of Egypt was the sky goddess Hathor, a mother goddess sometimes known as a deity of fertility, love, and beauty. Ptah, another ancient deity, was credited in some myths with creating the world and other gods. Thoth, a **patron** of wisdom and arts, was the **scribe** of the gods. He was said to have invented **hieroglyphics,** astronomy, mathematics, and medicine, as well as to have written the Egyptian Book of the Dead. Anubis, a god of the dead, presided over funerals and guided dead souls through the **underworld.**

Major Myths and Themes

incantation chant, often part of a magical formula or spell

Very few actual Egyptian myths have been preserved from ancient times. Modern scholars have reconstructed stories from such sources as hymns, ritual texts, magical **incantations,** images on temple walls, and decorations on tombs and coffins. Some myths about major deities were known and valued throughout Egypt. But many gods and the legends about them had only regional significance. Even the widespread myths often changed or adapted to new situations over the centuries, resulting in numerous variations of a particular story.

primeval from the earliest times

Creation Myths. The Egyptian creation myth has many versions. According to one account, the world was originally a dark, endless chaos of **primeval** waters. The forces of chaos were represented by an *ogdoad* consisting of four pairs of deities: Nun and Naunet, the god and goddess of the primeval waters; Kek and Ketet, the forces of darkness; Heh and Hehet, the spirits of boundlessness; and Amun and Amaunet, the invisible powers. In some versions of the myth, the god Ptah is associated with Nun and plays a central role in creation.

Within the waters of chaos, the spirit of creation waited to take form. When a primeval mound rose above the waters, Amun (or Ra) emerged and used divine powers to establish order *(ma'at)* out of the chaos. The spirit of creation (Amun or Ra—or sometimes Ptah) then made other gods and humans to inhabit the world. Some accounts say that the gods were formed from the sweat of the creator spirit and that humans came from his tears.

Related Entries
Other entries related to Egyptian mythology are listed at the end of this article.

Another part of the Egyptian creation myth concerned the formation of the Great Ennead of Heliopolis. The first of these nine gods was Ra-Atum, who emerged from the primeval waters and created Shu, the god of air, and Tefnet, the goddess of moisture. Shu and Tefnet united to produce the earth god Geb and sky goddess Nut. Geb and Nut stayed very close together, leaving no room for anything to exist between them. Finally Shu separated the two, providing space for other creatures. Geb and Nut eventually had two pairs of male-female twins: Osiris and Isis and Set and Nephthys. The birth of these gods and goddesses completed the ennead.

Solar Myths. Another group of Egyptian myths involved the sun gods and the daily cycle of their movement. According to one story, the sun god was born each day at dawn and crossed the sky

Egyptian Deities

Deity	Role
Amun	supreme god, combined with the sun god Ra to form a new deity called Amun-Ra, who was king of the gods and creator of the universe
Anubis	god of the dead
Aten	personification of the sun and later an all-powerful and creator god under the pharaoh Akhenaten
Atum	god of the sun and creation
Geb	god of the earth
Hathor	mother goddess associated with fertility and love, goddess of the sky
Horus	sun god and sky god, ruler of Egypt, identified with the pharaoh
Isis	mother goddess
Nut	goddess of the sky and mother goddess
Osiris	god of the underworld and judge of the dead
Ptah	creator god, patron of sculpting and metalworking
Ra (Re)	sun god, combined with the supreme god Amun to form a new deity called Amun-Ra, who was king of the gods and creator of the universe
Set	god of violent and chaotic forces
Thoth	god of wisdom and knowledge, patron of scribes

The ancient Egyptians believed that kings were living gods. Here, King Horemheb's tomb at the Valley of the Kings in Thebes is decorated with the figures of many gods.

in a boat filled with other gods and spirits. At nightfall, he descended to the underworld, where he traveled throughout the night, only to be born again the next day. During his passage through the sky and the underworld, the sun god faced dangers from a giant snake named Apep (or Apophis) and other enemies who tried to interrupt his journey.

The Egyptians celebrated the sun's cycle daily in temples and sang hymns and incantations to help ensure that the sun god would escape danger and continue his journey. They believed that the movements of the sun god made it possible for the world to be created anew each day.

Myth and Magic

Magic played an important role in Egyptian religion, often providing a way to avoid or control misfortune. Magical spells might include versions of myths. All gods had secret, divine names that carried magical powers. One spell told the story of how Isis discovered the secret name of Ra, which she then used to increase her own magical skills. Many spells were used to treat the bites of snakes and scorpions, generally regarded as symbols of the forces of chaos. The god Thoth, a patron of wisdom, was closely connected with magic.

Myths of Osiris. According to Egyptian mythology, Osiris was one of the most important pharaohs. In time, his cult rivaled those of Ra and Amun, and myths about Osiris were widespread. Most of the stories involve three basic themes: the struggle between good and evil, the cycle of birth and rebirth, and the judgment of the dead.

As pharaoh, Osiris civilized the Egyptian people by introducing agriculture, establishing laws, and teaching them to worship the gods. Osiris decided to travel around in the world to bring civilization to other peoples. During his absence, he left his sister-wife, Isis, in charge.

By the time Osiris returned to Egypt, his evil brother Set had concocted a plot to kill him. Set had crafts workers build a beautifully decorated box to the measurements of Osiris's body. At a lavish banquet, Set displayed the box and announced that he would give it to the person whose body fit in it exactly. When Osiris lay in the box, Set and his supporters closed the top and

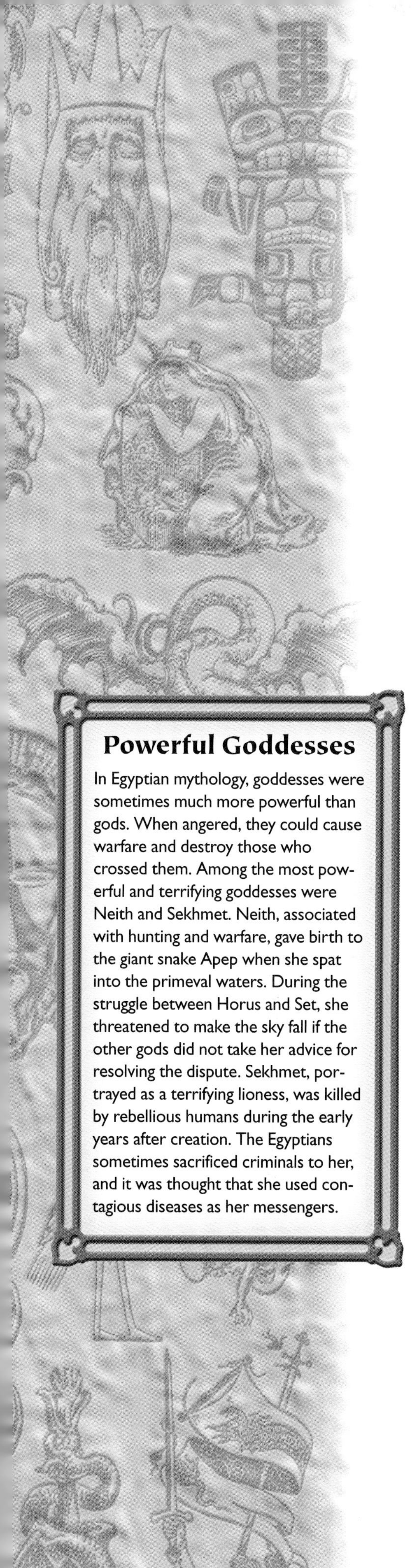

nailed it shut. Then they carried the box to the Nile River and threw it in the water.

When Isis heard of Set's treachery, she was overcome with grief and set out to find her husband's body. During the course of her travels, she learned that the box had floated to the shores of the land of Byblos and had become trapped in the branches of a tree. The tree had grown to a great size, and the king of Byblos had cut it down to make a pillar for one of the rooms in his palace.

Isis went to Byblos and recovered the box. Then she brought it back to Egypt and hid it. However, Set discovered the box and cut Osiris's body into many pieces, scattering them all over Egypt. Accompanied by her son Horus and sister Nephthys, Isis gathered the pieces and used her magical powers to bring the dead Osiris back to life. Osiris then became the king of the gods and the underworld.

To avenge his father and to punish Set for his evil deeds against Osiris, Horus fought his uncle three times. Their battles represented a struggle between good and evil. Horus won each battle, and in the end, the gods decided that he was the rightful heir to the thrones of both Upper and Lower Egypt. Set was forced to accept this judgment. With Horus as pharaoh, Isis went to live with Osiris in the underworld, where he ruled as lord of the dead.

The underworld and the idea of the afterlife played a central role in Egyptian religion. When humans died, their souls began a difficult journey through the underworld. Spells and incantations helped them on their way, and these eventually were collected in a group of texts known as the Book of the Dead.

When the dead person's soul reached Osiris's throne room, it was placed on a scale balanced by a white feather symbolizing truth. Osiris, assisted by Horus, Anubis, and Thoth, sat in judgment. Individuals found innocent of various sins could live among the gods until their bodies were one day resurrected and reunited with the soul. Those found guilty were condemned to eternal torment.

Powerful Goddesses

In Egyptian mythology, goddesses were sometimes much more powerful than gods. When angered, they could cause warfare and destroy those who crossed them. Among the most powerful and terrifying goddesses were Neith and Sekhmet. Neith, associated with hunting and warfare, gave birth to the giant snake Apep when she spat into the primeval waters. During the struggle between Horus and Set, she threatened to make the sky fall if the other gods did not take her advice for resolving the dispute. Sekhmet, portrayed as a terrifying lioness, was killed by rebellious humans during the early years after creation. The Egyptians sometimes sacrificed criminals to her, and it was thought that she used contagious diseases as her messengers.

Legacy of Egyptian Mythology

The influence of Egyptian mythology and religion extended beyond the kingdom's borders. The ancient Greeks and Romans adopted some of Egypt's gods and myths, suitably modified to fit their cultures. Egyptian cults, particularly that of Isis, also spread to Greece and Rome. In his book *The Golden Ass,* Roman philosopher Lucius Apuleius mentions festivals of Isis, and the Roman historian Plutarch wrote down one of the most complete versions of the myth of Osiris and Isis.

Egyptian mythology has inspired modern writers, artists, and composers as well. The novel *The Egyptian* (1949) by Finnish author Mika Waltari refers to the supremacy of Aten over other gods. The opera *Aida* (1869) by Italian composer Giuseppe Verdi is set in ancient Egypt and mentions the god Ptah. ***See also*** **AFTERLIFE; AMUN; ANIMALS IN MYTHOLOGY; ANUBIS; ATEN; ATUM; CREATION STORIES; HATHOR; HORUS; ISIS; NUT; OSIRIS; PTAH; RA (RE); SET; THOTH; UNDERWORLD.**

El

deity god or goddess

In the mythology of the ancient Near East, El was the supreme god of the Canaanites†. He was the creator **deity,** the father of gods and men, and the highest judge and authority in all divine matters and human affairs. In the Old Testament of the Bible, the creator deity is referred to as El, Elohim (a form of El), or Yahweh.

In Canaanite mythology, El was usually represented as an elderly man with a long beard. He was believed to live on Mount Saphon, near the ancient Syrian city of Ugarit. A highly respected deity, El was all-knowing and all-powerful, wise and compassionate. He was sometimes referred to as "the Bull" and was generally shown as a seated figure wearing a crown with bull's horns. The bull suggested El's strength and creative force.

Despite his religious significance, El did not play an active role in Canaanite mythology. Most myths were about the actions of others and involved El indirectly. For example, one story from Ugarit concerned Aqhat, son of King Danel. In return for the king's hospitality, the craftsman god Kothar gave Aqhat his bow and arrows. The goddess Anat wanted the bow and tried to buy it with gold and silver. When Aqhat refused, the goddess offered to give him **immortality** in exchange for the bow. Aqhat rudely rejected her offer, telling the goddess that she could not make immortal a man destined to die.

immortality ability to live forever

Angry about having her offer rejected, Anat asked for and received El's permission to have Aqhat killed. The young man's death brought drought and crop failure. Anat cried over his death and said she would bring him back to life so that the earth might be fertile again. Unfortunately, the tablets containing this myth are in such bad condition that the ending of the story is difficult to interpret. ***See also*** **Anat; Semitic Mythology.**

El Dorado

The legend of El Dorado was about a fabulously wealthy city of gold and the king who ruled over it. The story sprang up shortly after the first Spanish explorers landed in Central and South America.

Local people told tales of a rich king who plastered his body with gold dust and then dived into a sacred lake to wash it off. Afterward, he would toss gold into the lake as an offering to the gods. The Spanish called the king El Dorado—The Gilded One—because his body was gilded, or covered, in gold. As the tale spread, the city he ruled came to be called El Dorado. Eventually, the meaning of the name changed to include any mythical region that contained great riches.

An early version of the El Dorado legend placed the city near Lake Guatavita not too far from modern Bogotá, Colombia. The story was based on the Muisca people who performed a ceremony similar to that in the legend. The Muisca king, covered with gold dust, boarded a raft in the lake and made offerings to the gods. Both Spaniards and Germans searched the region in 1538 but failed to find El Dorado. They looked in a number of other places as well.

*†See **Names and Places** at the end of this volume for further information.*

Local inhabitants usually claimed that El Dorado was somewhere far away in the hope that the Europeans would search elsewhere and leave them in peace. Men as famous as Sir Walter Raleigh spent years in South America looking for legendary golden cities such as Manoa and Omagua. Other places mentioned in stories were Paititi, a land of gold located in Paraguay, and the City of the Ceasars, an invisible golden city in Chile. Several bloody expeditions were launched to find these imaginary kingdoms. One of the most tragic was led by a rebel soldier named Lope de Aguirre, a brutal madman who proclaimed himself king and was murdered by one of his followers.

El Dorado made its way into literature. In *Candide,* a novel by the French writer Voltaire, the main character accidentally discovers the rich city. Edgar Allan Poe's poem *Eldorado* refers to the legend, as does *Paradise Lost* by English poet John Milton.

Electra

Titan one of a family of giants who ruled the earth until overthrown by the Greek gods of Olympus

In Greek mythology, there are two figures called Electra. The earlier Electra was one of seven daughters of the **Titan** Atlas† and Pleione. The seven sisters together were known as the Pleiades and eventually became a constellation, or group of stars, by the same name. According to the story, Electra was the mother of Dardanus, the founder of the city of Troy†. When the Greeks destroyed Troy during the Trojan War†, she left her place in the constellation to avoid seeing the city's destruction.

The second Electra appears in plays by the Greek writers Aeschylus, Sophocles†, and Euripides†. In their works, Electra was the daughter of Agamemnon, the leader of the Greeks in the Trojan War, and his wife, Clytemnestra. While Agamemnon was away at war, Clytemnestra took a lover named Aegisthus, and they plotted to murder Agamemnon when he returned. They also wanted to kill Orestes, Agamemnon's young son, but his sister Electra rescued him and sent him away to live in safety.

Electra helped her brother Orestes plan the murder of Clytemnestra and Aegisthus to avenge the death of their father.

As an adult, Orestes returned home with his cousin Pylades to avenge his father's murder. Although Orestes disguised himself to enter the palace, Electra recognized him. She helped her brother and Pylades murder Clytemnestra and Aegisthus. It was said that Electra later married Pylades.

Stories concerning Electra also appear in the play *Mourning Becomes Electra,* written by Eugene O'Neill in 1931, and the 1909 opera *Elektra* by Richard Strauss. In psychology, an "Electra complex" refers to a woman whose unresolved love for her father harms her relationships with other men. ***See also*** **AGAMEMNON; CLYTEMNESTRA; ORESTES; PLEIADES.**

Elves

See ***Dwarfs and Elves.***

Elysium

immortal able to live forever

underworld land of the dead

In Greek and Roman mythology, Elysium was the place of rest for the dead who were blessed by the gods. It was also known as the Elysian Fields or the Elysian Plain. Originally, only heroes whom the gods had made **immortal** went to Elysium. Eventually, it became the destination of anyone who had lived a righteous life.

Writers disagree about the location of Elysium. The Greek poet Homer† said it was located at the ends of the earth by the banks of the Oceanus River. Hesiod† and Pindar† claimed Elysium was in the Isles of the Blessed, which were to be found in the Western Ocean. Later Greek and Roman mythology placed Elysium in the **underworld.** In Virgil's *Aeneid*†, the hero Aeneas† sees his father in the Elysian Fields. The major street in Paris known as the Champs Elysées takes its name from this mythical place. ***See also* AFTERLIFE.**

Enkidu

immortal able to live forever

epic long poem about legendary or historical heroes, written in a grand style

underworld land of the dead

The "wild man" Enkidu is an important character in the *Epic of Gilgamesh,* a collection of stories about a Sumerian† king who wanted to become **immortal.** As the rival and then the best friend of the hero Gilgamesh, Enkidu represents the force of untamed nature, a force that civilized, city-dwelling society both feared and admired.

Having decided to make a "strong and courageous man" who would be "just like Gilgamesh," the gods created Enkidu from a pinch of clay thrown onto a plain. Enkidu came into life full-grown, hairy, and wild. He lived like an animal, eating grass and drinking with the beasts at water holes.

Hearing of the untrappable wild man, Gilgamesh sent a woman to tame him and teach him the ways of civilization. After seven days with her, Enkidu could no longer live as an animal, innocent of human ways. He began shaving and wearing clothes, and the animals fled from him. Enkidu had taken his first step into human society. In this part of the **epic,** he becomes a symbol of the shift from primitive to civilized life that had occurred across Mesopotamia† centuries earlier.

Enkidu went to Gilgamesh's city, Uruk, where he challenged the king to a wrestling match. Drawn together by mutual respect and the desire for companionship, the two men became the closest of friends. They accomplished great feats of courage and strength together, but after they killed a divine bull, the gods punished them by sending illness to Enkidu. The "wild man" wasted and died. At the end of the epic, Enkidu returned from the **underworld,** the "House of Darkness and Dust," to tell Gilgamesh of the dismal fate that awaits all who enter the land of the dead. ***See also* GILGAMESH.**

Enlil

In the mythology of ancient Mesopotamia†, Enlil ("lord of the wind") was the storm god and the god of earth and air. He was one of a trio of major gods that included Anu and Ea, the gods of heaven and water. Enlil played an important role in creation, separating

†*See **Names and Places** at the end of this volume for further information.*

heaven from earth, causing seeds to grow on the land, and bringing order and harmony to the universe.

deity god or goddess

underworld land of the dead

A complex **deity** who destroyed as well as created, Enlil appeared in many Mesopotamian myths. In one story, he was sent to the **underworld** as punishment for raping the goddess Ninlil. She followed him there and gave birth to their son, the moon god Nanna. Because Nanna would die in the underworld, Enlil devised a scheme that allowed his son to escape and return to the heavens so that he could light up the night sky.

Another well-known myth revealed Enlil's destructive nature. According to this tale, the other gods rebelled against Enlil because he made them work too hard. As a solution, the gods decided to create humans to labor for them. This seemed fine for a while, but as the human population increased, their noise kept Enlil awake at night. Angered by this disruption, Enlil sent disease, drought, and a great flood to reduce the number of people on the earth.

Enlil also appeared in stories in the role of preserver and creator. As the source of rain, he nourished fields and crops. He also introduced humans to the pickax and taught them how to use it to build cities. In some myths, Enlil was associated with agriculture, fertility, and the seasons. ***See also*** **ANU; FLOODS; SEMITIC MYTHOLOGY.**

Enuma Elish

epic long poem about legendary or historical heroes, written in a grand style

Enuma Elish was the creation myth of the people of Babylonia, a civilization of the ancient Near East. Written in the form of an **epic,** Enuma Elish gives the Babylonian account of the origin of the world. The myth is similar to the biblical story of creation in the book of Genesis.

The poem, inscribed on seven tablets, probably dates from around 1100 B.C., although earlier, unrecorded versions of it may have existed long before that time. Its title, meaning "When on high," comes from the first line of the epic, which begins: "When on high the heaven had not been named/Firm ground below had not been called by name."

deity god or goddess
primeval from the earliest times
chaos great disorder or confusion
patron special guardian, protector, or supporter

Enuma Elish tells how the Babylonian **deities** were born from a **primeval** goddess named Tiamat, a vast ocean of formless **chaos,** sometimes described as a dragon. Marduk, the **patron** god of the city of Babylon, defeated Tiamat and her army of monsters. He then divided her corpse into two parts, one of which became heaven and one earth. He also killed Tiamat's ally, Kingu, and created human beings from Kingu's blood to serve the gods. Marduk's victory brought order to the universe.

Enuma Elish had political as well as religious meaning for the Babylonians. By identifying the heroic creator god as Marduk of Babylon, the myth justified the city's dominance over the region. For hundreds of years, celebrations to mark the beginning of the new year in Babylon included a recital of *Enuma Elish* in many of the city's main temples. ***See also*** **CREATION STORIES; MARDUK; TIAMAT.**

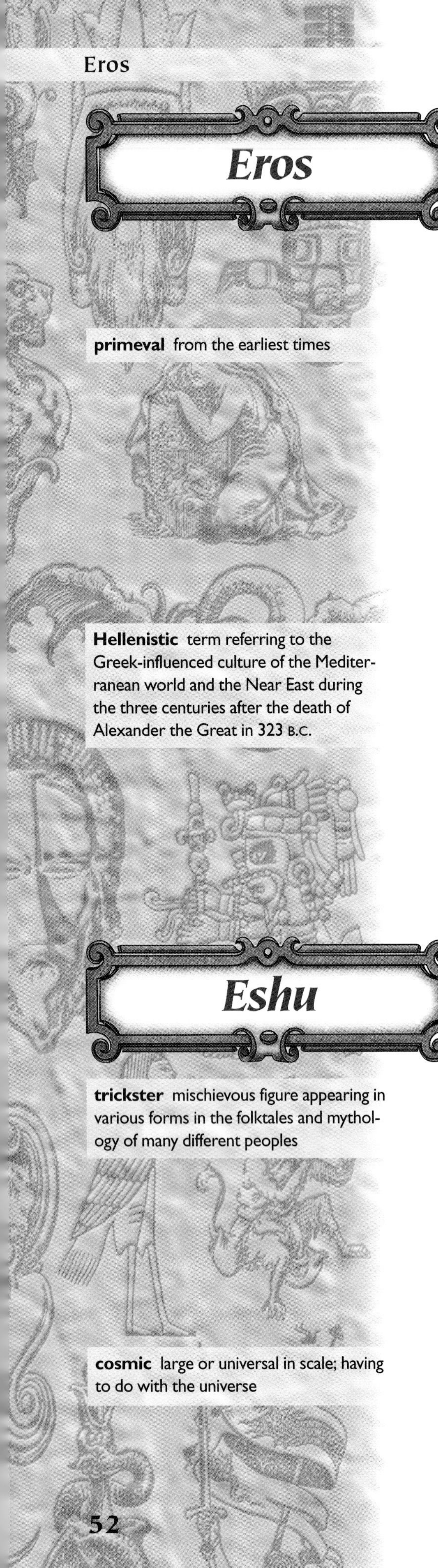

Eros

In Greek mythology, Eros was the god of erotic, or sexual, love. The Romans called him Amor or Cupid, from the words *amor* meaning "love" and *cupido* meaning "desire." His role in mythology changed over time, as did images of him in sculpture and other works of art.

primeval from the earliest times

Many different accounts of Eros's birth exist. One of the oldest is found in the *Theogony* (History of the Gods), written by the Greek Hesiod† around 700 B.C. Hesiod claimed that Eros, like Gaia the earth goddess, was one of the offspring of the **primeval** emptiness called Chaos. He believed Eros to be one of the first powers in the universe, representing the force of attraction and harmony that filled all of creation.

In later times, the Greeks spoke of Eros as the son of Aphrodite (Venus), the goddess of love, and Ares (Mars)†. Eros became specifically identified with passionate love and fertility. The Greeks portrayed him as a handsome young man with a bow and arrow. The people he struck with his arrows were bound to fall in love. Eros himself fell in love with a beautiful human woman named Psyche.

Hellenistic term referring to the Greek-influenced culture of the Mediterranean world and the Near East during the three centuries after the death of Alexander the Great in 323 B.C.

During **Hellenistic** times, another image of Eros became popular—that of a mischievous, chubby, winged boy or infant. He was often seen holding his bow and arrow and wearing a blindfold to show that he shot his arrows at random. Artists sometimes multiplied him into many small winged figures. After the rise of Christianity, these little cupids became identified with baby angels. Eros appears throughout literature in works such as the *Aeneid* by Virgil† and the *Metamorphoses* by Ovid† as well as in the poems *Endymion* and *Ode to Psyche* by the English poet John Keats. ***See also*** **APHRODITE; GREEK MYTHOLOGY; PSYCHE; VENUS.**

Eshu

Eshu, also known as Elegba or Legba, is a **trickster** god of the Yoruba people of Nigeria in West Africa. He is unpredictable, sly, and fond of pranks that can be cruel and disruptive. Eshu, who knows all the languages spoken on earth, serves as a messenger between the gods and people. He also carries up to heaven the sacrifices that people offer to the gods.

trickster mischievous figure appearing in various forms in the folktales and mythology of many different peoples

According to one story, Eshu became the messenger after playing a trick on the High God. He stole yams from the god's garden, used the god's slippers to make footprints there, and then suggested that the god had stolen the yams himself. Annoyed, the High God ordered Eshu to visit the sky every night and tell him what happened on earth during the day.

Eshu enjoys confusion. Many stories tell of tricks he plays that cause arguments between friends or between husbands and wives. In one myth he lured the sun and moon into changing places, which upset the **cosmic** order. As the god of change, chance, and uncertainty, Eshu is sometimes paired with Ifa, a god representing order. In one tale Eshu claimed that he would ruin Ifa, who laughingly replied, "If you transform yourself, I shall do the same, and if I die, you will die, for so it has been ordained in heaven." In this way,

cosmic large or universal in scale; having to do with the universe

†*See* ***Names and Places*** *at the end of this volume for further information.*

This carved wood sculpture shows Eshu, the trickster god of the Yoruba people of Nigeria in West Africa.

order and disorder are forever paired, and neither can exist without the other. ***See also*** **African Mythology; Tricksters.**

Eurydice

nymph minor goddess of nature, usually represented as young and beautiful
underworld land of the dead

In Greek mythology, Eurydice was a dryad, or tree **nymph,** who became the bride of Orpheus, a legendary hero known for his musical skills. While walking in the countryside one day soon after their wedding, Eurydice met Aristaeus, the son of the god Apollo†. Aristaeus tried to seize her. Eurydice fled but was bitten by a poisonous snake and died. Overcome with grief at his wife's death, Orpheus decided to go to the **underworld** and bring her back.

Orpheus gained entrance to the underworld by charming its guardians with his singing and playing of the lyre. The beauty of

his music persuaded Hades, the ruler of the underworld, to allow Eurydice to return to the world of the living, but Hades made one condition. Orpheus and Eurydice must not look back as they left his realm. The couple set out on the long, difficult journey back to earth. Toward the end of their trip, just as the darkness of the underworld gave way to the light of earth, Orpheus turned back to Eurydice to share his joy with her. But as he looked at her, Eurydice disappeared, returning to the underworld forever. The story of Orpheus and Eurydice appears in various poems, plays, and operas. ***See also*** **Greek Mythology; Hades; Orpheus; Underworld.**

Excalibur

In Arthurian legends, Excalibur was King Arthur's magic sword. There are two accounts of how Arthur obtained Excalibur. According to one version, the sword had been plunged into a stone and remained firmly fixed there. It was said that whoever pulled the sword from the stone would be the next king of England. Some of the strongest men in the land attempted to pull the sword out, but none succeeded until the young Arthur pulled it out with ease. In the other story, Arthur received Excalibur from the Lady of the Lake, a mysterious figure who lived in an enchanted underwater realm.

King Arthur kept Excalibur for many years, and it served him well. In time, however, Arthur was mortally wounded during a rebellion led by his nephew Mordred. As he lay dying, the king ordered a companion, Sir Bedivere, to cast Excalibur into a nearby lake. Reluctant to throw away such a valuable weapon, Sir Bedivere twice failed to follow Arthur's order and hid the sword instead. However, Arthur knew that his friend had disobeyed his wishes and ordered him again to cast away the sword. Sir Bedivere finally threw Excalibur far out over the water. An arm clothed in white rose from the water, grasped the sword, waved it in the air, and disappeared beneath the water. The Lady of the Lake had taken back Excalibur. ***See also*** **Arthur, King; Arthurian Legends; Camelot; Celtic Mythology; Lady of the Lake.**

Fates

deity god or goddess
destiny future or fate of an individual or thing

allot to assign a portion or share

The Fates were three female **deities** who shaped people's lives. In particular, they determined how long a man or woman would live. Although a number of cultures held the notion of three goddesses who influenced human **destiny,** the Fates were most closely identified with Greek mythology.

The Greek image of the Fates developed over time. The poet Homer†, credited with composing the *Iliad* and the *Odyssey,* spoke of Fate as a single force, perhaps simply the will of the gods. Another poet, Hesiod†, portrayed the Fates as three old women. They were called the Keres, which means "those who cut off," or the Moirai, "those who **allot.**" They may have originated as goddesses who were present at the birth of each child to determine the course of the child's future life.

The parentage of the Fates is something of a mystery. Hesiod described them as daughters of Nyx, or night, but he also said that

†*See* ***Names and Places*** *at the end of this volume for further information.*

they were the children of Zeus, the chief of the gods, and Themis, the goddess of justice. The Fates had power over Zeus and the gods, and many ancient authors, including the Roman poet Virgil†, stressed that even the king of the gods had to accept the decisions of the Fates. Occasionally, however, fate could be **manipulated.** One myth says that Apollo† tricked the Fates into letting his friend Admetus live beyond his assigned lifetime. Apollo got the Fates drunk, and they agreed to accept the death of a substitute in place of Admetus.

manipulate to influence or control in a clever or underhanded way

Hesiod called the Fates Clotho ("the spinner"), Lachesis ("the allotter"), and Atropos ("the unavoidable"). In time, the name Clotho, with its reference to spinning thread, became the basis for images of the three Fates as controlling the thread of each person's life. Clotho spun the thread, Lachesis measured it out, and Atropos cut it with a pair of shears to end the life span. Literary and artistic works often portray the Fates performing these tasks.

The Romans called the Fates Parcae, "those who bring forth the child." Their names were Nona, Decuma, and Morta. Nona and Decuma were originally goddesses of childbirth, but the Romans adopted the Greek concept of the three weavers of Fate and

In Greek mythology, the Fates were three goddesses who shaped people's lives. They determined how long a man or woman would live.

triad group of three

added a third goddess to complete the **triad.** In addition, they sometimes referred to fate or destiny as a single goddess known as Fortuna.

A triad of goddesses linked with human destiny appears in various forms in mythology. In addition to the Moirai, the Greeks recognized a triad of goddesses called the Horae, who were associated with the goddess Aphrodite†. Their names were Eunomia (Order), Dike (Destiny), and Irene (Peace.) The Norse† called their three Fates the Norns: Urth, the past; Verthandi, the present; and Skuld, the future. Sometimes the Norns were referred to as the Weird Sisters, from the Norse word *wyrd,* meaning "fate." The Celts† had a triad of war goddesses, collectively known as the Morrigan, who determined the fate of soldiers in battle. The image of a triple goddess may be linked to very ancient worship of a moon goddess in three forms: a maiden (the new moon), a mature woman (the full moon), and a crone (the old moon).

Fatima

prophet one who claims to have received divine messages or insights

Born in the holy city of Mecca in Arabia in about 605, Fatima was the daughter of the **prophet** Muhammad, the founder of Islam. Generations of Muslims have revered her as one of four "perfect women." (They also place Mary, the mother of Jesus, in this group.) Fatima is especially important to the Shiite sect of Islam.

Muhammad had other sons and daughters, but they all died young or failed to produce heirs. Fatima stayed close to her father and nursed him at his deathbed. When the prophet died, a split developed over Muslim leadership. Fatima's support for her husband Ali's claim as leader led to the establishment of the Shiite sect. Later Shiites viewed Hasan and Husayn, the sons of Fatima and Ali, as the rightful heirs to Muhammad and the Islamic tradition.

Although Fatima was a historical figure, many aspects of her life took on the dimensions of myth, and she has become the subject of various legends. In one, for example, Fatima was a virgin who had three sons, and she possessed miraculous powers. Some stories describe her as the incarnation, or human form, of the Arabian moon goddess. Fatima appears as the holy woman in a story about Aladdin, *Thousand and One Nights.*

Faust

The legend of Faust is well known in Germany and western Europe. The hero of the tale, a German magician named Faust, or Faustus, agreed to sell his soul to the devil in exchange for youth, knowledge, earthly pleasures, and magical powers.

The legend is based on a historical figure, a wandering German scholar who lived between about 1480 and 1540. Contemporary accounts describe him as a magician with an evil reputation who was associated with black magic. Although a relatively minor figure, he inspired many stories that developed into the Faust legend.

To acquire greater wisdom, power, and pleasure, Faust turned away from God and made a pact with the devil, Mephistopheles. But in selling his soul, he gained eternal damnation. Faust's tale

*†See **Names and Places** at the end of this volume for further information.*

serves as a warning for those seeking to fulfill their earthly desires without the help of God.

The legend became the basis for *Doctor Faustus,* a 1604 play by English writer Christopher Marlowe; *Faust,* a two-part drama by German poet Johann von Goethe, published in 1808 and 1832; and *Doctor Faustus,* a 1947 novel by German author Thomas Mann. The story has also inspired musical works, including the operas *The Damnation of Faust* (1846) by Hector Berlioz and *Faust* (1859) by Charles Gounod. ***See also*** **Devils and Demons; Hell.**

Fenrir

Fenrir, a monstrous wolf, was one of three terrible children of the Norse† **trickster** god Loki and the giantess Angrboda. Their other children—Jormungand, a giant serpent, and Hel, the goddess of the dead—were thrown out of Asgard, the home of the gods, by Odin†. But Odin felt that the gods should look after Fenrir.

trickster mischievous figure appearing in various forms in the folktales and mythology of many different peoples

In time, Fenrir grew incredibly large, and only Odin's son Tyr was brave enough to approach and feed him. The gods finally decided to chain the beast, but Fenrir broke the two huge chains they made to restrain him. Asked by the gods to create something that would hold Fenrir, the dwarfs produced a silky ribbon called Gleipnir. To make it, they used the sound of a cat moving, the beard of a woman, the roots of a mountain, the sinews of a bear, the breath of a fish, and the spit of a bird.

The gods took Fenrir to an isolated island and challenged him to prove that he was stronger than Gleipnir. Because the ribbon seemed so weak, Fenrir suspected it was magical. He allowed himself to be bound with it only after Tyr agreed to put his hand in Fenrir's mouth. When Fenrir found that he could not break Gleipnir, he bit off Tyr's hand. The gods put a sword in Fenrir's open mouth to quiet him.

chaos great disorder or confusion

According to legend, Fenrir will be released during the **chaos** just before Ragnarok, the final battle in which the gods of Asgard will be killed. Fenrir will swallow Odin during the battle and then be killed himself. ***See also*** **Animals in Mythology; Norse Mythology; Ragnarok; Tyr.**

Finn

Finn, also known as Finn MacCumhail or Finn MacCool, is the hero of a series of Irish legends known as the Fionn (or Fenian) Cycle. Finn was the son of Cumhail, who led a band of warriors called the Fianna. Members of this group were chosen for their bravery and strength and took an oath to fight for the king and defend Ireland from attack. In time, Finn became the leader of the Fianna and was the greatest warrior of all.

As a boy, Finn became the pupil of a druid, a Celtic priest. The druid had been told that he would gain all the world's knowledge if he caught and ate a certain salmon. He caught the fish and instructed Finn to cook but not to eat it. While preparing the fish, Finn touched it and burned his thumb. He sucked the thumb

to ease the pain and received the knowledge that was meant for the druid.

Finn later traveled to Tara, the court of the Irish king, Cormac MacArt. Every year a demon came and destroyed Tara. Finn managed to kill the demon and save the hall. As a reward, the king named Finn the leader of the Fianna. Under his leadership, the Fianna performed many amazing deeds, such as traveling to the **underworld** and defeating **supernatural** enemies. Always a select group, the Fianna became even more exclusive when Finn invented tests of strength and courage for all those who wanted to join.

underworld land of the dead
supernatural related to forces beyond the normal world; magical or miraculous

Several legends concern Finn's death. However, some stories say he is not dead at all, just sleeping in a cave or a hollow tree, and that he will awaken when Ireland once again needs his help. ***See also*** **Celtic Mythology; Druids.**

Finnish Mythology

Finnish mythology, like that of many other cultures, tells the stories of gods and legendary heroes. Most of the myths date from pre-Christian times and were passed from generation to generation by storytellers. A work called the *Kalevala,* which the Finnish people consider their national **epic,** contains many of the legends. Compiled by Finnish scholar Elias Lönnrot in the early 1800s, the *Kalevala* is based on traditional poems, songs, and **incantations** that Lönnrot collected over a long period of time.

epic long poem about legendary or historical heroes, written in a grand style
incantation chant, often part of a magical formula or spell

Major Themes and Characters. The word *Kalevala,* which means "land of the descendants of Kaleva," is an imaginary region associated with Finland. The epic's 50 poems or songs—also known as cantos or runes—recount the stories of various legendary heroes and of gods and goddesses and describe mythical events such as the creation of the world.

Vainamoinen, one of the heroes in the *Kalevala,* is a wise old **seer** who can work magic through the songs that he sings. His mother is Ilmatar, the virgin spirit of air, who brought about creation. Another great hero of the epic, Lemminkainen, appears as a handsome, carefree, and romantic adventurer.

seer one who can predict the future

Vainamoinen and Lemminkainen have certain experiences and goals in common. In their adventures, both men meet Louhi, the evil mistress of Pohjola (the Northland), and both of them seek to wed Louhi's daughter, the beautiful Maiden of Pohjola. A third suitor for the maiden's hand, Ilmarinen, is a blacksmith who constructs a *sampo,* a mysterious object like a mill that can produce prosperity for its owner.

A number of other figures become involved with these leading characters. Kuura, another hero, joins Lemminkainen on his journey to Pohjola. Joukahainen, an evil youth, challenges Vainamoinen to a singing contest. His sister Aino, who is offered in marriage to Vainamoinen, drowns herself rather than wed the aged hero. Another character, Kullervo, commits suicide after unknowingly raping his own sister. Marjatta, the last major character introduced in the *Kalevala,* is a virgin who gives birth to a king.

This painting, *The Curse of Kullervo,* by Akseli Gallén-Kallela, illustrates a story from the Finnish national epic known as the *Kalevala.*

Principal Myths. The *Kalevala* begins with the story of Ilmatar, who descends from the heavens to the sea, where she is tossed about for 700 years. During that time, a seabird lays eggs on her knee. When Ilmatar moves, the eggs break, and the pieces form the physical world and the sun and the moon. She then has a son, Vainamoinen, who begins life as a wise old man.

Soon after Vainamoinen's birth, the evil Joukahainen challenges him to a singing contest after hearing that the hero is noted for his magic songs. Vainamoinen accepts the challenge and wins the contest, causing Joukahainen to sink into a swamp. Fearing that he will drown, Joukahainen offers Vainamoinen his sister Aino in exchange for his rescue.

Vainamoinen plans to marry Aino, and her parents encourage the match. But she refuses to wed the old man. When her mother tries to persuade her to change her mind, Aino goes to the sea and drowns herself. Vainamoinen follows the girl and finds her in the form of a fish. He catches the fish, but she slips back into the water and escapes.

Unhappy that he has lost Aino, Vainamoinen sets off for Pohjola, the Northland, in search of another wife. Along the way Joukahainen, still bitter over losing the singing contest, shoots at the hero but only hits his horse. Vainamoinen falls into the sea and escapes. He finally arrives at Pohjola, where the evil Louhi promises him her daughter, the Maiden of Pohjola, if he will build a magic *sampo* for her. Unable to do this by himself, Vainamoinen seeks help from Ilmarinen, the blacksmith. However, after Ilmarinen completes the *sampo,* Louhi gives her daughter to him instead of to Vainamoinen.

The next section of the *Kalevala* recounts the adventures of the hero Lemminkainen, who marries Kyllikki, a woman from the island of Saari. But she is unfaithful to him, and he leaves her and goes to Pohjola to find a new wife. When he reaches his destination, Louhi promises him her daughter if he can complete several tasks. While Lemminkainen is working on the last task, he is killed by a blind cattle herder whom he has insulted. The herder cuts the hero's body into many pieces, but Lemminkainen's mother manages to collect the pieces and restore him to life with magic spells.

Meanwhile, Louhi gives her daughter to Ilmarinen as a bride. Angry at not being invited to the wedding, Lemminkainen storms Louhi's castle, kills her husband, and then returns home. Discovering that his house has been burned by raiders from Pohjola, Lemminkainen returns there with his companion Kuura. They try to destroy the land but are defeated.

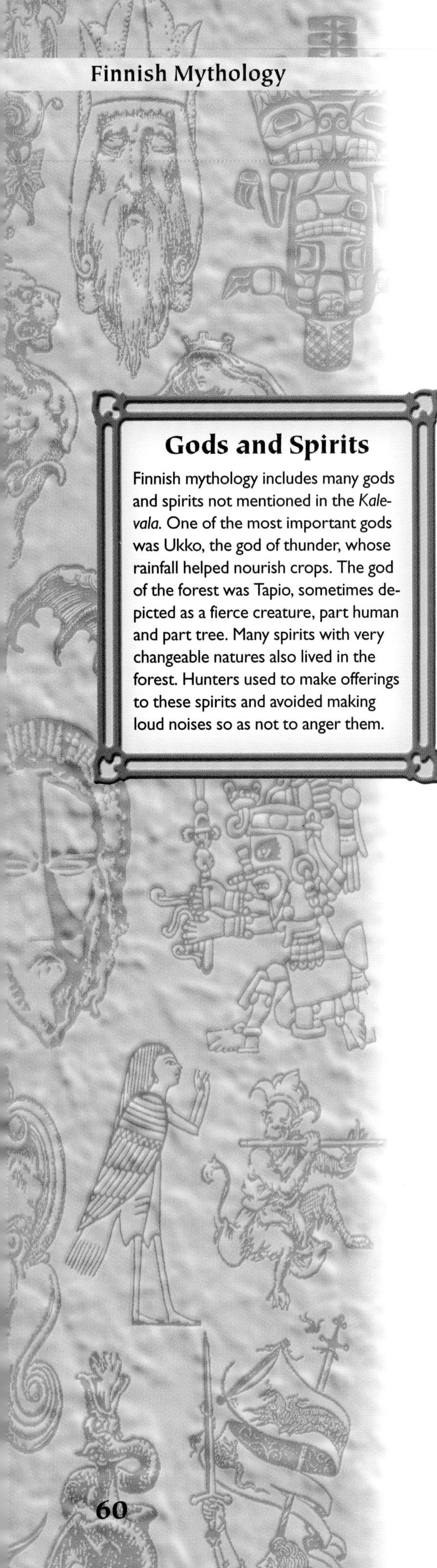

The *Kalevala* next tells the tragic tale of Kullervo, who is sent by his family to the home of Ilmarinen and the Maiden of Pohjola. The Maiden takes a strong dislike to the youth, and one day she puts a stone in his bread. In revenge, Kullervo kills the Maiden and flees. After wandering for some time, he finds his family and works for them. On his way home one day, he meets a woman and rapes her. Later he finds out that the woman is his sister. When the sister discovers that she has been raped by her own brother, she throws herself into a river and drowns. Later Kullervo kills himself because of what he has done.

In the next section of the epic, the three heroes—Vainamoinen, Ilmarinen, and Lemminkainen—travel together to Pohjola to steal the magic *sampo,* which has brought great riches to the evil Louhi. They succeed in stealing the mysterious object, but Louhi and her forces pursue them. A great battle takes place, during which the *sampo* is lost in the sea. Furious at the loss, Louhi tries to destroy Vainamoinen and his land. In the end, however, Vainamoinen emerges victorious.

The last story of the *Kalevala* deals with the virgin Marjatta and the birth of her son. As the time approaches for the boy to be baptized, Vainamoinen arrives to investigate. He decides that the boy must be put to death, but the boy scolds him severely. Later the boy is baptized and becomes king. An angry Vainamoinen leaves

Gods and Spirits

Finnish mythology includes many gods and spirits not mentioned in the *Kalevala.* One of the most important gods was Ukko, the god of thunder, whose rainfall helped nourish crops. The god of the forest was Tapio, sometimes depicted as a fierce creature, part human and part tree. Many spirits with very changeable natures also lived in the forest. Hunters used to make offerings to these spirits and avoided making loud noises so as not to anger them.

Major Characters of the *Kalevala*

Character	Role
Aino	Joukahainen's sister, drowns herself after being offered in marriage to Vainamoinen
Ilmarinen	blacksmith, makes a magical object called a *sampo* that brings prosperity to its owner
Ilmatar	virgin spirit of the air and creator goddess
Joukahainen	evil youth, challenges Vainamoinen to a singing contest
Kuura	hero, joins Lemminkainen on his journey to Pohjola
Lemminkainen	hero, handsome adventurer
Louhi	evil woman and mother of the Maiden of Pohjola
Maiden of Pohjola	beautiful young woman sought in marriage by Ilmarinen, Lemminkainen, and Vainamoinen
Vainamoinen	hero, wise old seer who sings magical songs

the land. Most of the characters and tales in the *Kalevala* reflect pre-Christian ideas, but the story of Marjatta and of Vainamoinen's flight suggests a transition from **pagan** to Christian beliefs.

pagan term used by early Christians to describe non-Christians and non-Christian beliefs

Influence of the Kalevala. The *Kalevala* helped create a national identity for the Finnish people by presenting a common mythology filled with familiar heroes and gods. The work also inspired many literary and artistic works by Finns and others.

Among the most famous individuals to make use of the *Kalevala* was Finnish composer Jean Sibelius, who wrote a number of symphonies and other musical works based on its characters and tales. Another Finnish composer, Robert Kajanus, also created several pieces of music inspired by the *Kalevala,* and Finnish artist Akseli Gallén-Kallela painted many works based on its stories. The American poet Henry Wadsworth Longfellow used the rhythmic patterns of the *Kalevala* as the basis for his poem *The Song of Hiawatha.* Some of the scenes and events in the poem are modeled after the Finnish work as well. ***See also*** **HIAWATHA.**

Fire

In ancient times, people considered fire one of the basic elements of the universe, along with water, air, and earth. Fire can be a friendly, comforting thing, a source of heat and light, as anyone who has ever sat by a campfire in the dark of night knows. Yet fire can also be dangerous and deadly, racing and leaping like a living thing to consume all in its path. In mythology, fire appears both as a creative, cleansing force and as a destructive, punishing one, although positive aspects of fire generally outweigh negative ones.

Symbols and Themes. People in all parts of the world tell myths and legends about fire. Numerous stories explain how people first acquired fire, either through their own daring or as a gift from an animal, god, or hero.

The ability to make and control fire—which is necessary for cooking, making pottery and glass, and metalworking—sets people apart from the animals. The Admiralty Islanders of the Pacific Ocean have a myth in which a snake asks his human children to cook some fish. The children simply heat the fish in the sun and eat it raw, so the snake gives them fire and teaches them to use it to cook their food.

Because fire warms and gives off light like the sun, it often represents the sun or a sun god in mythology. In some tales, it is linked with the idea of the hearth, the center of a household. Fire can also be a symbol of new life, as in the case of the phoenix, the mythical bird that is periodically destroyed by flames to rise reborn from its own ashes.

Fire's energy is not always a good thing. Flames can bring punishment and suffering, as in the Christian image of hell as a place of fiery torment. Some myths of **apocalypse** predict that the world will end in fire—but it may be a purifying, cleansing fire that will allow the birth of a fresh new world.

apocalypse prediction of a sudden and violent end of the world

Many cultures have myths and rituals involving fire. Here, Australian Aborigines with complex designs painted on their bodies dance in front of a fire.

trickster mischievous figure appearing in various forms in the folktales and mythology of many different peoples

deity god or goddess

Because fire can be treacherous and destructive, mythical figures associated with it may be **tricksters,** not always to be trusted. The Norse god Loki's shifty and malicious character may have been based on the characteristics of a forest fire. Another **deity** associated with fire is the Greek Hephaestus (Vulcan), god of metalworking, who is usually portrayed as deformed and sullen.

ritual ceremony that follows a set pattern

Rituals. In many cultures, people practice **rituals** related to fire. These rituals are often based on myths and legends about fire or fire gods. In ancient Rome, a sacred flame associated with the goddess Vesta represented national well-being. Women called the Vestal Virgins had the holy duty of keeping that flame alive. The Aztecs of ancient Mexico believed that the fire god Huehueteotl kept earth and heaven in place. At the end of each cycle of 52 years, they extinguished all fires, and Huehueteotl's priests lit a new flame for the people to use. In northern Europe, which has long, dark, cold winters, fire was especially honored. **Pagan** fire festivals such as lighting bonfires on May 1 have continued into modern times in European communities.

pagan term used by early Christians to describe non-Christians and non-Christian beliefs

Many cultures have practiced cremation, the burning of the dead. In cremation, fire represents purification, a clean and wholesome end to earthly life. The Pima people of the southwestern United States say that fire appeared in the world to solve the problem of how people should dispose of the dead.

† *See* ***Names and Places*** *at the end of this volume for further information.*

immortal able to live forever

hierarchy organization of a group into higher and lower levels

Fire Myths. Agni, the god of fire in Hindu mythology, represents the essential energy of life in the universe. He consumes things, but only so that other things can live. Fiery horses pull Agni's chariot, and he carries a flaming spear. Agni created the sun and the stars, and his powers are great. He can make worshipers **immortal** and purify the souls of the dead from sin. One ancient myth about Agni says that he consumed so many offerings from his worshipers that he was tired. To regain his strength, he had to burn an entire forest with all its inhabitants.

Chinese mythology includes stories of Hui Lu, a magician and fire god who kept 100 firebirds in a gourd. By setting them loose, he could start a fire across the whole country. There was also a **hierarchy** of gods in charge of fire. At its head was Lo Hsüan, whose cloak, hair, and beard were red. Flames spurted from his horse's nostrils. He was not unconquerable, however. Once when he attacked a city with swords of fire, a princess appeared in the sky and quenched his flames with her cloak of mist and dew.

The bringers of fire are legendary heroes in many traditions. Prometheus† of Greek mythology, one of the most famous fire bringers, stole fire from the gods and gave it to humans. Similar figures appear in the tales of other cultures.

Native Americans believe that long ago some evil being hid fire so that people could not benefit from it. A hero had to recover it and make it available to human beings. In many versions of the story Coyote steals fire for people, but sometimes a wolf, woodpecker, or other animal does so. According to the Navajo, Coyote tricked two monsters that guarded the flames on Fire Mountain. Then he lit a bundle of sticks tied to his tail and ran down the mountain to deliver the fire to his people.

African traditions also say that animals gave fire to humans. The San of South Africa believe that Ostrich guarded fire under his wing until a praying mantis stole it. Mantis tricked Ostrich into spreading his wings and made off with the fire. The fire destroyed Mantis, but from the ashes came two new Mantises.

Indians of the Amazon River basin in Brazil say that a jaguar rescued a boy and took him to its cave. There the boy watched the jaguar cooking food over a fire. The boy stole a hot coal from the fire and took it to his people, who then learned to cook.

Legends in the Caroline Islands of the Pacific link fire to Olofat, a mythical trickster hero who was the son of the sky god and a mortal woman. As a youth, Olofat forced his way into heaven to see his father. Later Olofat gave fire to human beings by allowing a bird to fly down to earth with fire in its beak.

A myth from Assam, in northern India, says that after losing a battle with Water, Fire hid in a bamboo stalk. Grasshopper saw it and told Monkey, who figured out how to use Fire. But a man saw Monkey and decided that he should have Fire, so he stole it from Monkey. Like many stories, this myth portrays ownership of fire as a human quality. Even partial control over such a powerful force of nature is one of the things that gives human society its identity. ***See also*** **FLOODS; HELL; HUEHUETEOTL; LOKI; PHOENIX; PROMETHEUS; VESTA; VULCAN.**

Fighting Sorcery with Fire

In Europe and America, individuals accused of being witches were once burned at the stake. Many cultures have held the belief that fire destroys sorcery, or black magic. The Assyrians of ancient Mesopotamia† called upon fire to undo the effects of evil witchcraft aimed at them. They used these words:

> *Boil, boil, burn, burn! . . . As this goat's skin is torn asunder and cast into the fire, and as the blaze devours it . . . may the curse, the spell, the pain, the torment, the sickness, the sin, the misdeed, the crime, the suffering, that oppress my body, be torn asunder like this goat's skin! May the blaze consume them today.*

Firebird

tsar Russian ruler

The firebird is a magical bird with golden feathers and crystal eyes that appears in many Russian folk stories. Several of the tales involve young Prince Ivan, son of the **tsar.**

In one story, the firebird stole apples from the tsar's garden. The tsar promised his kingdom to the son who could catch the firebird. The youngest son, Ivan, found a magic gray wolf, which helped him capture the bird. While Ivan and the wolf were on their journey, they met a beautiful princess and a horse with a golden mane. When Ivan's two jealous brothers saw them, they killed Ivan and took the horse and princess for themselves. The wolf found Ivan and brought him back to life just in time to stop Ivan's older brother from marrying the princess. When their father heard the full story, he imprisoned his two evil sons and allowed Ivan to marry the princess.

In another tale, Ivan captured the firebird in a castle garden but set it free in exchange for a magic feather from the firebird. Thirteen princesses came out of the castle and told Ivan that the owner was an evil magician who turned people into stone. But Ivan, who fell in love with one of the princesses, ignored the warning and decided to face the magician and his demons. The magic feather protected Ivan, and the firebird cast a spell on the demons. When the bird showed the prince an egg that contained the magician's soul, Ivan broke the egg, killing the magician and freeing the princesses.

The stories inspired Russian composer Igor Stravinsky to write a ballet called *The Firebird* in 1910. ***See also*** **ANIMALS IN MYTHOLOGY; BIRDS IN MYTHOLOGY.**

First Man and First Woman

In the mythology of the Navajo of North America, First Man and First Woman, known as Altsé hastiin and Altsé asdzáá, respectively, were beings who prepared the world for the creation of people. Created when the winds blew life into two special ears of corn, the couple led the creatures that would become the Navajo on a journey from a series of lower worlds up to the surface of the earth. In some stories, First Man and First Woman are joined by two other original leaders: First Boy and First Girl.

In each of the lower worlds, the followers of First Man and First Woman discovered different resources. The couple taught their followers how to survive in the unfamiliar surroundings and urged them to learn new skills, such as planting beans and corn for food. The two helped their people overcome various crises, including a great flood that surged over the land in powerful waves. They also had to deal with the troublesome Coyote, who quarreled and played many tricks on the people.

In one of the lower worlds, First Man and First Woman had a bitter dispute about whether men and women need each other to live. As a result of their dispute, First Man led all of the men away from the women for four years. Following this period of separation, some of the young women gave birth to terrible monsters that preyed on the people. Eventually, the men and women realized that they needed each other, and they agreed to live together again.

† *See* ***Names and Places*** *at the end of this volume for further information.*

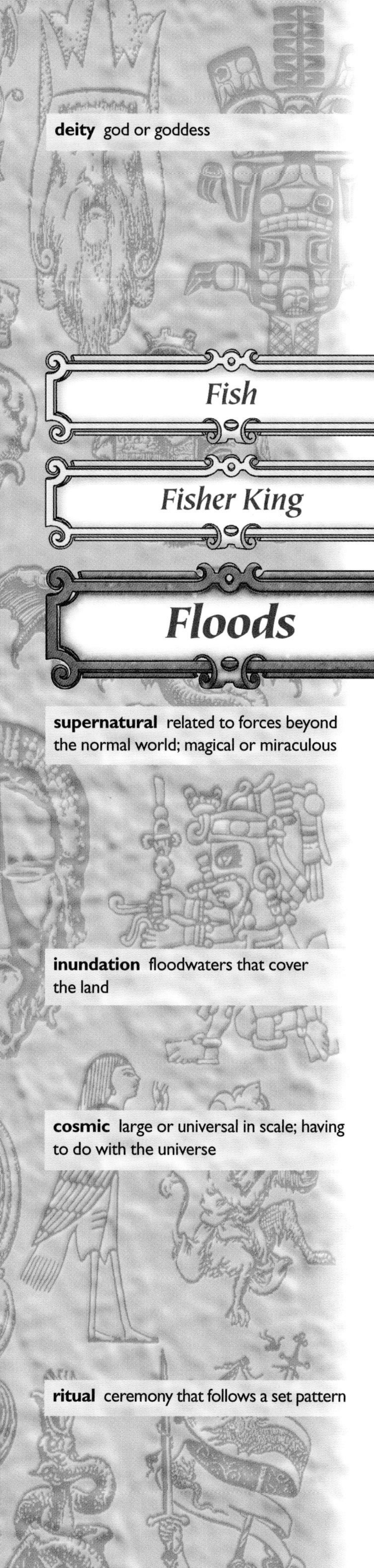

First Man and First Woman also raised the Navajo **deity** Changing Woman (Asdzáá nádleehé), whom they found as a child. They gave Changing Woman the medicine bundle of creation, a bag or collection of sacred objects that became the source of her power. Changing Woman and her sister, White Shell Woman (Yolgai asdzáá), gave birth to twins who became warriors and killed the monsters that threatened their people. ***See also*** **CHANGING WOMAN; CORN; CREATION STORIES; FLOODS; NATIVE AMERICAN MYTHOLOGY.**

deity god or goddess

Fish

See *Animals in Mythology*.

Fisher King

See *Holy Grail*.

Floods

Floods are among the most powerful and devastating of natural events. Long after the water has subsided, people remember and talk about the loss and destruction. Moreover, the scale of devastation is often so great as to convince people that the flooding is the work of **supernatural** beings.

supernatural related to forces beyond the normal world; magical or miraculous

Small wonder, then, that flood myths occur in cultures around the world. One of the most common tells of a great flood that occurred in the distant past. The biblical story of Noah and the ark he built to save certain people and animals from the flood is just one version of a much older myth from Mesopotamia†. Similar stories appear wherever people have experienced floods.

Some scholars believe that memories of real disasters, such as the violent and unpredictable floods that occurred along Mesopotamia's Tigris and Euphrates Rivers, underlie mythological accounts of catastrophic rains and **inundations.** These stories give meaning and purpose to events in the natural world. In myths, floods become part of a cycle of destruction and rebirth.

inundation floodwaters that cover the land

Flood Themes

Mythological floods are not local. They take place on a **cosmic** scale, generally covering the whole world. Though the direct cause of the rising waters may be heavy rainfall, gods or other supernatural beings are responsible. Often the flood is sent as punishment for the wrongdoings of humankind.

cosmic large or universal in scale; having to do with the universe

In some traditions, a flood reproduces the original mythological conditions of creation—the formless, empty expanse out of which the world was created. The inundation not only destroys the old world but also sets the stage for a brand new one. In myths in which the flood was sent to punish people for their sins, the new world that follows the flood is purified. The religious **ritual** of baptism reenacts the flood myth on an individual level. The baptismal water is believed to wash away sins, allowing people to be reborn in a purified state. In India, Hindus bathe in the sacred Ganges River to purify themselves.

ritual ceremony that follows a set pattern

deity god or goddess

According to many myths of the great flood, a few virtuous individuals survived the inundation, perhaps with the help or advice of a friendly **deity.** Those survivors repopulated the world, becoming the parents of the present human race. In this way, flood myths are often myths of human origins as well.

Flood Myths

Although the details of the stories differ, flood myths from around the world have many similarities. The themes of punishment, survival, and rebirth or renewal occur frequently.

Ancient Near East. The basic flood myth of the ancient Near East, in which the flood was sent as a divine punishment, originated among the Sumerian cities in southern Mesopotamia. Over a period of several thousand years, the Babylonians, the Hebrews, and other civilizations developed their own versions.

In this illustration of a story from India, a fish tells the first man, Manu, to prepare for a great flood. Manu follows the fish's instructions and survives the flood.

† *See **Names and Places** at the end of this volume for further information.*

The Sumerian myth tells how the human race, which the gods had created to do their work, became so numerous and noisy that the god Enlil sent a flood to destroy it. However, another god, Enki, wanted to save King Ziusudra (King Atrahasis in some versions). Forbidden by Enlil to warn the king, Enki spoke to the king's reed house. The king overheard the warning, built a boat, and saved his family and a collection of animals.

The Babylonian version of the flood myth appears in the *Epic of Gilgamesh.* In this account, the survivor is a man called Utnapishtim. Warned of the flood by a dream in which he heard a god whispering to his reed house, Utnapishtim built a boat, took aboard his family and a selection of craftspeople and animals, and rode out a terrible storm that raged for six days and six nights. Finally the boat landed on a mountaintop, the only land above the flood. Utnapishtim and his wife become **immortal** as a reward for following the advice of the god in the dream.

immortal able to live forever

The Hebrew version of the story, told in the book of Genesis in the Bible, places greater emphasis on the sinfulness of humankind. The flood was not a cruel whim or mistake of the gods but a deliberate punishment. Like Utnapishtim, Noah was a good man who received a warning and instructions to build a boat. He and his family, and two of every sort of living thing, survived the flood and landed upon the peak of Mount Ararat.

Egypt. The Egyptian flood myth begins with the sun god Ra, who feared that people were going to overthrow him. He sent the goddess Hathor, who was his eye, to punish the people. But she killed so many that their blood, flowing into the Nile River and the ocean, caused a flood. Hathor greedily drank the bloody water. Feeling that things had gone too far, Ra ordered slaves to make a lake of beer, dyed red to look like blood. Hathor drank the beer, became very drunk, and failed to finish the task of wiping out humanity. The survivors of her bloodbath started the human race anew.

Ancient Greece. The Greek flood myth says that Zeus, father of the gods, sent a mighty inundation to destroy the human race. Some versions say that Zeus was angry at the **Titan** Prometheus† for stealing the gift of fire from the gods and giving it to people. Others say that the flood was punishment for human sinfulness. Prometheus warned his son Deucalion to escape the flood by building a boat. Deucalion and his wife survived, and when the flood waters retreated, they were the only humans left on earth. The couple began the race of people who inhabit the world today. The story of the flood, along with many other Greek myths, appears in the *Metamorphoses*† by the Roman poet Ovid.

Titan one of a family of giants who ruled the earth until overthrown by the Greek gods of Olympus

China. For thousands of years, the Chinese people have suffered from the flooding of the two great rivers that flow through their land, the Chang Jiang (Yangtze) and the Huang He (Yellow) Rivers. Taming the rivers was one of the chief goals of early Chinese

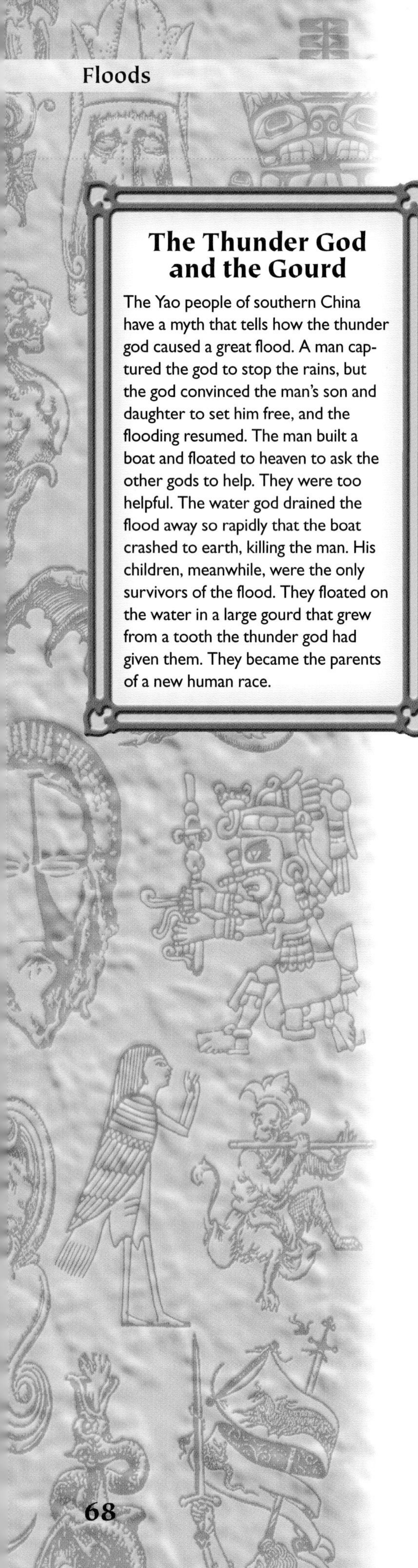

civilization. The story of Yu, one of several Chinese flood myths, celebrates a victory in the long struggle against floods.

In the myth, a man named Gun tried for nine years to dam the destructive waters that covered the land. Because he failed, the supreme god executed him. Gun's son, Yu, took up the task of taming the waters. Instead of building a dam, he decided to drain away the floodwaters through channels. A winged dragon flew in front of him, marking with his tail where Yu should dig the channels. Yu worked for many years, too busy even to see his family. In the end, however, he tamed the rivers, making the land along them suitable for farming. As his reward, Yu became emperor of China.

The Thunder God and the Gourd

The Yao people of southern China have a myth that tells how the thunder god caused a great flood. A man captured the god to stop the rains, but the god convinced the man's son and daughter to set him free, and the flooding resumed. The man built a boat and floated to heaven to ask the other gods to help. They were too helpful. The water god drained the flood away so rapidly that the boat crashed to earth, killing the man. His children, meanwhile, were the only survivors of the flood. They floated on the water in a large gourd that grew from a tooth the thunder god had given them. They became the parents of a new human race.

India. The flood legend of India begins with a creator god named Manu washing himself with water from a jar. A fish in the jar asked for Manu's protection and promised to save him from a great flood that would occur in the future. Manu raised the fish until it was one of the largest fish in the world, and then he released it into the sea. The fish told Manu what year the flood would come and advised him to build a ship. Manu built the ship, and when the flood came, the fish towed it to a mountaintop. Manu alone survived the flood. The fish is generally identified as one form of the god Vishnu†.

Native America. In many Native American myths, floods occur as punishment for human misdeeds. The Chiricahua Apache maintain that the Great Spirit sent a flood to drown the whole earth because people did not worship him. According to the Navajo, a series of floods forced the people to emerge from deep in the earth through several higher worlds. The final flood was caused by Water Monster, who became angry when Coyote stole his child. This flood, which drove the people to the surface of the present world, ended when Coyote returned the Water Monster's baby. The Cheyenne say that the gods use floodwaters to control people's movements.

Floods also have positive powers. In myths of the Arikara and Caddo people, floods wipe out evil giants and make the world safe for humans. Several Indian mythologies in Mexico and the American West tell of cycles of destruction in which one whole world creation was destroyed by flood, while others ended in fire, ice, wind, or other disasters. The Aztecs believed that the first age of creation ended in a flood. In the Mayan creation story, a flood washes away the wooden people made by the gods in an early attempt to create human beings.

Australia. Several groups among the Aborigines, the native people of Australia, believe that a vast flood swept away a previous society. Perhaps these myths grew out of conditions at the end of the last Ice Age, when sea levels rose and coastal regions flooded.

One group of Aborigines says that their ancestral heroes, the *Wandjina,* caused the flood and then re-created society in its present form. Another version of the myth tells that a huge half-human

†*See **Names and Places** at the end of this volume for further information.*

snake called Yurlunggur brought on the flood to punish two sisters for sexual misbehavior, that is, for breaking tribal rules concerning proper partners. Yurlunggur swallowed the sisters, but after the floodwaters withdrew, he spat them out and allowed them to start a new society. ***See also*** **Creation Stories; Gilgamesh; Manu; Noah; Utnapishtim; Wandjina; Yu.**

Flowers in Mythology

From new life to death, from purity to passion, flowers have had many meanings in myths and legends. Swelling from tender bud to full bloom, flowers are associated with youth, beauty, and pleasure. But as they wilt and die, flowers represent fragility and the swift passage from life into death. Specific flowers such as roses and lilies have assumed symbolic significance in mythology.

Roles of Flowers

Many plants bloom for only a few weeks, often in the spring or early summer, and the individual flowers tend to be short-lived. At their peak, flowers are delicate, colorful, and frequently sweet-scented. From these qualities emerge the symbolic meanings of flowers and, in some cultures, **floral** goddesses.

floral having to do with flowers

Symbolism. Many cultures connect flowers with birth, with the return of spring after winter, with life after death, and with joyful youth, beauty, and merriment. Yet because they fade quickly, flowers are also linked with death, especially the death of the young. Together the two sets of associations suggest death followed by heavenly rebirth, which may be one reason for the tradition of placing or planting flowers on graves. People also offer flowers to their gods at shrines and decorate churches with them.

In many societies, certain colors of flowers have acquired symbolic meanings. White blossoms, for example, represent both purity and death, while red ones often symbolize passion, energy, and blood. Yellow flowers may suggest gold or the sun. In the Chinese Taoist tradition the highest stage of **enlightenment** was pictured as a golden flower growing from the top of the head.

enlightenment in Buddhism, a spiritual state marked by the absence of desire and suffering

The shapes of flowers also have significance. Blossoms with petals projecting outward like rays of light from the sun have been associated with the sun and with the idea of the center—of the world, the universe, or consciousness.

Goddesses. The Aztecs, who dominated central Mexico before the early 1500s, had a goddess of sexuality and fertility named Xochiquetzal, which means "flower standing upright." She carried a bouquet of flowers and wore a floral wreath in her hair. Fragments of surviving poetry show that the Aztecs recognized the double symbolism of flowers as emblems of both life and death:

> The flowers sprout, and bud, and grow, and glow. . . . Like a flower in the summertime, so does our heart take refreshment and bloom. Our

This Roman fresco of A.D. 79 shows the goddess Flora gathering flowers.

underworld land of the dead

divination act or practice of foretelling the future

discus heavy, circular plate hurled over distance as a sport

body is like a flower that blossoms and quickly withers. . . . Perish relentlessly and bloom once more, ye flowers who tremble and fall and turn to dust.

The Greeks also had a floral goddess, Chloris, who was married to Zephyrus, the god of the west wind. The Romans called her Flora and honored her each year with a celebration known as the Floralia. She was often portrayed holding flowers or scattering them; her blossom-crowned image appeared on coins of the Roman republic.

Stories and Meanings

Many flowers from around the world appear in mythology. The anemone, carnation, hyacinth, lily, lotus, narcissus, poppy, rose, sunflower, and violet are among those that are associated with stories or customs from various cultures.

Anemone. Greek mythology linked the red anemone, sometimes called the windflower, to the death of Adonis. This handsome young man was loved by both Persephone, queen of the **underworld,** and Aphrodite, goddess of love. Adonis enjoyed hunting, and one day when he was out hunting alone, he wounded a fierce boar, which stabbed him with its tusks. Aphrodite heard the cries of her lover and arrived to see Adonis bleeding to death. Red anemones sprang from the earth where the drops of Adonis's blood fell. In another version of the story, the anemones were white before the death of Adonis, whose blood turned them red.

Christians later adopted the symbolism of the anemone. For them its red represented the blood shed by Jesus Christ on the cross. Anemones sometimes appear in paintings of the Crucifixion.

Carnation. Composed of tightly packed, fringed petals of white, yellow, pink, or red, carnations have many different meanings. To the Indians of Mexico, they are the "flowers of the dead," and their fragrant blooms are piled around corpses being prepared for burial. For the Koreans, three carnations placed on top of the head are a form of **divination.** The flower that withers first indicates which phase of the person's life will contain suffering and hardship. To the Flemish people of Europe, red carnations symbolized love, and a kind of carnation called a pink was traditionally associated with weddings.

Hyacinth. The Greek myth of Hyacinthus and Apollo tells of the origin of the hyacinth, a member of the lily family. Hyacinthus, a beautiful young man of Sparta†, was loved by the sun god Apollo. One day the two were amusing themselves throwing a **discus** when the discus struck Hyacinthus and killed him. Some accounts say that Zephyrus, the god of the west wind, directed the discus out of jealousy because he also loved Hyacinthus.

†*See **Names and Places** at the end of this volume for further information.*

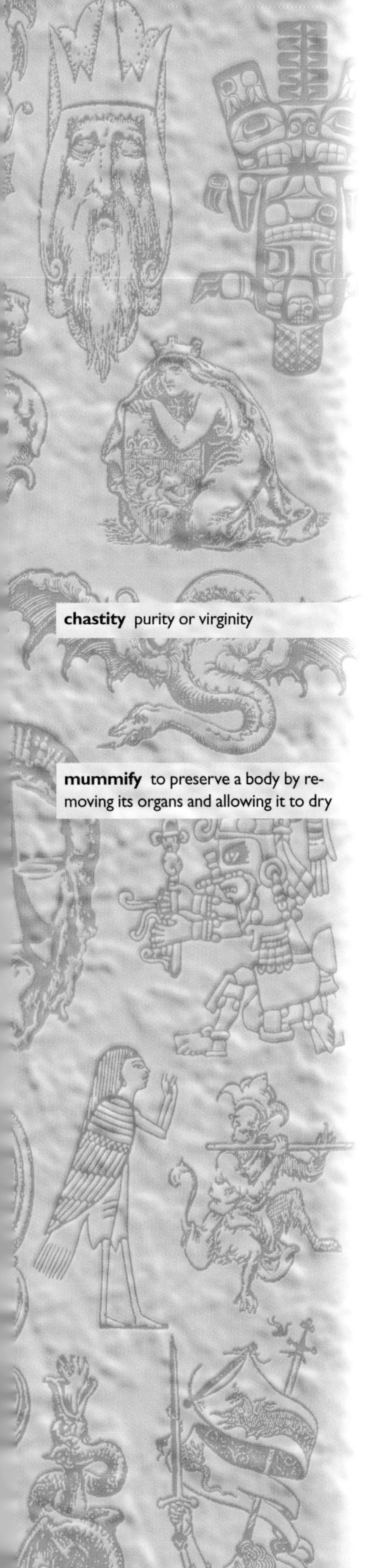

While Apollo was deep in grief, mourning the loss of his companion, a splendid new flower rose out of the bloodstained earth where the young man had died. Apollo named it the hyacinth and ordered that a three-day festival, the Hyacinthia, be held in Sparta every year to honor his friend.

Lily. To the ancient Egyptians, the trumpet-shaped lily was a symbol of Upper Egypt, the southern part of the country. In the ancient Near East, the lily was associated with Ishtar, also known as Astarte, who was a goddess of creation and fertility as well as a virgin. The Greeks and Romans linked the lily with the queen of the gods, called Hera by the Greeks and Juno by the Romans. The lily was also one of the symbols of the Roman goddess Venus.

In later times, Christians adopted the lily as the symbol of Mary, who became the mother of Jesus while still a virgin. Painters often portrayed the angel Gabriel handing Mary a lily, which became a Christian symbol of purity. Besides being linked to Mary, the lily was also associated with virgin saints and other figures of exceptional **chastity.**

chastity purity or virginity

Lotus. The lotus shares some associations with the lily. Lotus flowers, which bloom in water, can represent female sexual power and fertility as well as birth or rebirth. The ancient Egyptians portrayed the goddess Isis being born from a lotus flower, and they placed lotuses in the hands of their **mummified** dead to represent the new life into which the dead souls had entered.

mummify to preserve a body by removing its organs and allowing it to dry

The lotus often appears in Hindu and Buddhist stories. Here, Buddha sits on a throne of lotus blossoms.

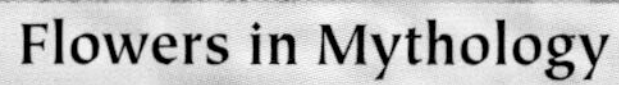

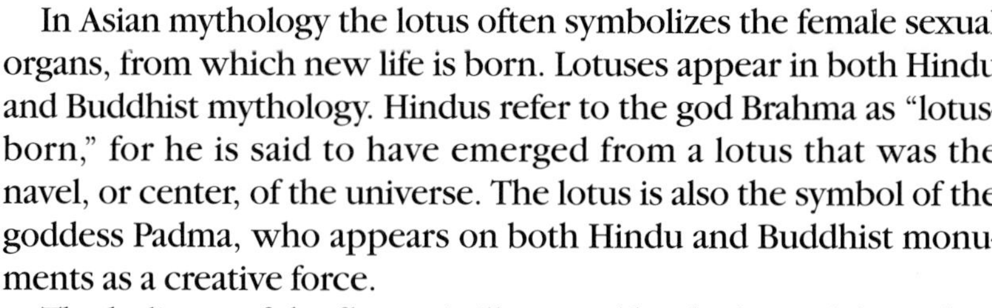

The Language of Flowers

In Europe during the late 1800s, the idea that flowers represented feelings grew into a system of communicating through flower arrangements. Code books guided those who wanted to compose or read floral messages. According to one book, the apple blossom meant "Will the glow of love finally redden your delicate cheeks?" Field clover signified "Let me know when I can see you again." A red rose petal meant "Yes!", a white one "No!" Spurge, a green flower, carried the message: "Your nature is so cold that one might think your heart made of stone." Users of this elaborate language needed not only a code book but also the ability to recognize blooms.

nymph minor goddess of nature, usually represented as young and beautiful

In Asian mythology the lotus often symbolizes the female sexual organs, from which new life is born. Lotuses appear in both Hindu and Buddhist mythology. Hindus refer to the god Brahma as "lotus-born," for he is said to have emerged from a lotus that was the navel, or center, of the universe. The lotus is also the symbol of the goddess Padma, who appears on both Hindu and Buddhist monuments as a creative force.

The holiness of the flower is illustrated by the legend that when the Buddha walked on the earth he left lotuses in his trail instead of footprints. One myth about the origin of Buddha relates that he first appeared floating on a lotus. According to a Japanese legend, the mother of Nichiren (Lotus of the Sun) became pregnant by dreaming of sunshine on a lotus. Nichirin founded a branch of Buddhism in the 1200s. The phrase "Om mani padme hum," which both Hindus and Buddhists use in meditation, means "the jewel in the lotus" and can refer to the Buddha or to the mystical union of male and female energies.

Narcissus. The Greek myth about the narcissus flower involves the gods' punishment of human shortcomings. Like the stories of Adonis and Hyacinth, it involves the transfer of life or identity from a dying young man to a flower.

Narcissus was an exceptionally attractive young man who scorned the advances of those who fell in love with him, including the **nymph** Echo. His lack of sympathy for the pangs of those he rejected angered the gods, who caused him to fall in love with his own reflection as he bent over a pool of water. Caught up in self-adoration, Narcissus died—either by drowning as he tried to embrace his own image or by pining away at the edge of the pool. In the place where he had sat gazing yearningly into the water, there appeared a flower that the nymphs named the narcissus. It became a symbol of selfishness and coldheartedness. Today psychologists use the term *narcissist* to describe someone who directs his or her affections inward rather than toward other people.

Poppy. A type of poppy native to the Mediterranean region yields a substance called opium, a drug that was used in the ancient world to ease pain and bring on sleep. The Greeks associated poppies with both Hypnos, god of sleep, and Morpheus, god of dreams. Morphine, a drug made from opium, gets its name from Morpheus.

Rose. The rose, a sweet-smelling flower that blooms on a thorny shrub, has had many meanings in mythology. It was associated with the worship of certain goddesses and was, for the ancient Romans, a symbol of beauty and the flower of Venus. The Romans also saw roses as a symbol of death and rebirth, and they often planted them on graves.

When Christians adopted the rose as a symbol, it still carried connections with ancient mother goddesses. The flower became associated with Mary, the mother of Christ, who was sometimes

†*See **Names and Places** at the end of this volume for further information.*

addressed as the Mystic or Holy Rose. In time, the rose took on additional meanings in Christian symbolism. Red roses came to represent the blood shed by the martyrs who died for their faith; white ones stood for innocence and purity. One Christian legend says that roses originally had no thorns. But after the sin of Adam and Eve—for which they were driven out of the Garden of Eden—the rose grew thorns to remind people that they no longer lived in a state of perfection.

Sunflower. Some flowers turn their heads during the day, revolving slowly on their stalks to face the sun as it travels across the sky. The Greek myth of Clytie and Apollo, which exists in several versions, explains this movement as the legacy of a lovesick girl.

Clytie, who was either a water nymph or a princess of the ancient city of Babylon†, fell in love with Apollo, god of the sun. For a time the god returned her love, but then he tired of her. The forlorn Clytie sat, day after day, slowly turning her head to watch Apollo move across the sky in his sun chariot. Eventually, the gods took pity on her and turned her into a flower. In some versions of the myth, she became a heliotrope or a marigold, but most accounts say that Clytie became a sunflower.

Violet. The violet, which grows low to the ground and has small purple or white flowers, appeared in an ancient Near Eastern myth that probably inspired the Greek and Roman myth of Venus and Adonis. According to this story, the great mother goddess Cybele loved Attis, who was killed while hunting a wild boar. Where his blood fell on the ground, violets grew.

The Greeks believed that violets were sacred to the god Ares† and to Io, one of the many human loves of Zeus†. Later, in Christian symbolism, the violet stood for the virtue of humility, or humble modesty, and several legends tell of violets springing up on the graves of virgins and saints. European folktales associate violets with death and mourning. ***See also*** **ADONIS; ATTIS; FRUIT IN MYTHOLOGY; HYPNOS; ISHTAR; ISIS; NARCISSUS; PLANTS IN MYTHOLOGY; TREES IN MYTHOLOGY.**

Flying Dutchman

The Flying Dutchman, a ghost ship in several maritime legends, was a sign of bad luck, particularly for sailors. In most versions, the ship appeared off the Cape of Good Hope, the southern tip of Africa. The legend was inspired by the story of a Dutch sea captain named Vanderdecken who boasted that he could complete the journey around the cape during a fierce storm. He swore that he would do so or keep trying forever. As punishment for his rashness, he was condemned to sail around the cape until the end of time. A similar version of the legend involves another captain who was forced to sail across the ocean forever because he had sold his soul to the devil. In 1843 the composer Richard Wagner wrote an opera based on the tale of the Flying Dutchman, which spread the story's popularity.

Freyja

deity god or goddesss
trickster mischievous figure appearing in various forms in the folktales and mythology of many different peoples

In Norse† mythology, Freyja was the goddess of love and fertility, associated with affairs of the heart. According to one Norse source, "all lovers would do well to invoke her." Her identification with love and passion led other **deities** to condemn her behavior. The **trickster** god Loki claimed that Freyja was the lover of all of the gods and accused her of sleeping with her twin brother, Freyr, the god of fertility and prosperity.

One story about Freyja explained how she acquired her favorite possession, the Necklace of the Brisings, made by four dwarfs. She agreed to spend a night with each of the dwarfs in exchange for the necklace. However, Loki later crept into Sessrumnir, Freyja's heavenly home, while Freyja was sleeping and stole the precious necklace.

In addition to being concerned with matters of love, Freyja had links with death and the world of the dead. Half of all the warriors who died in battle were given to her; the other half went to Odin, ruler of the gods. Freyja was associated with Frigg, goddess of marriage. Some scholars have suggested that the two goddesses represent different aspects of the same deity, who oversaw both love and motherhood. ***See also* Freyr; Frigg; Loki; Norse Mythology.**

Freyr

In Norse† mythology, Freyr was the god of fertility and prosperity and the twin of Freyja, the goddess of love and fertility. He and his sister were the children of the sea god Njord and the female giant Skadi. Freyr belonged to the race of gods known as the Vanir. When these gods went to war with another group of gods called the Aesir, Freyr was taken hostage. The Aesir eventually released Freyr, and the Norse came to consider him a member of both groups of gods.

Freyr used many magical items during his adventures. These included a horse named Blodughofi and a magnificent boar, Gullinbursti, which pulled his chariot. Thus, both boars and horses were associated with Freyr. From the dwarfs, Freyr received a ship that could travel in any direction regardless of which way the wind was blowing. When Freyr was not using the ship, he could fold it up and put it in his pocket. Another magnificent treasure was a sword that could fight by itself.

One of the best-known legends about Freyr explains how he fell in love with a female giant named Gerda. From the moment he saw her, Freyr decided to make her his bride. He sent his servant Skirnir to try to convince Gerda to marry him. She refused at first but later agreed. Freyr gave his magic sword to Skirnir in return for winning Gerda for him. ***See also* Dwarfs and Elves; Freyja; Norse Mythology.**

Frigg

In Norse† mythology, Frigg was the wife of Odin, father of the gods. She was associated with marriage and the birth of children. In earlier Germanic mythology, Frigg was called Frija, from which the word *Friday* comes. For many years, Germans considered Friday a lucky day to be married.

*† See **Names and Places** at the end of this volume for further information.*

Even though her main role was guardian of marriage, Frigg did not live with Odin. Instead, she made her home in a place called Fensalir and was attended by several maids. One of the best-known stories about Frigg concerns her attempt to make her son Balder **immortal.** She obtained promises from every thing under the sky, except one, not to harm him. The one thing she neglected to ask was the mistletoe plant, which she considered too small and weak to be of any danger. However, the **trickster** god Loki found this out and tricked Balder's blind brother into throwing mistletoe at Balder to kill him. ***See also*** **BALDER; LOKI; ODIN.**

immortal able to live forever

trickster mischievous figure appearing in various forms in the folktales and mythology of many different peoples

Fruit in Mythology

Fruit appears in myths from around the world. Often it is a symbol of abundance, associated with goddesses of fruitfulness, plenty, and the harvest. Sometimes, however, fruit represents earthly pleasures, **gluttony,** and temptation. Specific kinds of fruit have acquired their own symbolic meanings in the myths and legends of different cultures.

gluttony excessive eating or drinking

Apple. Apples are brimming with symbolic meanings and mythic associations. In China they represent peace, and apple blossoms are a symbol of women's beauty. In other traditions, they can signify wisdom, joy, fertility, and youthfulness.

Apples play an important part in several Greek myths. Hera, queen of the gods, owned some precious apple trees that she had received as a wedding present from Gaia, the earth mother. Tended by the Hesperides, the Daughters of Evening, and guarded by a fierce dragon, these trees grew in a garden somewhere far in the west. Their apples were golden, tasted like honey, and had magical powers. They could heal, they renewed themselves as they were eaten, and if thrown, they always hit their target and then returned to the thrower's hand.

For the eleventh of his 12 great labors, the hero Hercules† had to obtain some of these apples. After a long, difficult journey across North Africa, he enlisted the help of the giant Atlas, who entered the garden, strangled the dragon, and obtained the fruit. Hercules took the apples to Greece, but Athena† returned them to the Hesperides.

A golden apple stolen from Hera's garden caused the Trojan War†, one of the key events in Greek mythology. Eris, the goddess of **discord,** was angry not to be included among the gods asked to attend a wedding feast. Arriving uninvited, she threw one of the apples, labeled "For the Fairest," onto a table at the feast. Hera, Athena, and Aphrodite† each assumed that the apple was meant for her. They asked Paris, a prince of Troy, to settle the matter, and he awarded the apple to Aphrodite. In revenge, Hera and Athena supported the Greeks in the war that led to the fall of Troy. People still use the phrase "apple of discord" to refer to something that provokes an argument.

discord disagreement

In Norse† mythology, apples are a symbol of eternal youth. Legend says that the goddess Idun guarded the magical golden apples

trickster mischievous figure appearing in various forms in the folktales and mythology of many different peoples

immortality ability to live forever

that kept the gods young. But after the **trickster** god Loki allowed Idun to be carried off to the realm of the giants, the gods began to grow old and gray. They forced Loki to recapture Idun from the giants. Celtic† mythology also mentions apples as the fruit of the gods and of **immortality.**

Today the apple is often associated with an episode of temptation described in Genesis, the first book of the Bible. Adam and Eve, the first man and woman, lived in a garden paradise called Eden. God forbade them to eat the fruit of one tree that grew in the garden—the tree of the knowledge of good and evil. When they gave in to temptation and tasted the fruit, God drove them out of the Garden of Eden for breaking his commandment. Many people picture the forbidden fruit as an apple because it has been portrayed that way for centuries in European artworks. However, the apple was unknown in the Near East when the Bible was written there. The biblical description of the tree in the Garden of Eden does not name a specific fruit, and in some traditions, the forbidden fruit has been imagined as a fig, a pear, or a pomegranate.

Breadfruit. The breadfruit—a round fruit that can be baked and eaten like bread—is an important staple food in Polynesia. Myths about the origin of the breadfruit are found on several Polynesian islands. One story told in Hawaii takes place during a famine. A man named Ulu, who died in the famine, was buried beside a spring.

This painting of the 1400s illustrates the Greek myth about a beauty contest involving the goddesses Hera, Athena, and Aphrodite. The goddess judged most beautiful by Paris, a Trojan prince, would receive a golden apple.

† *See **Names and Places** at the end of this volume for further information.*

The Horn of Plenty

The cornucopia, a curved horn with fruits and flowers spilling from its open mouth, is a common symbol of abundance and the earth's bounty. The symbol's origin lies in Greek mythology. Legend says that Zeus, the king of the gods, was raised by a foster mother named Amalthaea, who was either a goat or a goddess who tended a goat. Either way, she fed the infant god goat's milk. One day one of the goat's horns broke off. Amalthaea filled the horn with fruits and flowers and gave it to Zeus, who graciously placed it in the sky, where it became a constellation.

During the night, his family heard the rustle of flowers and leaves drifting to the ground. Next came a thumping sound of falling fruit. In the morning, the people found a breadfruit tree growing near the spring, and the fruit from the tree saved them from the famine.

Cherry. Cherries can symbolize fertility, merrymaking, and festivity. In Japan, where cherry blossoms are the national flower, cherries represent beauty, courtesy, and modesty. The ancient Chinese regarded the fruit as a symbol of immortality. One Chinese legend tells of the goddess Xi Wang Mu, in whose garden the cherries of immortality ripen every thousand years. Because cherry wood was thought to keep evil spirits away, the Chinese placed cherry branches over their doors on New Year's Day and carved cherry wood statues to stand guard in front of their homes.

Coconut. People in tropical regions consume the milk and meat of the coconut and use the oil and empty shells for various purposes. According to a legend from Tahiti, the first coconut came from the head of an eel named Tuna. When the moon goddess Hina fell in love with the eel, her brother, Maui, killed it and told her to plant the head in the ground. However, Hina left the head beside a stream and forgot about it. When she remembered Maui's instructions and returned to search for the head, she found that it had grown into a coconut tree.

Fig. Native to the Mediterranean region, the fig tree appears in some images of the Garden of Eden. After eating the forbidden fruit, Adam and Eve covered their nakedness with leaves that are usually said to be from the fig tree, and Islamic tradition mentions two forbidden trees in Eden—a fig tree and an olive tree. In Greek and Roman mythology, figs are sometimes associated with Dionysus (Bacchus to the Romans), god of wine and drunkenness, and with Priapus, a **satyr** who symbolized sexual desire.

The fig tree has a sacred meaning for Buddhists. According to Buddhist legend, the founder of the religion, Siddhartha Gautama or the Buddha, achieved **enlightenment** one day in 528 B.C. while sitting under a bo tree, a kind of fig tree. The bo or bodhi tree remains a symbol of enlightenment.

satyr woodland deity that was part man and part goat or horse

enlightenment in Buddhism, a spiritual state marked by the absence of desire and suffering

Pear. In Greek and Roman mythology, pears are sacred to three goddesses: Hera (Juno to the Romans), Aphrodite (Venus to the Romans), and Pomona, an Italian goddess of gardens and harvests.

The ancient Chinese believed that the pear was a symbol of immortality. (Pear trees live for a long time.) In Chinese the word *li* means both "pear" and "separation," and for this reason, tradition says that to avoid a separation, friends and lovers should not divide pears between themselves.

Plum. The blossom of the plum tree, even more than the fruit, has meaning in East Asia. Appearing early in the spring before the trees have leaves, the blossoms are a symbol of a young woman's

early beauty. The cover on a bridal bed is sometimes called a plum blossom blanket. The blossom has another meaning as well. Its five petals represent the five traditional Chinese gods of happiness.

Pomegranate. For thousands of years, the pomegranate, a juicy red fruit with many seeds, has been a source of food and herbal medicines in the Near East and the eastern Mediterranean. Its many seeds made it a symbol of fertility, for out of one fruit could come many more. To the Romans, the pomegranate signified marriage, and brides decked themselves in pomegranate-twig wreaths.

underworld land of the dead

Pomegranate seeds appear in the Greek myth of the goddess Demeter, protector of grain, crops, and the earth's bounty, and her daughter Persephone. One day Persephone was picking flowers when Hades, the king of the **underworld,** seized her and carried her to his dark realm to be his bride. Grief-stricken, Demeter refused to let crops grow. All of humankind would have starved if Zeus had not ordered Hades to release Persephone. Hades let her go, but first he convinced her to eat some pomegranate seeds. Having once eaten the food of the underworld, Persephone could never be free of the place. She was fated to spend part of each year there. For those months, the world is plunged into barrenness, but when Persephone returns to her mother, the earth again produces flowers, fruit, and grain.

Strawberry. Strawberries have special meaning to the Seneca of the northeastern United States. Because strawberries are the first fruit of the year to ripen, they are associated with spring and rebirth. The Seneca also say that strawberries grow along the path to the heavens and that they can bring good health. ***See also*** **ADAM AND EVE; ATALANTA; DEMETER; FLOWERS IN MYTHOLOGY; PERSEPHONE; TREES IN MYTHOLOGY.**

Furies

underworld land of the dead

primeval from the earliest times

deity god or goddess
pantheon all the gods of a particular culture

In Greek and Roman mythology, the Furies were female spirits of justice and vengeance. They were also called the Erinyes (angry ones). Known especially for pursuing people who had murdered family members, the Furies punished their victims by driving them mad. When not punishing wrongdoers on earth, they lived in the **underworld** and tortured the damned.

According to some stories, the Furies were sisters born from the blood of Uranus, the **primeval** god of the sky, when he was wounded by his son Cronus†. In other stories, they were the children of Nyx (night). In either case, their primeval origin set them apart from the other **deities** of the Greek and Roman **pantheons.**

Most tales mention three Furies: Allecto (endless), Tisiphone (punishment), and Megaera (jealous rage). Usually imagined as monstrous, foul-smelling hags, the sisters had bats' wings, coal-black skin, and hair entwined with serpents. They carried torches, whips, and cups of venom with which to torment wrongdoers. The Furies could also appear as storm clouds or swarms of insects.

† *See **Names and Places** at the end of this volume for further information.*

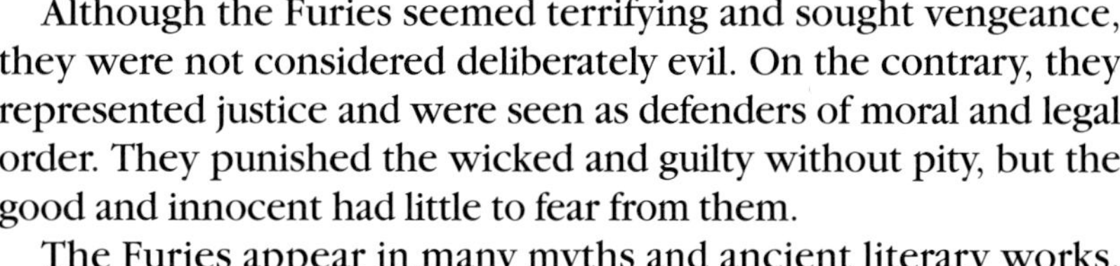

Although the Furies seemed terrifying and sought vengeance, they were not considered deliberately evil. On the contrary, they represented justice and were seen as defenders of moral and legal order. They punished the wicked and guilty without pity, but the good and innocent had little to fear from them.

The Furies appear in many myths and ancient literary works. They have a prominent role in *Eumenides,* a play written by the Greek dramatist Aeschylus. This play tells of the Furies' pursuit of Orestes, who had killed his mother, Clytemnestra, in revenge for her part in murdering his father, King Agamemnon† of Mycenae.

In *Eumenides,* Orestes' act was depicted as just, and the god Apollo† protected him in his sacred shrine at Delphi†. But the Furies still demanded justice. Finally, the gods persuaded the Furies to allow Orestes to be tried by the Areopagus, an ancient court in the city of Athens. The goddess Athena†, the **patron** of Athens, cast the deciding ballot.

patron special guardian, protector, or supporter

Athena then calmed the anger of the Furies, who became known afterward as the Eumenides (soothed ones) or Semnai Theai (honorable goddesses). Now welcomed in Athens and given a home there, they helped protect the city and its citizens from harm. The Furies also had shrines dedicated to them in other parts of Greece. In some places, the Furies were linked with the three Graces, goddess sisters who represented beauty, charm, and goodness—qualities quite different from those usually associated with the Furies. ***See also*** **GRACES; ORESTES; URANUS.**

Gaia

In Greek mythology, the goddess Gaia represented the earth. Also called Gaea or Ge by the Greeks and Terra or Tellus by the Romans, she was a maternal figure who gave birth to many other creatures and **deities.** Gaia was the child of Chaos, an early deity who produced the gods of the **underworld,** night, darkness, and love. Gaia gave birth to Uranus, who represented the sky; Pontus, the sea; and Oure, the mountains.

deity god or goddess
underworld land of the dead

Gaia had numerous other children who appear in a variety of myths. She mated with her son Uranus to create gods, including the **Titans,** and giants such as the Cyclopes. She was also the mother of Aphrodite†, Echo, the Furies, and the serpent that guarded the Golden Fleece. When Gaia's son, the Titan Cronus†, had children, Gaia and Uranus warned him that one of his offspring would challenge and defeat him. Cronus therefore swallowed each child at birth. However, his wife, Rhea, managed to trick him and save the youngest one, Zeus†.

Titan one of a family of giants who ruled the earth until overthrown by the Greek gods of Olympus

Gaia is mentioned in Virgil's *Aeneid*† and the *Theogony*† by the Greek poet Hesiod. She was widely worshiped at temples in Greece, including the shrine of the **oracle** at Delphi†. The Greeks also took oaths in Gaia's name and believed that she would punish them if they failed to keep their word. ***See also*** **AENEID, THE; CYCLOPES; DELPHI; ECHO; FURIES; GOLDEN FLEECE; TITANS; URANUS; VENUS; ZEUS.**

oracle priest or priestess or other creature through whom a god is believed to speak; also the location (such as a shrine) where such words are spoken

Galahad

Holy Grail sacred cup said to have been used by Jesus Christ at the Last Supper

According to Arthurian legend†, Galahad was the purest and noblest knight in King Arthur's court and the only one ever to see the **Holy Grail.** The son of Lancelot—another celebrated knight—and Elaine, Galahad was raised by nuns and arrived at the court as a young man.

When the knights took their seats at the Round Table, Galahad sat in a special seat known as the Siege Perilous. It was said that only the knight destined to find the Holy Grail could occupy this seat safely. All others who had sat in it had instantly perished. When Galahad remained unharmed, it became clear that he would accomplish great deeds. In some stories, the knight also proved his worth by drawing a special sword from a stone. An inscription on the stone stated that only the best knight in the land could withdraw the sword.

After Galahad's arrival at Arthur's court, the knights began their search for the Holy Grail. Galahad set off alone but later joined forces with two other knights, Perceval and Bors. Their travels took them to the city of Sarras, where they were imprisoned by a cruel king. However, when the king was dying, he released the knights, and the people of the city chose Galahad to be their next king.

After ruling Sarras for a year, Galahad had a vision in which the Holy Grail was revealed to him. Content with having achieved his life's goal, he prayed to be allowed to die then. According to the legend, his request was granted and "a great multitude of angels bore his soul up to heaven." ***See also*** **ARTHURIAN LEGENDS; HOLY GRAIL; LANCELOT; ROUND TABLE.**

Galatea

nymph minor goddess of nature, usually represented as young and beautiful

Galatea, whose name means "milk white," was a sea **nymph** in Greek mythology. She was loved by the Cyclops† Polyphemus, an ugly giant with one eye in the middle of his forehead. But Galatea rejected him and instead fell in love with a youth named Acis. Polyphemus saw Acis with his beloved, chased the youth, and crushed him with an enormous stone. As Acis died, a stream of water burst forth from the stone and flowed down to the sea, where it mingled with the waves behind which Galatea had hidden herself. The story of Galatea pursued by Polyphemus appears in a Renaissance painting by Raphael.

In another legend, Galatea was a statue of a woman carved by the sculptor Pygmalion. After Pygmalion fell in love with his creation, the goddess Aphrodite† agreed to bring it to life. ***See also*** **CYCLOPES; NYMPHS; PYGMALION; VENUS.**

Ganesha

deity god or goddess

Ganesha, the god of good fortune and wisdom, is one of the most popular Hindu **deities.** People call upon him at the beginning of any task, because his blessing supposedly ensures success. Ganesha is portrayed as a short man with a pot belly, four hands, and an elephant's head with one tusk. He is the son of Shiva, the Hindu god of destruction, and his wife, Parvati.

†See ***Names and Places*** *at the end of this volume for further information.*

Ganesha, the Hindu god of good fortune and wisdom, appears here with the head of an elephant. He is seated on a throne flanked by two lions.

Several legends tell how Ganesha came to have an elephant's head. One says that Parvati was so proud of her son that she asked all the gods to look at him, even the god Sani. Sani's gaze burned to ashes everything he saw, including Ganesha's head. Brahma, the god of creation, instructed Parvati to give her son the first head she found, which turned out to be that of an elephant. According to another account, Shiva struck off Ganesha's head and later attached an elephant's head to his son's body.

Ganesha's single tusk is also the subject of various stories. In one tale, he lost his second tusk in a fight with Parasurama, a form of the god Vishnu†. Another myth claims that Ganesha lost the tusk after using it to write the **epic** the *Mahabharata*. ***See also*** **HINDUISM AND MYTHOLOGY, MAHABHARATA, THE.**

epic long poem about legendary or historical heroes, written in a grand style

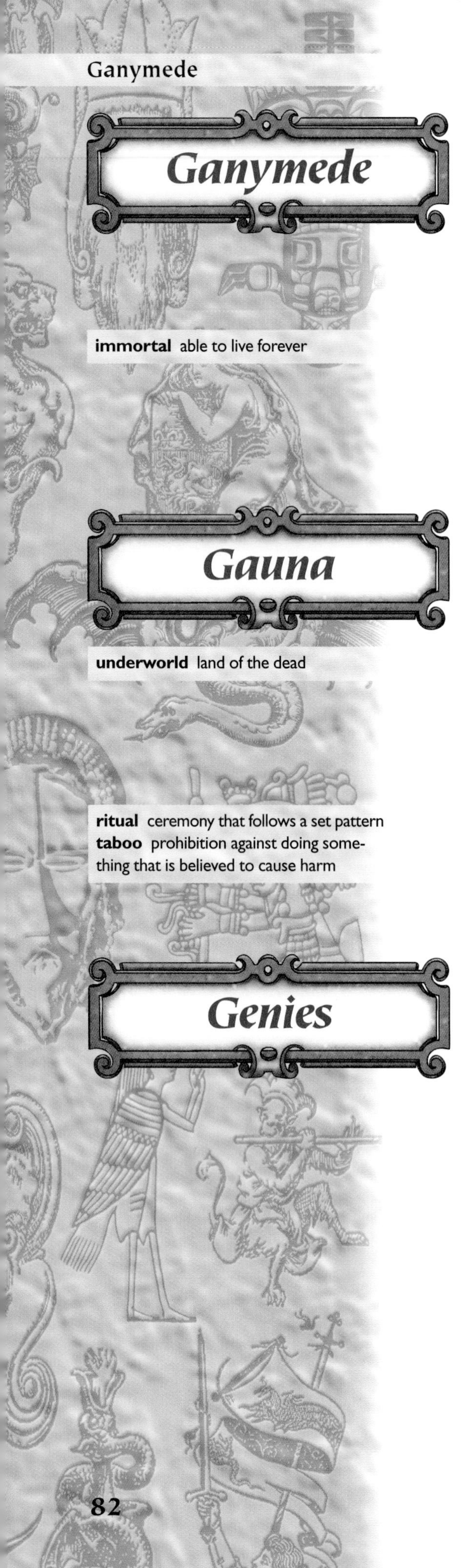

Ganymede

Greek myths describe Ganymede as a handsome boy who was kidnapped by the gods to serve as a cupbearer on Mount Olympus†. Born in Troy†, where his father was king, Ganymede came to the attention of Zeus†, who was captivated by his appearance. In some stories, it is Zeus disguised as an eagle—or an eagle sent by Zeus—who seizes the boy and carries him up to the home of the gods.

immortal able to live forever

In return for his son, Ganymede's father received a group of **immortal** horses from Zeus. Some versions of the tale say that the gift was a vine made of gold. Later Zeus placed Ganymede in the sky in the constellation Aquarius. Images of Ganymede sometimes show him carrying a cup or accompanied by an eagle. ***See also*** **Zeus.**

Gauna

The Bushpeople of southern Africa believe that Gauna is the leader of the spirits of the dead. He is the enemy of Cagn, the god who created the world. Though not as powerful as Cagn, Gauna is strong enough to cause trouble for people and animals.

underworld land of the dead

Gauna lives in the **underworld,** where he rules the tormented ghosts of the dead. At his command, these spirits haunt family members who are still living. Gauna regularly visits the earth to seize people and imprison them in the underworld. He hates the world created by Cagn and tries to interfere with the affairs of the living.

ritual ceremony that follows a set pattern
taboo prohibition against doing something that is believed to cause harm

To avoid being troubled by Gauna, the Bushpeople practice various **rituals** and **taboos** that they learned from Cagn. For example, they stay away from graves for fear that the dead people buried inside will reach out and pull them down into the underworld. ***See also*** **African Mythology; Cagn; Underworld.**

Genies

Genies (also called jinn or genii) are spirits in cultures of the Middle East and Africa. The term *genie* comes from the Arabic word *jinni,* which referred to an evil spirit that could take the shape of an animal or person. It could be found in every kind of nonliving thing, even air and fire. Jinn (the plural of jinni) were said to have magical powers and are favorite figures in Islamic literature. To the Mende people of Sierra Leone in Africa, genii are spirits who occasionally try to possess living men. The Mende use magic to fight genii who enter the living.

In ancient Rome, the term *genii,* the plural form of the Latin word *genius,* referred to the spirits that watched over every man. The genius was responsible for forming a man's character and caused all actions. Believed to be present at birth, genius came to be thought of as great inborn ability. Women had a similar spirit known as a *juno.* Some Romans also believed in a spirit, called an evil genius, that fought the good genius for control of a man's fate. In later Roman mythology, genii were spirits who guarded the household or community. ***See also*** **African Mythology; Roman Mythology; Semitic Mythology.**

†*See* ***Names and Places*** *at the end of this volume for further information.*

George, St.

martyr person who suffers or is put to death for a belief
piety faithfulness to beliefs

persecute to harass or punish individuals or groups

patron special guardian, protector, or supporter

St. George was a Christian **martyr** who lived in the Middle East in the A.D. 200s. Over the centuries, legends grew up about his courage and **piety.** The most popular tale described how St. George killed a terrifying dragon.

The dragon was threatening the local citizens in a city. The people decided to cast lots each day to choose one person for the dragon to eat, thus sparing the rest of the population. One day the king's daughter was selected to be the dragon's victim. As the dragon prepared to devour her, St. George arrived. He charged forward, made the sign of the cross, and killed the dragon. Impressed with both his faith and his strength, the people of the city decided to convert to Christianity.

Other tales concern St. George's martyrdom, which took place in Palestine†. The Roman government there was **persecuting** Christians, and St. George openly opposed their policies. The Romans tortured him for his resistance and beheaded him in about A.D. 300.

The legends about St. George spread to Europe during the Crusades, when armies of Europeans traveled to the Middle East. In the 1300s, George became **patron** saint of England. He is often pictured in Christian art carrying a sword and shield and wearing armor decorated with a red cross. ***See also* DRAGONS.**

This painting by Raphael shows St. George slaying a dragon that had been devouring a city's inhabitants.

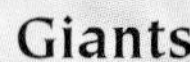

Giants

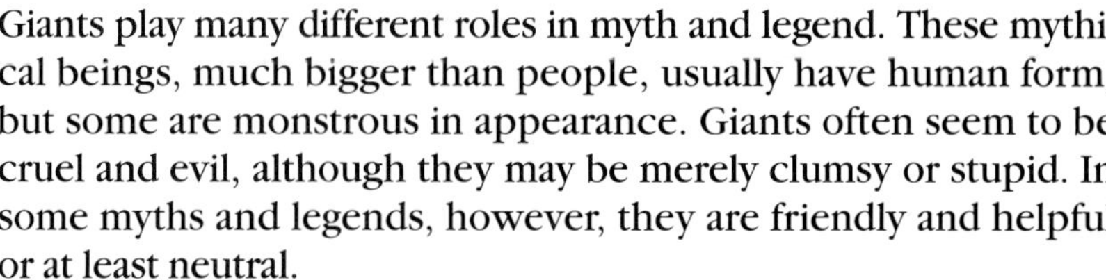

Giants play many different roles in myth and legend. These mythical beings, much bigger than people, usually have human form, but some are monstrous in appearance. Giants often seem to be cruel and evil, although they may be merely clumsy or stupid. In some myths and legends, however, they are friendly and helpful or at least neutral.

chaos great disorder or confusion

supernatural related to forces beyond the normal world; magical or miraculous

Giants can represent powerful natural forces that frighten and threaten humans. In the mythology of the Native American Lakota people, Waziya is a northern giant who blows the winter wind. In some traditions, a giant appears as a symbol of **chaos,** threatening to disrupt the orderly natural world or social community.

The evil giants of myth generally need to be defeated, either by humans or by **supernatural** beings such as gods. Although immensely powerful, these creatures fall when faced with bravery and cleverness. This victory of wit over brute strength occurs in the biblical story of David, who kills the giant Goliath with a stone from his sling, and in the English folktale of Jack the Giant-Killer, who vanquishes the giant Blunderbore.

Occasionally, cruel and kind giants appear in the same myth. The Mensa people of Ethiopia tell a story about a man who tries to steal cattle from one of the Rom, a tribe of giants. Enraged, the giant tries to kill the man. As the man flees, another giant befriends him and hides him in his cloak. Unfortunately, the man is crushed when the two giants come to blows.

Greek Giants. The word *giant* comes from the Greek Gigantes (meaning earthborn), a race of huge creatures who were the offspring of Gaia, the earth, and Uranus, the heavens. These giants were half man, half monster, with serpents' tails instead of legs. After Gaia became angry with Zeus, the father of the Olympian gods, the giants and the Olympians engaged in a war to the death known as the Gigantomachy.

The gods needed the help of a human hero because the giants could not be killed by gods. Zeus therefore fathered a son, the mighty Hercules†, whose mother was a human. The two sides met in battle at the home of the giants, a place called Phlegra (Burning Lands). The giants hurled huge rocks and mountaintops and brandished burning oak trees. The gods fought back strongly, and Hercules picked off the giants one by one with his arrows. Many Greek sculptors and artists depicted the Gigantomachy, with the

Many stories in Native American mythology describe giants with monstrous features. This wooden mask of a giant was made by the Tsimshian people of the northwest coast of North America.

†*See **Names and Places** at the end of this volume for further information.*

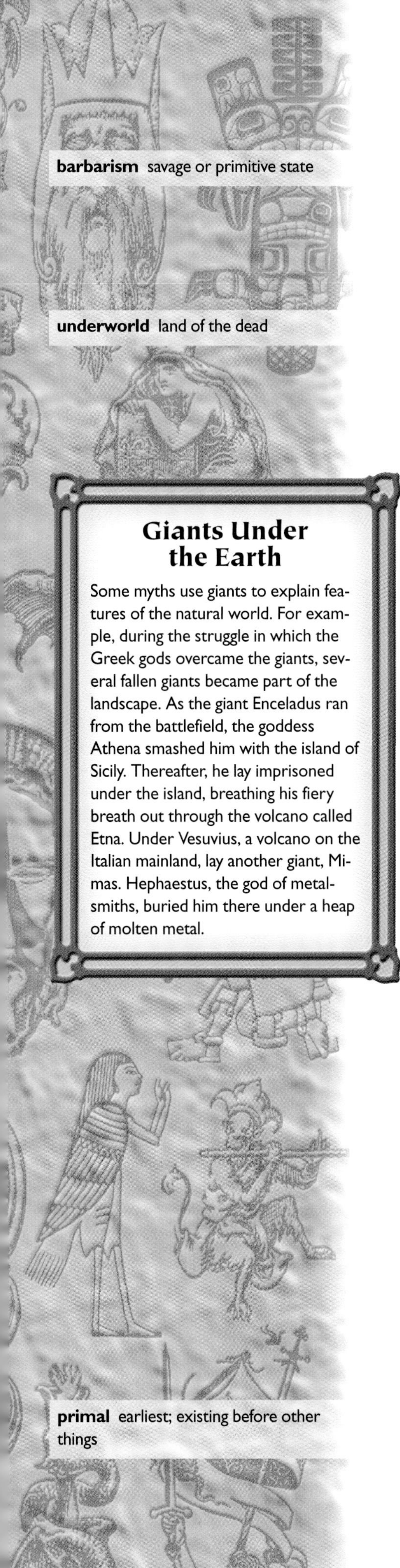

barbarism savage or primitive state

underworld land of the dead

Giants Under the Earth

Some myths use giants to explain features of the natural world. For example, during the struggle in which the Greek gods overcame the giants, several fallen giants became part of the landscape. As the giant Enceladus ran from the battlefield, the goddess Athena smashed him with the island of Sicily. Thereafter, he lay imprisoned under the island, breathing his fiery breath out through the volcano called Etna. Under Vesuvius, a volcano on the Italian mainland, lay another giant, Mimas. Hephaestus, the god of metalsmiths, buried him there under a heap of molten metal.

primal earliest; existing before other things

gods' victory over the giants, as the triumph of Greek civilization over **barbarism,** or of good over evil.

Two special groups of giants, also the children of Gaia, were the Cyclopes† and the Hundred-Armed giants. The three Cyclopes each had one eye in the middle of the forehead. The three Hundred-Armed giants each had 50 heads and 100 arms. Both groups were loyal to Zeus. The Hundred-Armed giants were the jailors of Tartarus, the place of punishment in the **underworld.**

Norse Giants. Giants appear in numerous myths of northern Europe. The giants' realm was a place called Jotunheim, located in Midgard, the center of the three-tiered Norse† universe. There they dwelt in a huge castle called Utgard.

Norse myths, like Greek myths, say that the gods fought and conquered the race of giants. Yet the gods and the giants were not always enemies. Friendship and even marriage could occur between them. Male deities mated with female giants. The mother of the thunder god Thor was a giantess named Jord, for example. However, the gods violently resisted all attempts by giants to mate with goddesses. The giant Hrungir built a wall around Asgard, the home of the gods, and for payment desired the goddess Freyja. But he received only a crushing blow from Thor's hammer.

Many myths concern Thor's conflict with the giants. In one tale, he journeyed to Utgard to challenge the giants. The giants beat Thor and his companions at several tests of strength but only by using trickery. In one contest, Thor lost a wrestling match to an old woman who was in fact Age, which overcomes all. Though the gods were not always good and the giants were not always bad, the struggle between the two groups constitutes one of the underlying themes of Norse mythology and often symbolizes the struggle of good against evil.

Native American Giants. Most Native American giants are evil and dangerous. Some start fights among humans so that in the confusion they can steal the men's wives. Others steal children, sometimes to eat them. Many Native American giants have monstrous or inhuman features. Tall Man, a giant of the Seminole people, smells bad, while giants in Lakota stories look like oxen.

The Shoshone Indians of the American West tell stories of Dzoavits, an ogre or hideous giant who stole two children from Dove. Eagle helped Dove recover her children. When the angry Dzoavits chased Dove, other animals protected her. Crane made a bridge from his leg so she could cross a river. Weasel dug an escape tunnel for her, and Badger made a hole where Dove and her children could hide. After tricking Dzoavits into entering the wrong hole, Badger sealed him in with a boulder.

Ancestral Giants. The myths of various cultures associate giants with **primal** times. Sometimes giants figure in the creation of the world. Norse mythology says that the first thing to appear out of chaos was the frost giant Ymir, father of both giants and people,

who had to die so that the earth could be formed from his body. The giant Pan Gu fills a similar role in Chinese mythology. Aboriginal people in northwestern Australia have stories about the two Bagadjimbiri brothers, both giants and creator gods, who made the landscape and people. When they died, their bodies became water snakes and their spirits became clouds. According to the Akamba people of Kenya, a giant hunter named Mwooka created the mountains and rivers.

Myths from many parts of the world say that in some remote time human ancestors were giants and that they have shrunk down to their present size over a very long period. Other stories tell of giants living among people at an earlier time in history. Gog and Magog are two giants of British myth. Brutus, the legendary founder of Britain, is said to have conquered them. In Jewish myth, a race of giants lived in the world along with people before the great Flood that wiped out most living things. One giant, Og, survived the Flood by hitching a ride on Noah's Ark. Later, however, he came into conflict with Noah's descendants, and the prophet Moses had to kill him. ***See also*** **Cyclopes; Monsters; Pan Gu.**

Gilgamesh

immortal able to live forever

epic long poem about legendary or historical heroes, written in a grand style

The best-known and most popular hero in the mythology of the ancient Near East, Gilgamesh was a Sumerian† king who wished to become **immortal.** Endowed with superhuman strength, courage, and power, he appeared in numerous legends and myths, including the *Epic of Gilgamesh.* This **epic,** written more than 3,000 years ago, seems to be the earliest work of literature. It is an adventure story that explores human nature, dealing with values and concerns that are still relevant today.

Historical Figure and Mythical Hero

demigod one who is part human and part god

Although most tales about Gilgamesh are obviously myths, they may be based on an actual historical figure. Ancient lists of Sumerian kings identify Gilgamesh as an early ruler of the city of Uruk around 2600 B.C. These same texts, however, also say that Gilgamesh was a **demigod** and reigned for 126 years.

According to legendary accounts, Gilgamesh was the son of the goddess Ninsun and of either Lugalbanda, a king of Uruk, or of a high priest of the district of Kullab. Gilgamesh's greatest accomplishment as king was the construction of massive city walls around Uruk, an achievement mentioned in both myths and historical texts.

Gilgamesh first appeared in five short poems written in the Sumerian language sometime between 2000 and 1500 B.C. The poems—"Gilgamesh and Huwawa," "Gilgamesh and the Bull of Heaven," "Gilgamesh and Agga of Kish," "Gilgamesh, Enkidu, and the Nether World," and "The Death of Gilgamesh"—relate various incidents and adventures in his life.

However, the most famous and complete account of Gilgamesh's adventures is found in the *Epic of Gilgamesh.* Originally written between 1500 and 1000 B.C., the epic weaves various tales

*†See **Names and Places** at the end of this volume for further information.*

of Gilgamesh together into a single story. Its basic theme is the king's quest for fame, glory, and immortality through heroic deeds. One of the best-known parts of the epic is the tale of a great flood, which may have inspired the story of Noah and the flood in the Bible.

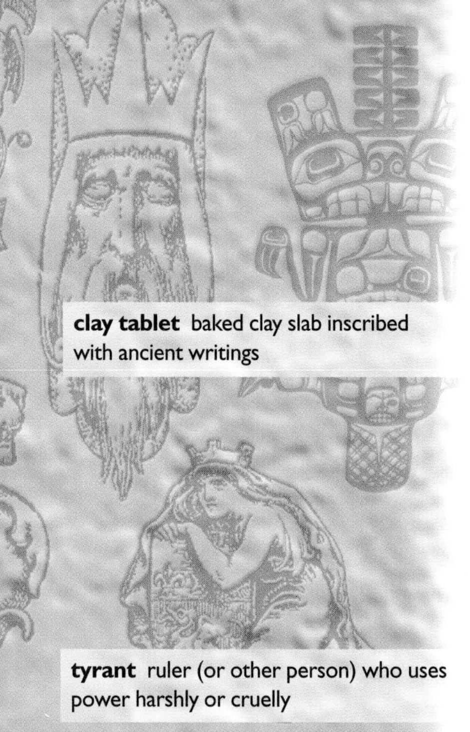

clay tablet baked clay slab inscribed with ancient writings

The epic appears on 12 **clay tablets** found at the site of the ancient Assyrian city of Nineveh. The tablets came from the library of King Ashurbanipal, the last great king of Assyria, who reigned in the 600s B.C.

The Epic of Gilgamesh

tyrant ruler (or other person) who uses power harshly or cruelly

The *Epic of Gilgamesh* begins with a brief account of Gilgamesh's ancestry, his youth, and his accomplishments as king. Although acknowledged to be a wise man and a courageous warrior, Gilgamesh is criticized as a **tyrant** who mistreats the people of Uruk. The nobles of the city complain bitterly of Gilgamesh's behavior. Their complaints attract the attention of the gods, who decide to do something about it.

Enkidu. The gods create a rival for Gilgamesh—a man named Enkidu who is as strong as the king and who lives in the forest with the wild animals. Their plan is for Enkidu to fight Gilgamesh and teach him a lesson, leading the king to end his harsh behavior toward his people. When Gilgamesh hears about Enkidu, he sends a woman from the temple to civilize the wild man by showing him how to live among people.

Gilgamesh was a Sumerian king and popular hero in the mythology of the ancient Near East. This carving shows the legendary figure.

After learning the ways of city life, Enkidu goes to Uruk. There he meets the king at a marketplace and challenges him to a wrestling match. The king and the wild man struggle, and Gilgamesh is so impressed by Enkidu's strength, skill, and courage that he embraces his rival, and the two men become close friends. Because of this loving friendship, Gilgamesh softens his behavior toward the people of Uruk and becomes a just and honorable ruler.

One day Gilgamesh and Enkidu decide to travel to a distant cedar forest to battle the fierce giant Humbaba (or Huwawa) who guards the forest. Knowing that he cannot live forever like the gods, Gilgamesh hopes that he will gain the next best thing—lasting fame—by slaying the monster. Together the two heroes kill Humbaba, and Enkidu cuts off the monster's head.

The Insulted Goddess. Impressed with Gilgamesh's courage and daring, the goddess Ishtar offers to marry him. He refuses, however, and insults the goddess by reminding her of her cruelty toward previous lovers. Enraged by his refusal and insults, Ishtar persuades her father, the god Anu, to send the sacred Bull of Heaven to kill Gilgamesh. Anu sends the bull, but Gilgamesh and Enkidu kill the bull first. Enkidu further insults Ishtar by throwing a piece of the dead bull in her face.

That night, Enkidu dreams that the gods have decided that he must die for his role in killing the Bull of Heaven. His death will also be the punishment for his dear friend Gilgamesh. Enkidu falls ill

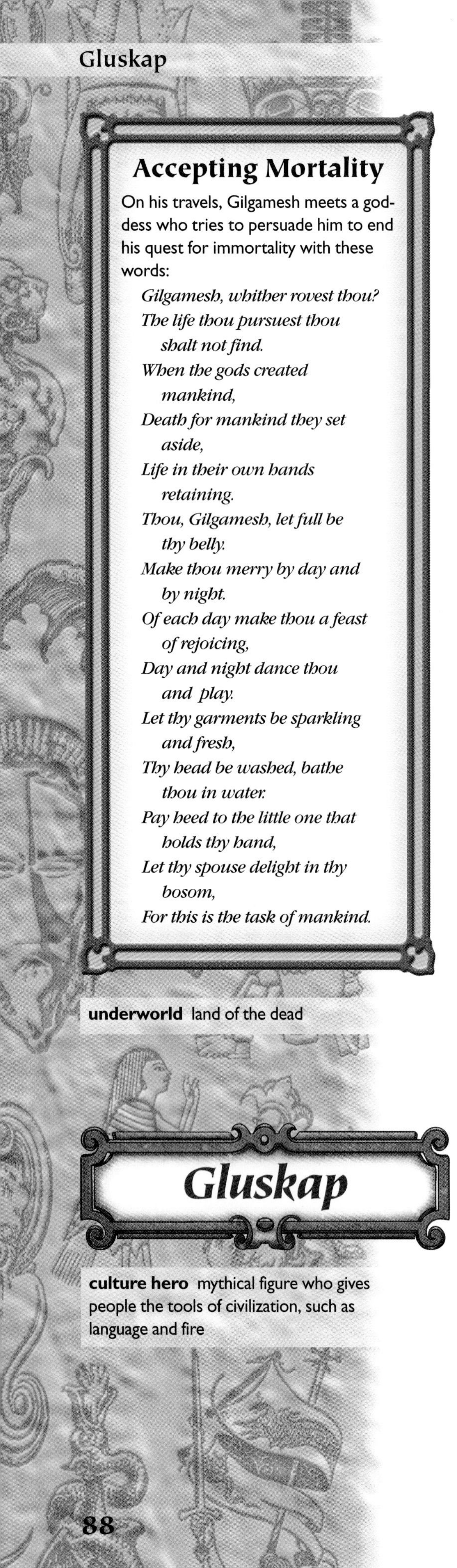

Accepting Mortality

On his travels, Gilgamesh meets a goddess who tries to persuade him to end his quest for immortality with these words:

Gilgamesh, whither rovest thou?
The life thou pursuest thou shalt not find.
When the gods created mankind,
Death for mankind they set aside,
Life in their own hands retaining.
Thou, Gilgamesh, let full be thy belly.
Make thou merry by day and by night.
Of each day make thou a feast of rejoicing,
Day and night dance thou and play.
Let thy garments be sparkling and fresh,
Thy head be washed, bathe thou in water.
Pay heed to the little one that holds thy hand,
Let thy spouse delight in thy bosom,
For this is the task of mankind.

underworld land of the dead

and has other dreams of his death and descent to the **underworld.** He grows weaker and weaker and finally dies after 12 days of suffering. Gilgamesh is overwhelmed with grief. He also fears his own death and decides that he must find a way to gain immortality.

Search for Utnapishtim. After Enkidu's funeral and burial, Gilgamesh sets out on a long and hazardous journey to seek a man named Utnapishtim. Utnapishtim had survived a great flood and was granted immortality by the gods. Gilgamesh travels through various strange lands and meets people who tell him to end his search and accept his fate as a mortal. Refusing to give up, Gilgamesh finally reaches the sea and persuades a boatman to take him across the waters to the home of Utnapishtim.

Utnapishtim tells Gilgamesh the story of the Great Flood and of the boat that he constructed to save his family and various animals. He then offers the hero a challenge: if Gilgamesh can stay awake for seven days, he will be given the immortality he desperately desires. Gilgamesh accepts the challenge but soon falls asleep. When he awakes seven days later, he realizes that immortality is beyond his reach, and with sorrow, he accepts his fate. Utnapishtim tells him not to despair because the gods have granted him other great gifts, such as courage, skill in battle, and wisdom.

In appreciation of Gilgamesh's courageous efforts to find him, Utnapishtim tells the hero where to find a plant that can restore youth. Gilgamesh finds the plant and continues on his journey. Along the way, while he bathes in a pool, a snake steals the plant. This explains the snake's ability to slough off its old skin and start afresh with a new one. Disappointed and tired, but also wiser and more at peace with himself, Gilgamesh returns to Uruk to await his death.

The last part of the *Epic of Gilgamesh,* thought to be a later addition, tells how the spirit of Enkidu returns from the underworld and helps Gilgamesh find some lost objects he received from Ishtar. Enkidu also tells his close friend about the afterlife and describes the grim conditions of the underworld. ***See also*** **Anu; Enkidu; Floods; Ishtar; Noah; Utnapishtim.**

Gluskap

culture hero mythical figure who gives people the tools of civilization, such as language and fire

Gluskap, a **culture hero** of the Algonquian-speaking people of North America, created the world and has helped his people in many situations. According to Native American mythology, Gluskap was responsible for making all the good things in the universe—the air, the earth, the animals, and the people—from his mother's body. His evil brother Malsum created the mountains and valleys and all the things that are a bother to humans, such as snakes.

There are many tales about Gluskap's adventures and how he serves his people, teaching them to hunt, fish, weave, and do many other useful things. In one story, a giant monster steals all the water and will not share it with anyone else. At the end of the story, Gluskap fights the monster and turns it into a bullfrog. In another myth, Gluskap frees all the rabbits in the world, which are

*† See **Names and Places** at the end of this volume for further information.*

being held prisoner by the Great White Hare. The rabbits then become food for his people. ***See also*** **ANIMALS IN MYTHOLOGY; NATIVE AMERICAN MYTHOLOGY.**

Godiva, Lady

Medieval legend says that a woman named Lady Godiva rode naked on her horse through the English city of Coventry centuries ago. Although a Lady Godiva really existed, no evidence links her with such a deed. The connection occurred when an older fragment of traditional mythology became attached to the name of a historical figure.

Lady Godiva was the wife of Leofric, lord of Coventry. According to the story, she felt that his taxes on the people were unfair. Irritated, he said that he would change them if she rode naked through the marketplace. She did so, wearing only her long hair. The townspeople respectfully stayed indoors, but a tailor named Tom sneaked a peek out his window and was struck blind. This story seems to be the origin of the expression "peeping Tom."

pagan term used by early Christians to describe non-Christians and non-Christian beliefs

The tale was first written down in the mid-1200s. It most likely combines the real woman's name with ancient folklore about **pagan** goddesses and processions through the countryside in their honor.

Gog and Magog

Gog and Magog appear as evil figures in the mythology of several different cultures. In the book of Revelation in the Bible, Gog and Magog are the evil powers that will battle God at the end of the world. In Islamic mythology, they appear as forces called Yajuj and Majuj that are fighting against Allah (God).

Britain's Gog and Magog were the last survivors of a race of evil giants. After slaying the other giants, the legendary hero Brut brought Gog and Magog back to London to serve as his gatekeepers. According to tradition, Brut, or Brutus, was the founder of London. London's Guildhall has housed monumental figures of Gog and Magog for nearly 500 years.

Golden Bough

In Roman mythology, the Golden Bough was a tree branch with golden leaves that enabled the Trojan hero Aeneas† to travel through the **underworld** safely. The bough was said to be sacred to Proserpina (Persephone), the queen of the underworld, and was associated with the goddess Diana†.

underworld land of the dead

epic long poem about legendary or historical heroes, written in a grand style

The story of Aeneas and the Golden Bough is found in the *Aeneid,* the **epic** by the Roman poet Virgil. According to this tale, the spirit of Anchises, Aeneas's dead father, appears and tells Aeneas to visit the underworld, where he will learn what the future holds in store for people. First, however, Aeneas must find the **oracle** known as the Sibyl of Cumae, who will lead him to the land of the dead.

oracle priest or priestess or other creature through whom a god is believed to speak; also the location (such as a shrine) where such words are spoken

Aeneas locates the oracle, who informs him that he cannot pass through the underworld safely without the Golden Bough. When Aeneas enters the forest to look for the sacred branch, two doves lead him to an oak tree that shelters the bough of shimmering

This painting by J. M. W. Turner illustrates a story from Roman mythology. The Sibyl of Cumae explains to Aeneas that he must obtain a sacred branch called the Golden Bough for safe passage through the underworld.

golden leaves. Aeneas gets the Golden Bough and returns to the Sibyl of Cumae.

Together Aeneas and the Sibyl enter the underworld. With the Golden Bough in his possession, the hero is able to pass safely through the various dangers and obstacles there. At the deadly and magical river Acheron, the boatman Charon sees the sacred bough and takes Aeneas and the Sibyl across the water to the kingdom of Hades†. There Aeneas finds the spirit of his father.

The Golden Bough also appears in other legends, particularly in connection with the goddess Diana. According to some accounts, it was a custom in the **cult** of Diana for a slave to cut a branch from a sacred tree and then kill the priest responsible for guarding the tree. The slave took the priest's place and was later killed himself in the same way. This custom inspired *The Golden Bough,* a multivolume study of religion and mythology written by Scottish scholar Sir James Frazer and published in 1890. ***See also*** **AENEAS; AENEID, THE; DIANA; PERSEPHONE; ROMAN MYTHOLOGY; SIBYLS, THE; TREES IN MYTHOLOGY; UNDERWORLD.**

cult group bound together by devotion to a particular person, belief, or god

Golden Fleece

One of the best-known stories in Greek mythology concerns the hero Jason and his quest for the Golden Fleece. The fleece, which came from a magic ram, hung in a sacred grove of trees in the distant land of Colchis. Jason's adventure, however, was only one part of the story of the Golden Fleece, which began years earlier.

According to legend, King Athamas of Boeotia in Greece had two children by his wife Nephele: a son, Phrixus, and a daughter,

*†See **Names and Places** at the end of this volume for further information.*

Helle. After a time, Athamas grew tired of Nephele and took a new wife, Ino, with whom he had two sons. Jealous of Phrixus and Helle, Ino plotted against them. First, she cunningly had seeds destroyed so that crops would not grow, resulting in a famine. She then arranged to have blame for the famine placed on her stepchildren and convinced Athamas that he must sacrifice Phrixus to Zeus† to restore the kingdom's prosperity.

Fearful for her children's lives, Nephele sought help from the god Hermes†, and he sent a winged ram with a fleece of gold to carry Phrixus and Helle to safety. While flying over the water on the ram, Helle fell off and drowned. But Phrixus reached the land of Colchis and was welcomed by its ruler, King Aeëtes. Phrixus sacrificed the ram to Zeus and gave the Golden Fleece to the king, who placed it in an oak tree in a sacred grove. It was guarded by a dragon that never slept.

The story of the Golden Fleece resumes some time later when Jason and the Argonauts, a band of Greek heroes, set out in search of the fleece aboard a ship called the *Argo.* Jason undertook this quest in order to gain his rightful place as king of Iolcus in Thessaly. The country had been ruled for a number of years by his uncle Pelias.

After many adventures, Jason and the Argonauts finally reached Colchis. However, King Aeëtes refused to give up the Golden Fleece unless Jason could harness two fire-breathing bulls to a plow, plant dragons' teeth in the ground, and defeat the warriors that sprang up from the teeth. Aeëtes had a daughter, Medea, who was a sorceress. She fell in love with Jason and helped him accomplish these tasks. Medea also helped Jason steal the Golden Fleece by charming the serpent that guarded it and putting the creature to sleep. Jason, Medea, and the Argonauts then set sail for Iolcus with the fleece. ***See also*** **ANIMALS IN MYTHOLOGY; ARGONAUTS; JASON; MEDEA.**

Golem

According to Jewish legend, a golem was a human-shaped object brought to life by a magic word. Usually the golem functioned like a robot and could perform simple tasks. However, in some tales, the golem became a violent monster that could not be controlled, even by its creator.

Although the idea of a golem goes back to biblical times, most legends about the creature appeared during the Middle Ages. Typically, the golem came to life when a special word such as *truth* or one of the names of God was written on a piece of paper and placed on the golem's forehead or in its mouth. At any point, the creator of the golem might end its life by removing the paper with the sacred word.

In a famous story from the 1500s, Rabbi Judah Low ben Bezulel of Prague created a golem from clay. In another legend, set in Poland, a golem made by Rabbi Elijah of Chelm became so powerful and dangerous that the rabbi hurriedly changed it back into a lifeless heap. ***See also*** **SEMITIC MYTHOLOGY.**

Gordian Knot

In Greek and Roman mythology, the Gordian knot was an extremely complicated knot tied by Gordius, the king of Phrygia in Asia Minor†. Located in the city of Gordium, the knot came to symbolize a difficult problem that was almost impossible to solve.

According to legend, Gordius was a peasant who married the fertility goddess Cybele. When Gordius became king of Phrygia, he dedicated his chariot to Zeus† and fastened it to a pole with the Gordian knot. Although the knot was supposedly impossible to unravel, an **oracle** predicted that it would be untied by the future king of Asia.

oracle priest or priestess or other creature through whom a god is believed to speak; also the location (such as a shrine) where such words are spoken

Many individuals came to Gordium to try to undo the knot, but they all failed. Then, according to tradition, the Greek conqueror Alexander the Great visited the city in 333 B.C. After searching unsuccessfully for the hidden ends of the Gordian knot, Alexander became impatient. In an unexpected move, he took out his sword and cut through the knot. Alexander then went on to conquer Asia, thus fulfilling the oracle's **prophecy.** Alexander's solution to the problem led to the saying, "cutting the Gordian knot," which means solving a complicated problem through bold action. ***See also*** **CYBELE; MIDAS.**

prophecy foretelling of what is to come; also something that is predicted

Gorgons

The Gorgons, three terrifying creatures in Greek mythology, were sisters named Stheno (strength), Euryale (wide-leaping), and Medusa (ruler or queen). Daughters of the sea god Phorcys and his sister and wife, Ceto, they lived in the west near the setting sun.

According to legend, the Gorgons were ugly monsters with huge wings, sharp fangs and claws, and bodies covered with dragonlike scales. They had horrible grins, staring eyes, and writhing snakes for hair. Their gaze was so terrifying that anyone who looked upon them immediately turned to stone. Two of the Gorgons, Stheno and Euryale, were **immortal,** but Medusa was not. In one of the more famous Greek myths, the hero Perseus† kills and beheads her with help from Athena†. The goddess later placed an image of Medusa's head on her armor.

immortal able to live forever

The Gorgons had three sisters known as the Graeae ("the gray ones"). These old women—Enyo, Pemphredo, and Deino—shared one eye and one tooth, and they took turns using them. The Graeae guarded the route that led to their sisters, the Gorgons. Perseus, however, stole their eye and tooth, forcing them to help in his quest to find and kill Medusa. ***See also*** **GREEK MYTHOLOGY; MEDUSA; PERSEUS.**

The three Gorgons were called Stheno, Euryale, and Medusa. Their gaze was so terrifying that anyone who looked at them turned to stone. Caravaggio painted this shield with the face of Medusa in the 1590s.

†*See* ***Names and Places*** *at the end of this volume for further information.*

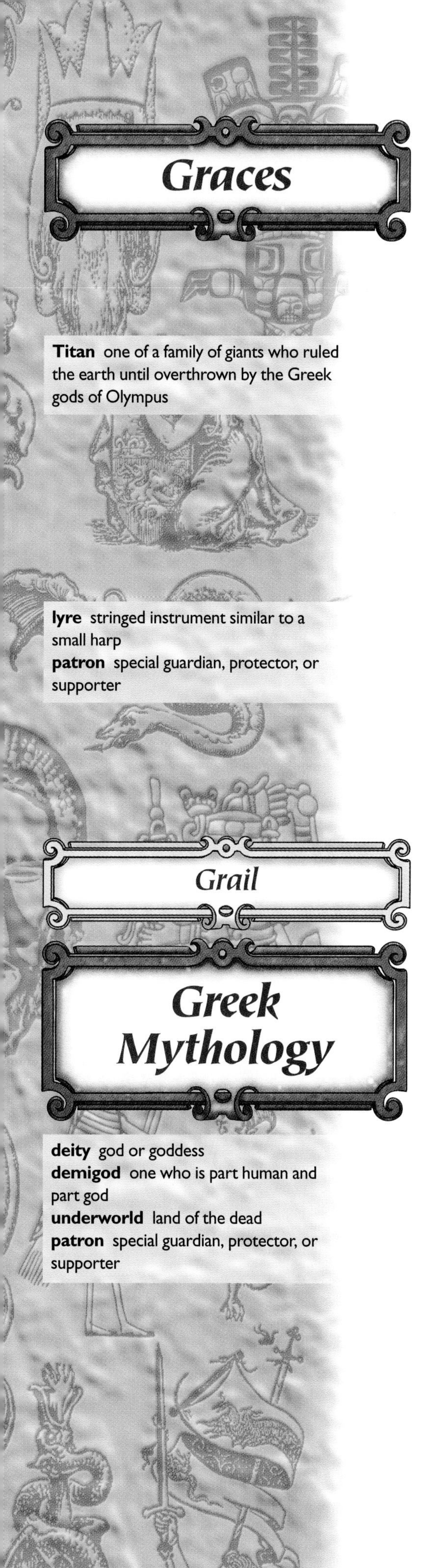

Graces

In Greek and Roman mythology, the Graces (or Charites) were minor goddesses who symbolized beauty, charm, and goodness. The number of Graces varied, though most myths included three sisters: Aglaia (brightness or splendor), Thalia (good cheer or blossoming one), and Euphrosyne (mirth or joyfulness). Other Graces sometimes mentioned were Cleta (sound), Pasithea (shining), and Peitho (persuasion).

Titan one of a family of giants who ruled the earth until overthrown by the Greek gods of Olympus

According to most stories, the Graces were the children of Zeus† and Eurynome, a daughter of the **Titans** Oceanus and Tethys. In some myths, however, the Graces' parents were Zeus and Hera†. The Graces always appeared as a group rather than as separate individuals. They were also frequently linked with the Muses, another group of female goddesses.

The main role of the Graces was to bestow beauty, charm, and goodness on young women and to give joy to people in general. They were usually associated with Aphrodite, the goddess of love, and appeared among the attendants of the gods Apollo†, Dionysus†, and Hermes†. They entertained the gods by dancing to the music of Apollo's **lyre.** At times, the Graces were considered **patrons** of music, dance, and poetry.

lyre stringed instrument similar to a small harp
patron special guardian, protector, or supporter

The Graces provided inspiration to artists throughout the centuries. Most works of art portray them with their hands entwined and their bodies either nude or partially draped with flowing robes. One of the most famous paintings of the Graces is *Primavera* by Botticelli, an Italian artist of the late 1400s. ***See also*** **Apollo; Greek Mythology; Muses; Roman Mythology.**

Grail

See *Holy Grail.*

Greek Mythology

The mythology of the ancient Greeks included a dazzling array of **deities, demigods,** monsters, and heroes. These figures inhabited a realm that stretched beyond the Greek landscape to the palaces of the gods on snow-capped Mount Olympus, as well as to the dismal **underworld.** In time, Greek mythology became part of European culture, and many of its stories became known throughout the world.

deity god or goddess
demigod one who is part human and part god
underworld land of the dead
patron special guardian, protector, or supporter

Despite their awesome powers, the Greek gods and goddesses were much like people. Their actions stemmed from recognizable passions, such as pride, jealousy, love, and the thirst for revenge. The deities often left Mount Olympus to become involved in the affairs of mortals, interacting with men and women as **patrons,** enemies, and sometimes lovers. They were not above using tricks and disguises to influence events, and their schemes and plots often entangled people.

Heroes and ordinary humans in Greek myths frequently discovered that things were not what they appeared to be. The underlying moral principle, though, was that the gods rewarded honorable behavior and obedience, and people who dishonored themselves or defied the gods usually paid a high price.

city-state independent state consisting of a city and its surrounding territory

epic long poem about legendary or historical heroes, written in a grand style

destiny future or fate of an individual or thing

Titan one of a family of giants who ruled the earth until overthrown by the Greek gods of Olympus

Roots and Sources

Geography helped shape Greek mythology. Greece is a peninsula surrounded by sea and islands. Rugged mountains and the jagged coastline break the land into many small, separate areas. Ancient Greece never became a unified empire. Instead, it consisted of small kingdoms that after about 800 B.C. became **city-states.** Because travel was easier by sea than by land, the Greeks became a nation of seafarers, and they traded and established colonies all over the Mediterranean and the Near East.

Greek mythology is a patchwork of stories, some conflicting with one another. Many have been passed down from ancient times in more than one version. The roots of this mythology reach back to two civilizations that flourished before 1100 B.C.: the Mycenaean, on the Greek mainland, and the Minoan, on the nearby island of Crete. The ancient beliefs merged with legends from Greek kingdoms and city-states and myths borrowed from other peoples to form a body of lore shared by most Greeks.

For hundreds of years, these myths passed from generation to generation in spoken form. Then, around the time the classical Greek culture of the city-states arose, people began writing them down. The works of Hesiod† and Homer†, which date from the 700s B.C., are key sources for the mythology of ancient Greece. Hesiod's *Theogony* tells of creation and of the gods' origins and relationships. The *Iliad*† and the *Odyssey*†, **epics** said to have been written by Homer, show the gods influencing human **destiny.** In addition, Pindar†, a poet of around 600 B.C., wrote poems called odes that contain much myth and legend.

Non-Greek sources also exist. The Romans dominated the Mediterranean world after the Greeks and adopted elements of Greek mythology. The Roman poet Ovid's poem the *Metamorphoses*† retells many Greek myths.

The Greek Pantheon

The word *pantheon,* which refers to all the gods of a particular culture, comes from the Greek *pan* (all) and *theoi* (gods). The pantheon of the ancient Greeks consisted of the Olympian gods and other major deities, along with many minor deities and demigods.

Olympian Gods. The principal deities, six gods and six goddesses, lived on Mount Olympus, the highest peak in Greece. Zeus (called Jupiter by the Romans) was the king of the gods and reigned over all the other deities and their realms. He was the protector of justice, kingship, authority, and the social order. His personal life was rather disorderly, however. Many myths tell of his love affairs with various goddesses, **Titans,** and human women—and their effects.

Hera (Roman Juno), queen of the gods, was Zeus's sister and wife. She could cause all kinds of trouble when her husband pursued other women. Although the patron of brides, wives, and mothers

†*See **Names and Places** at the end of this volume for further information.*

nymph minor goddess of nature, usually portrayed as young and beautiful

Major Greek and Roman Deities

Greek Deity	Roman Name	Role
Olympian Gods and Goddesses		
Aphrodite	Venus	goddess of love and beauty
Apollo	Apollo	god of the sun, arts, and medicine; ideal of male beauty
Ares	Mars	god of war
Artemis	Diana	goddess of hunting and protector of wild animals
Athena	Minerva	goddess of wisdom, warfare, and crafts
Demeter	Ceres	goddess of grain, farming, and soil
Hephaestus	Vulcan	god of fire, volcanoes, and industry
Hera	Juno	queen of the gods, protector of marriage and childbirth
Hermes	Mercury	messenger of the gods, patron of travelers, merchants, and thieves
Hestia	Vesta	goddess of the hearth
Poseidon	Neptune	god of the sea
Zeus	Jupiter	king of the gods, protector of justice and social order
Other Major Deities		
Dionysus	Bacchus	god of wine and revelry
Hades	Pluto	king of the underworld
Persephone	Proserpina	queen of the underworld
Prometheus	———	giver of fire and crafts to humans

in childbirth, Hera could be cruel and vengeful toward Zeus's mistresses and their children.

Poseidon (Roman Neptune), Zeus's brother, was god of the sea and of earthquakes. He was married to Amphitrite, a sea **nymph,** but like Zeus, he fathered many children outside his marriage. Among his descendants were nymphs, sea gods, and monsters such as the Hydra†.

Demeter (Roman Ceres), a sister of Zeus, was the goddess of grain, farming, and soil. She had a daughter, Persephone, by Zeus.

This frieze shows the Gigantomachy, a legendary battle in Greek mythology between the Giants and the Olympian gods. The gods won by killing the Giants with the help of Hercules.

Before merging into the Olympian pantheon, Demeter and Hera were aspects of a much older deity called the Great Goddess, an earth goddess worshiped by the agricultural Greeks.

Aphrodite (Roman Venus), the goddess of love, beauty, and desire, greatly resembled Near Eastern goddesses such as Ishtar and Astarte. Her husband was Hephaestus (Roman Vulcan), god of fire, volcanoes, and invention. The other gods mocked Hephaestus because he was lame and also because of Aphrodite's **adulteries,** such as her love affair with the god of war, Ares (Roman Mars).

adultery sexual relationship between a married person and someone other than his or her spouse

Two Olympian goddesses were virgins who resisted sexual advances from gods and men. Athena (Roman Minerva), the daughter of Zeus and a female Titan, was the goddess of wisdom, military skill, cities, and crafts. Artemis (Roman Diana) was the goddess of hunting and the protector of wild animals. She and her twin brother, the handsome young god Apollo, were the children of Zeus and the Titan Leto. Apollo functioned as the patron of archery, music, the arts, and medicine and was associated with the sun, enlightenment, and **prophecy.** He also served as the ideal of male beauty.

prophecy foretelling of what is to come; also something that is predicted

Hermes (Roman Mercury) was the son of Zeus and yet another Titan. He served as the gods' messenger and also as the patron of markets, merchants, thieves, and storytelling. Hestia (Roman Vesta), another sister of Zeus, was goddess of the hearth, and her identity included associations with stability, domestic well-being, and the ritual of naming children.

Other Major Deities. Hades (Roman Pluto), the brother of Zeus and Poseidon, was god of the underworld, where the dead could receive either punishment or a blessed afterlife. Hades dwelt in his underground kingdom and not on Mount Olympus. He controlled **supernatural** forces connected with the earth and was also associated with wealth.

supernatural related to forces beyond the normal world; magical or miraculous

Dionysus (Roman Bacchus), born as a demigod, became the god of wine, drunkenness, and altered states of consciousness such as religious frenzy. Like plants that die each winter only to return in

† *See **Names and Places** at the end of this volume for further information.*

the spring, Dionysus is said to have died and been reborn, a parallel to Cretan and Near Eastern myths about dying-and-returning gods. Dionysus eventually took Hestia's place on Mount Olympus.

Major Themes and Myths

Stories about the gods—along with other supernatural beings, demigods, heroes, and ordinary mortals—illustrate the major themes of Greek mythology. They explain how the world came to be and offer examples of how people should and should not live. The myths provided support for the Greeks' idea of community, especially the city-state.

Origins of Gods and Humans. The theme of younger generations overcoming their elders runs through the history of the Greek gods. Creation began with Chaos, first imagined as the gap between earth and sky but later as formless confusion. The mother goddess, Gaia, the earth, came into being and gave birth to Uranus, the sky. Joining with Uranus, she became pregnant with six male and six female Titans. But before these children could be born, Uranus had to be separated from Gaia. Cronus†, the youngest Titan, cut off his father's sexual organs and threw them into the sea. Aphrodite was born from the foam where they landed.

The 12 Titans mated with each other and with nymphs. Cronus married his sister Rhea (Roman Cybele). Perhaps remembering what he had done to his own father, Cronus swallowed his children as they were born. When Rhea gave birth to Zeus, however, she tricked Cronus by substituting a stone wrapped in baby clothes for him to swallow. Later, when Zeus had grown up, a female Titan named Metis gave Cronus a drink that made him vomit up Zeus's brothers and sisters. They helped Zeus defeat the Titans and become the supreme deity. Zeus then married Metis. However, because of a prophecy that her children would be wise and powerful, he swallowed her so that her children could not harm him. Their daughter Athena sprang full-grown from Zeus's head.

The matings of the gods and goddesses produced the rest of the pantheon. As for human beings, one myth says that they arose out of the soil. Another says that Zeus flooded the earth and drowned all human beings because they did not honor the gods. Deucalion and Pyrrha, the son and daughter-in-law of Zeus's brother Prometheus, survived the flood in a boat. Afterward they created the present human race from stones, which they threw onto the muddy land.

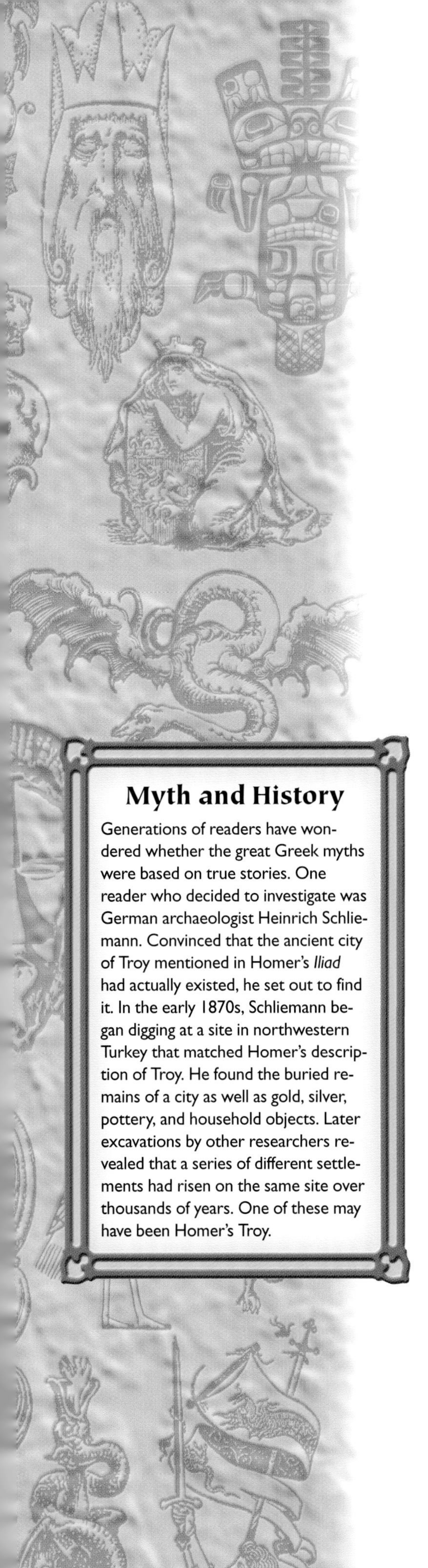

Myth and History

Generations of readers have wondered whether the great Greek myths were based on true stories. One reader who decided to investigate was German archaeologist Heinrich Schliemann. Convinced that the ancient city of Troy mentioned in Homer's *Iliad* had actually existed, he set out to find it. In the early 1870s, Schliemann began digging at a site in northwestern Turkey that matched Homer's description of Troy. He found the buried remains of a city as well as gold, silver, pottery, and household objects. Later excavations by other researchers revealed that a series of different settlements had risen on the same site over thousands of years. One of these may have been Homer's Troy.

The Ages of the World. According to the poet Hesiod, the world had seen four ages and four races of human beings before his time. The Titans created the people of the golden age, who lived in comfort and peace until they died and became good spirits. The Olympian gods created the silver race, a childish people whom Zeus destroyed for failing to honor the gods. Zeus then created the bronze race, brutal and warlike people who destroyed themselves with constant fighting.

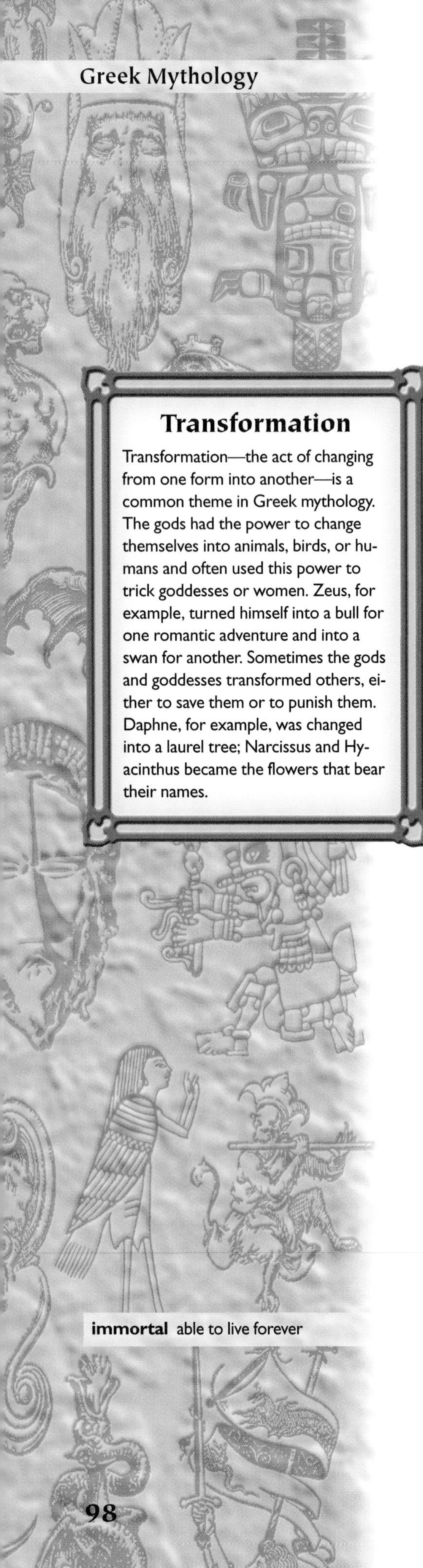

Zeus next created a race of heroes nobler than the men of the bronze age (no metal was associated with this age). The Greeks believed that distant but semihistorical events such as the Trojan War† had occurred during this fourth age, the age of heroes. Some heroes died, but Zeus took the survivors to the Isles of the Blessed, where they lived in honor. The fifth age, the age of iron, began when Zeus created the present race of humans. It is an age of toil, greed, and strife. When all honor and justice have vanished, Zeus will destroy this race like those before it.

The theme of this myth is decline, with the best times always in the past. Yet the Greeks also believed that one day the golden age would return again. Decline was only part of a long cycle.

Transformation

Transformation—the act of changing from one form into another—is a common theme in Greek mythology. The gods had the power to change themselves into animals, birds, or humans and often used this power to trick goddesses or women. Zeus, for example, turned himself into a bull for one romantic adventure and into a swan for another. Sometimes the gods and goddesses transformed others, either to save them or to punish them. Daphne, for example, was changed into a laurel tree; Narcissus and Hyacinthus became the flowers that bear their names.

War. The gods were born in strife and struggle, and the theme of war as an inescapable part of existence runs through Greek mythology. Many myths recount episodes in the Olympians' conflict with the Titans. Others are connected to the Trojan War, a long conflict in which both people and deities displayed such qualities as courage, stubbornness, pride, and anger. In addition to the war itself, the travels and adventures of warriors after the war ended are subjects of myth and legend.

Love. Many myths deal with the loves of Zeus, who sometimes disguised himself in order to enjoy sexual relations with mortal women. Other myths present examples of trust, loyalty, and eternal love—or of the pitfalls and problems of love and desire. The tragic myth of Pyramus and Thisbe illustrates a divine reward for lovers who could not live without each other. The story of Eros and Psyche revolves around the issue of trust. In another myth, the gods reward the elderly Baucis and Philemon for their devotion to each other and their kindheartedness toward strangers.

Love affairs in Greek myth do not always end happily. One story tells how Apollo fell in love with a nymph named Daphne, but like Artemis she cared more for hunting than for love. She ran from Apollo in terror, and when he was about to seize her, she asked her father, a river god, to save her. He changed her into a laurel tree, which is why the laurel was considered Apollo's sacred tree.

Heroes. Many Greek myths focus on the marvelous achievements of heroes who possessed physical strength, sharp wits, virtue, and a sense of honor. These heroes often had a god for a father and a human for a mother. One cycle of myths concerns the hero Hercules—Zeus's son by a mortal princess—renowned for his strength and for completing 12 remarkable feats. Unlike other heroes, who died and were buried, Hercules eventually became **immortal** and was worshiped as a god by both Greeks and Romans. Other heroes include Perseus, who killed the serpent-haired Medusa† and rescued a princess from a sea monster; Theseus, who defeated the man-eating Minotaur of Crete; Jason, who led a band of adventurers to capture the Golden Fleece; Achilles, a mighty warrior of the Trojan War; and Odysseus, who fought at Troy and

immortal able to live forever

†*See **Names and Places** at the end of this volume for further information.*

afterward faced many challenges from gods, men, and monsters during his long journey home.

The Underworld. Myths can give expression to a culture's ideas about death. Characters in Greek myths sometimes enter the underworld, the kingdom of the god Hades. Heroes may go there seeking advice or prophecies from the dead. Persephone, Demeter's daughter, was carried to the underworld by Hades, who fell in love with her. Her myth explains the seasons: plants grow and bear fruit while Persephone is aboveground with her mother but wither and die during the months she spends with Hades. The tale of Orpheus† and Eurydice explores the finality of death and the tempting possibility of a reunion with loved ones who have died.

Morality and Fate. Many Greek myths present visions of right and wrong behavior and the consequences of each. The myth of Baucis and Philemon, for example, illustrates the importance of hospitality and generosity toward all, for a humble stranger may be a deity in disguise with power to reward or punish. Another story tells how the handsome Narcissus, so vain and heartless that he could love only himself, drowned while gazing at his reflection in a stream. The myth of Icarus, who gains the ability to fly but soars so close to the sun that his wings melt, points out the dangers of tempting fate and rising above one's proper place in life. Such stories often involve unexpected changes or transformations. For example, the myth of King Midas, whose request for a golden touch turns his own daughter into a golden statue, warns of the perils of greed.

Like Icarus, those who claim godlike qualities, who defy the gods, or who perform outrageous acts suffer swift and severe punishment. Arachne was a mortal who boasted that she could weave better cloth than the goddess Athena, inventor of weaving. The goddess turned the boastful girl into a spider weaving its web. The gods devised eternal punishments in the depths of Hades for Sisyphus, who tried to cheat death, and for Tantalus, who killed his own son and fed him to the gods. They also punished Oedipus, who killed his father and married his mother, even though he did not know their identities when he did so.

The Legacy of Greek Mythology

Greek mythology has profoundly influenced Western culture. So universally familiar are its stories that words and sayings refer to them. The

This vase dating from around 490 B.C. shows Priam, the king of Troy, asking Achilles to return the body of his dead son Hector.

Greek Mythology

Other entries relating to Greek mythology include

Achilles	Aurora	Fates	Lethe	Philomela
Adonis	Baucis and Philemon	Furies	Medea	Pleiades
Aeolus	Bellerophon	Gaia	Medusa	Poseidon
Agamemnon	Boreas	Galatea	Menelaus	Priam
Ajax	Cadmus	Ganymede	Midas	Procrustes
Alcestis	Calliope	Golden Fleece	Minos	Prometheus
Amazons	Callisto	Gorgons	Minotaur	Proteus
Ambrosia	Calypso	Graces	Muses	Psyche
Androcles	Cassandra	Hades	Narcissus	Pygmalion
Andromache	Cassiopeia	Halcyone	Nemean Lion	Pyramus and Thisbe
Andromeda	Castor and Pollux	Harpies	Nike	Saturn
Antaeus	Centaurs	Hecate	Nymphs	Satyrs
Antigone	Cephalus and Procris	Hector	Odysseus	Scylla and Charybdis
Aphrodite	Cerberus	Hecuba	Oedipus	Sirens
Apollo	Circe	Helen of Troy	Orestes	Sisyphus
Arachne	Clytemnestra	Hera	Orion	Styx
Arcadia	Cybele	Hercules	Orpheus	Tantalus
Ares	Cyclopes	Hermaphroditus	Pan	Thanatos
Argonauts	Daedalus	Hermes	Pandora	Theseus
Argus	Daphnis and Chloe	Hero and Leander	Paris	Thetis
Ariadne	Delphi	Hydra	Pegasus	Tiresias
Artemis	Demeter	Hypnos	Peleus	Titans
Asclepius	Dionysus	Io	Penelope	Uranus
Astyanax	Echo	Iphigenia	Persephone	Vesta
Atalanta	Electra	Jason	Perseus	Vulcan
Athena	Eros	Jocasta	Phaedra	Zeus
Atlas	Eurydice	Laocoön	Phaethon	

discord disagreement

myth of Narcissus, for example, produced *narcissism,* or excessive vanity, and something that causes an argument may be called an "apple of discord," after an apple that Eris, the goddess of **discord,** used to start a dispute among Athena, Aphrodite, and Hera. Greek myths and legends span the sky in the names of constellations and planets.

Literature and drama have long drawn upon themes and stories from Greek myth. Besides the works of the ancient Greeks themselves—including the plays of Sophocles and Euripides—writers from ancient times to the present have found inspiration in Greek mythology. Roman authors Virgil (the *Aeneid*†) and Ovid (the *Metamorphoses*) used Greek stories and characters in their poems. References to Greek myths appear in the works of the medieval Italian poets Petrarch and Boccaccio and in those of the English poet Chaucer. Shakespeare's *A Midsummer Night's Dream* contains the story of Pyramus and Thisbe as a comic play-within-a-play. Modern writers who have drawn upon Greek mythology include James Joyce *(Ulysses)* and Mary Renault *(The Bull from the Sea).*

Artists from the Renaissance to the present have depicted scenes from Greek mythology. Botticelli's *Birth of Venus* (ca. 1480),

†*See* ***Names and Places*** *at the end of this volume for further information.*

Poussin's *Apollo and Daphne* (ca. 1630), and Renoir's *Diana* (1867) are just a few of many such paintings. The Greeks chanted songs and hymns based on myth at religious festivals, and Greek mythology has continued to inspire composers of the performing arts. Operas based on mythic stories include Monteverdi's *Ariadne,* Strauss's *Elektra,* and Offenbach's *Orpheus in the Underworld.* Marcel Camus' film *Black Orpheus* also came from the story of Orpheus and Eurydice. *Apollo* and *Orpheus* by Balanchine, *Ariadne* by Ailey, and *Clytemnestra* by Graham are four modern ballets that interpret Greek myths through dance. ***See also*** **Creation Stories; Homer; Iliad, The; Metamorphoses, The; Odyssey, The; Ovid; Roman Mythology; Trojan War.**

Griffins

The griffin was a creature that appeared in the mythology of Greece and the ancient Near East. A popular figure in art, it had the body of a lion and the head and wings of an eagle or other bird. Sometimes the griffin is shown with the tail of a serpent. With its eagle's head and lion's body, the griffin represented mastery of the sky and the earth. It became associated with strength and wisdom.

According to Greek mythology, griffins pulled the chariots of Zeus† and Apollo†. They also guarded the gold that lay near the lands of the Hyperboreans and the Arimaspians, mythical peoples of the far north, and represented Nemesis, the goddess of vengeance. To the ancient Hebrews, the griffin symbolized Persia because the creature appeared frequently in Persian art.

The griffin appeared in Christian art and mythology as well. At first, it symbolized Satan and was thought to threaten human souls. But the griffin later became a symbol of the divine and human nature of Jesus Christ. During the Middle Ages, Christian myths often spoke of the magical powers of griffins' claws, which if made into drinking cups were said to change color when they came in contact with poison. The griffin was also thought to prey on those who **persecuted** Christians. ***See also*** **Animals in Mythology; Greek Mythology; Persian Mythology; Semitic Mythology.**

persecute to harass or punish individuals or groups

Guinevere

Guinevere was the wife of King Arthur, the legendary ruler of Britain. She was a beautiful and noble queen, but her life took a tragic turn when she fell in love with Lancelot, one of Arthur's bravest and most loyal knights. The relationship between the queen and Lancelot eventually destroyed the special fellowship of the Knights of the Round Table.

Guinevere was the daughter of King Leodegran of Scotland. Arthur admired the king's lovely daughter and married her in spite of a warning from his adviser Merlin that Guinevere would be unfaithful to him. As a wedding gift, Leodegran gave Arthur a round table that would play a central role in his court.

After the marriage, Guinevere became acquainted with Lancelot, who performed various deeds to honor and rescue her. At first, Arthur took no notice of the growing attachment between

adultery sexual relationship between a married person and someone other than his or her spouse

the queen and Lancelot. Later, however, the king was forced to accuse his wife of **adultery** and to fight her lover. Several violent battles between Arthur and Lancelot followed, with groups of knights joining in on each side. Eventually, Guinevere returned to Arthur.

Another group of legends concerning Guinevere show the queen in a more loyal role. In these tales, King Arthur left his nephew Mordred in charge of the kingdom during a military campaign. Mordred began to plot against Arthur, planning to marry Guinevere and take over as ruler of Britain. The queen refused to cooperate with Mordred and locked herself in the Tower of London to avoid marrying him. When Arthur returned to reclaim his throne, the two men fought. Arthur killed Mordred but was fatally wounded.

Following the death of Arthur, Guinevere entered a convent, where she spent the rest of her life praying and helping the poor. Filled with remorse for the trouble she and her lover had caused, she vowed never to see Lancelot again. When Guinevere died, she was buried beside King Arthur. ***See also* ARTHUR, KING; ARTHURIAN LEGENDS; CAMELOT; LANCELOT; MERLIN; ROUND TABLE.**

Hades

Titan one of a family of giants who ruled the earth until overthrown by the Greek gods of Olympus

In Greek mythology, Hades was the god of the underworld, the kingdom of the dead. (The Romans called him Pluto.) Although the name *Hades* is often used to indicate the underworld itself, it rightfully belongs only to the god, whose kingdom was known as the land of Hades or house of Hades.

Hades was the son of Cronus† and Rhea, two of the **Titans** who once ruled the universe. The Titans had other children, the gods Zeus† and Poseidon† and the goddesses Demeter†, Hera†, and Hestia. When Hades was born, Cronus swallowed him as he had swallowed his other children at birth. However, Zeus escaped this fate, and he tricked Cronus into taking a potion that made him vomit up Hades and his siblings.

Together these gods and goddesses rebelled against the Titans and seized power from them. After gaining control of the universe, Hades, Poseidon, and Zeus drew lots to divide it among themselves. Zeus gained control of the sky, Poseidon took the sea, and Hades received the underworld.

The Underworld Kingdom. The kingdom of the dead was divided into two regions. At the very bottom lay Tartarus, a land of terrible blackness where the wicked suffered eternal torments. Among those imprisoned there were the Titans, who were guarded by giants with a hundred arms. The other region of the underworld, Elysium or the Elysian Fields, was a place where the souls of good and righteous people went after death.

To reach Hades' kingdom, the dead had to cross the river Styx. A boatman named Charon ferried the dead across the river, while the monstrous Cerberus, a multiheaded dog with a serpent's tail, guarded the entrance to the underworld to prevent anyone from leaving. Four other rivers flowed through the underworld: Acheron

†*See **Names and Places** at the end of this volume for further information.*

A well-known Greek myth tells of Hades kidnapping Persephone and taking her to the underworld. This vase painting shows Persephone and Hades as rulers of the underworld.

(river of woe), Lethe (river of forgetfulness), Cocytus (river of wailing), and Phlegethon (river of fire).

Hades supervised the judgment and punishment of the dead but did not torture them himself. That task was left to the Furies, the female spirits of justice and vengeance. Although portrayed as grim and unyielding, Hades was not considered evil or unjust. Still, the ancient Greeks rarely spoke his name aloud because it was thought to be unlucky. Moreover, they built no temples to honor Hades, and few Greeks or Romans worshiped the god of the underworld.

Hades and Persephone. Hades appears in very few myths. The best known concerns his kidnapping of Persephone, daughter of Demeter, the goddess of fertility and the earth. Hades saw the beautiful Persephone while he was riding in a chariot on earth and fell in love with her. When Hades asked Zeus for permission to marry Persephone, Zeus told him that Demeter would never agree. However, Zeus did agree to help Hades seize her.

One day while picking flowers, Persephone reached for a fragrant blossom, and the earth opened up before her. Hades emerged in a chariot, grabbed Persephone, and carried her to the underworld. When Demeter discovered that her daughter was missing, she searched all over, causing drought and devastation wherever she went. After finally learning what had happened, she threatened to starve all mortals as punishment to Zeus and the other gods.

Fearing the consequences of Demeter's anger, Zeus sent word to Hades that Persephone must be returned to her mother. Before letting her go, however, Hades gave Persephone a piece of fruit to eat. Persephone ate the fruit, not realizing that anyone who ate food in the kingdom of the dead must remain there.

Zeus intervened again and arranged for Persephone to spend part of every year with her mother and part with Hades. During the growing and harvest season, she may live on earth, but during the barren winter months she must return to Hades' kingdom and reign there as queen of the underworld. ***See also*** **CERBERUS; DEMETER; ELYSIUM; FURIES; GREEK MYTHOLOGY; LETHE; PERSEPHONE; STYX; TITANS; UNDERWORLD.**

Halcyone

Two separate Greek myths mention a figure named Halcyone (or Alcyone). In the first of these tales, Halcyone is one of seven sisters called the Pleiades. This story has different versions. In one, the death of two of the sisters drives all of the Pleiades to commit suicide. In the more familiar version, a giant named Orion chases the Pleiades for seven years. To allow them to escape, Zeus† changes

the sisters into a constellation, or group of stars. Orion also becomes a constellation, and he still chases the sisters in the night sky.

In the second tale, Halcyone is the daughter of Aeolus, god of the winds. There are two versions of this legend as well. In one myth, Halcyone and her husband, Ceyx, king of Thessaly, compare themselves to the gods by taking the names Zeus and Hera†. As punishment, the gods turn them into birds. In another story, Ceyx decides to sail across the sea to consult an **oracle** to find out if the gods are angry with him. Halcyone, fearing the dangers of such a voyage, begs him not to go. However, Ceyx sets out and, as Halcyone fears, drowns in a storm. Morpheus, the god of sleep and dreams, comes to Halcyone in a dream and tells her of her husband's death. Later when she sees his body washed up on shore, the gods transform both of them into kingfisher seabirds. Every winter Aeolus sends calm winds for a short time so that Halcyone can hatch her eggs in peace. From this story comes the expression "halcyon days," meaning a time of peace and joy. ***See also*** **Aeolus; Animals in Mythology; Birds in Mythology; Orion; Pleiades.**

oracle priest or priestess or other creature through whom a god is believed to speak; also the location (such as a shrine) where such words are spoken

Hamlet

Prince Hamlet of Denmark, the main character in Shakespeare's famous play *Hamlet,* is one of the most complex figures in Western literature. Faced with avenging the murder of his father by killing his uncle, Hamlet struggles with the conflict between good and evil, weakness and strength, and his own indecision.

Hamlet is based on a legendary character found in Danish and Icelandic myths and folktales. An early version appears in an Icelandic **saga** of the A.D. 800s. Later the *Prose Edda,* a book of Norse† mythology from the 1220s, mentions a man named Amloi or Amlothi, whose story is similar to that of Hamlet.

saga story recounting the adventures of historical and legendary heroes; usually associated with Icelandic or Norse tales of the Middle Ages

Another source for the legend is *Historiae Danicae* (Danish Histories), written by Saxo Grammaticus in the 1100s. The work contains a story about a figure named Amleth who, like Hamlet, slays the uncle who has murdered his father. Modern scholars have found characters in early Celtic† mythology that seem related to the legend of Hamlet as well.

In Shakespeare's play, first performed in about 1600, Hamlet's uncle Claudius has murdered Hamlet's father and married his mother. Although eager for revenge, Hamlet is reluctant to act. The play focuses on his emotional turmoil and eventual acceptance of his fate. Although Hamlet finally kills Claudius, his actions lead to his own death as well as the deaths of others, including his mother. ***See also*** **Celtic Mythology; Norse Mythology.**

In Act V of Shakespeare's play *Hamlet,* Prince Hamlet meets his friend Horatio and a gravedigger in a graveyard. They share their thoughts about life and death.

†*See* ***Names and Places*** *at the end of this volume for further information.*

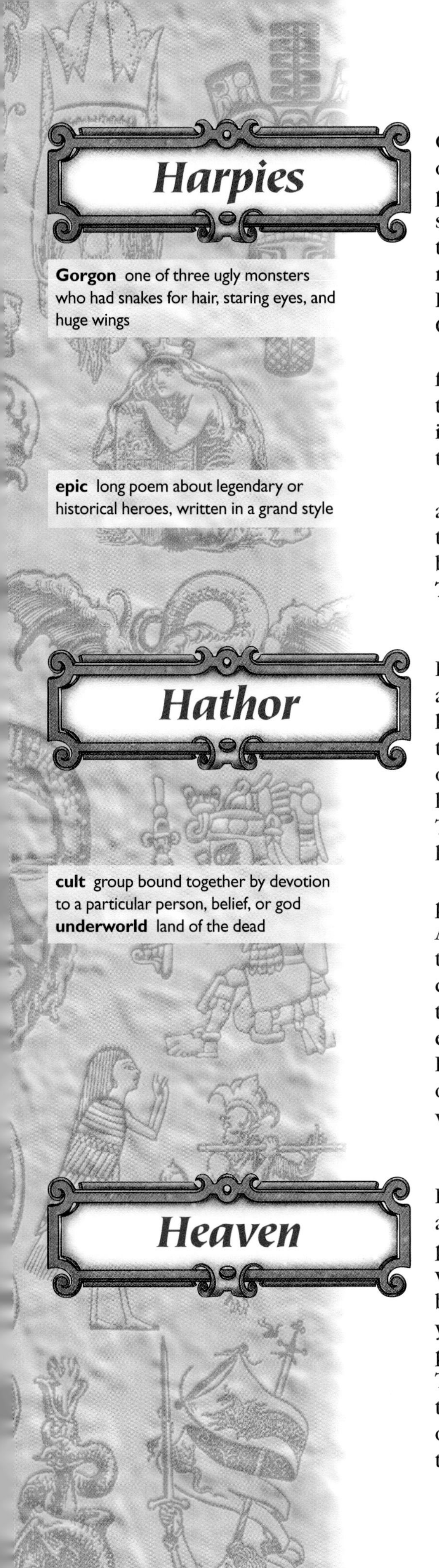

Harpies

Gorgon one of three ugly monsters who had snakes for hair, staring eyes, and huge wings

epic long poem about legendary or historical heroes, written in a grand style

Greek mythology contains two accounts of the Harpies. In the older version, the Harpies were spirits of the wind who snatched people and caused things to disappear. On one occasion, they seized the daughters of Pandareos, king of the city of Miletus, and took them off to be the servants of female spirits known as the Furies. Sometimes considered cousins of the **Gorgons,** the four Harpies were named Aello (hurricane), Celaeno (dark one), Ocypete (swift), and Podarge (racer).

The later story describes the Harpies as hideous birds with the faces of women. In the legend of Jason and the Argonauts, they terrorized Phineus, the king of Thrace, by blinding him and stealing his food. Phineus promised to tell the Argonauts their future if they would drive away the Harpies.

In Virgil's **epic** the *Aeneid,* the Harpies torment the hero Aeneas† and his companions, making it impossible for them to eat. Celaeno tells Aeneas that he and his followers will not return home until they become hungry enough to eat their tables. ***See also*** **Aeneas; Aeneid, The; Argonauts; Furies; Gorgons; Greek Mythology; Jason.**

Hathor

cult group bound together by devotion to a particular person, belief, or god
underworld land of the dead

Hathor was one of the most important and complex goddesses of ancient Egypt. A mother goddess who created and maintained all life on earth, Hathor was also worshiped as goddess of the sky, fertility, music, and dance and as the symbolic mother of the pharaoh, or ruler. The Egyptians associated the goddess with sexual love, and her festivals included singing, dancing, and drunken ceremonies. The ancient Greeks identified Hathor with their own goddess of love, Aphrodite.

Hathor was linked with the **cult** of the dead as well. In this role, she provided food to the dead when they arrived in the **underworld.** Anyone who carried her clothing would have a safe journey through the underworld. Many foreign lands around Egypt were considered to be under her protection, especially those from which the Egyptians obtained important resources, such as timber or minerals. In one inscription, she is called the "mistress of turquoise." Hathor is usually portrayed as a cow or a woman with a cow's head or horns. Some statues show her as a cow suckling the pharaoh with the milk of life. ***See also*** **Egyptian Mythology; Venus.**

Heaven

Heaven, as a sacred place or a state of being, appears in the myths and legends of cultures around the world. It can be the dwelling place of the god or gods, the place where people who have lived virtuously find their reward after death, or both. Heaven has often been described as a paradise of some kind, located above or beyond the limits of the ordinary world, perhaps high on a mountain peak or floating on a distant island. For example, the Hottentot god Tsuillgoab lives in a beautiful heaven in the clouds. Over the centuries, traditional ideas have changed, and many people now think of heaven more in terms of a state of spiritual existence or salvation than as a precise though otherworldly place.

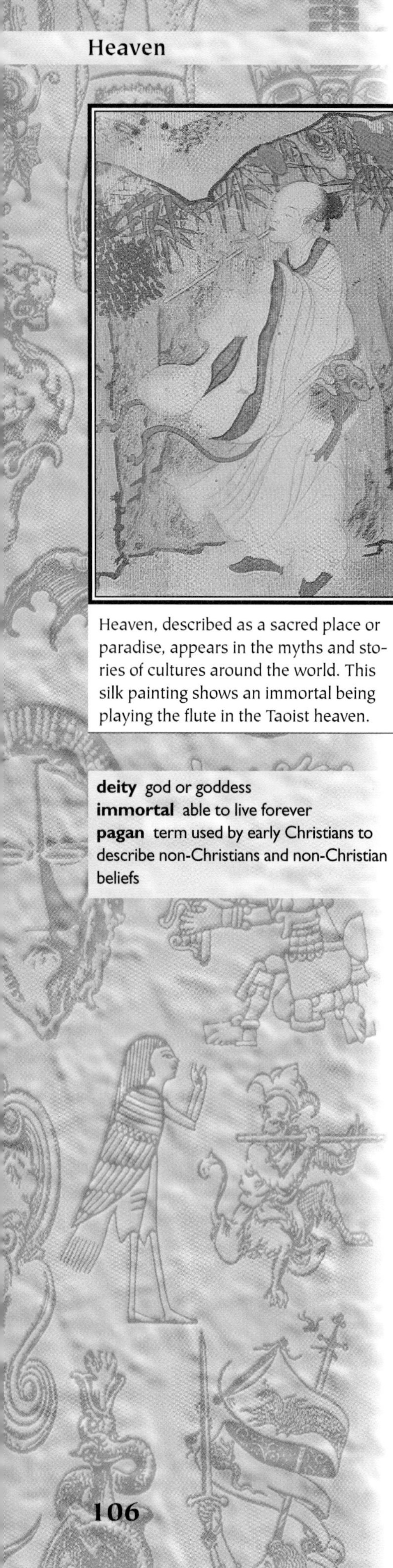

Heaven, described as a sacred place or paradise, appears in the myths and stories of cultures around the world. This silk painting shows an immortal being playing the flute in the Taoist heaven.

deity god or goddess
immortal able to live forever
pagan term used by early Christians to describe non-Christians and non-Christian beliefs

Buddhist View. A version of Buddhism based on Amida or Amitabha, the Buddha of Boundless Light, emerged in Japan in the 1100s. Followers of this sect believed in an eternal afterlife in a realm called the Pure Land or the Western Paradise. Anyone could enter the Pure Land through sincere spiritual devotion to Amida, who taught that the road to salvation lay in saving others from suffering. Other versions of Buddhism described the soul's ideal fate not as arriving in a heaven but as achieving nirvana, a state of being in which individual desires have ceased to exist.

Chinese View. Traditional Chinese religion and mythology included multiple concepts of heaven. Tian, associated with the sky, was both heaven and a **deity** who was the supreme power over gods, men, and nature and the source of order in the universe. The Chinese believed that their rulers' authority came from Tian, and they called their king or emperor Tianzi, Son of Heaven.

The Taoist tradition of Chinese mythology spoke of Penglai Shan (Mount Penglai), a mountain with eight peaks. On each was perched the palace of one of eight **immortal** beings. Like many heavens, Penglai was described in terms of precious things: it had trees of coral that bore pearls instead of fruit. No human could enter Penglai because it was surrounded only by air.

Pre-Christian European View. Before Christianity became the dominant religion of Europe, **pagan** cultures had various ideas about the dwelling places of the gods and the destinations of human souls after death. Some of these are comparable to heavens. In Norse† mythology, for example, the gods lived in Asgard, the topmost realm of existence. Like the human world below, Asgard had farms, orchards, and estates. The souls of heroes who had died in battle went to Valhalla, the "hall of the slain," where they spent their afterlife in joyous fighting and feasting.

Myths of the Slavic peoples of eastern Europe mentioned a paradise called Buyan, described as either a silent and peaceful underwater city or an island washed by a river of healing. The Celtic† peoples had myths of an island paradise called Avalon. Some legends say that King Arthur was carried there after he fell in battle. The Greeks imagined their deities as dwelling in a palatial heaven high above the mortal world on Mount Olympus. The blessed dead, however, went to Elysium, or the Elysian Fields, a green gardenlike afterworld.

Jewish View. The ancient Hebrew religion featured an afterlife, but it did not include a heaven or a hell. By about 200 B.C., however, the influence of other cultures had introduced the ideas of reward and punishment after death. Heaven came to be seen as a place where the righteous dead would dwell with God. Certain Jewish traditions pictured heaven as a mountain with seven tiers or layers. According to some accounts, King Solomon's throne, which had six steps leading to the throne itself, provided the model for the structure of heaven.

† *See **Names and Places** at the end of this volume for further information.*

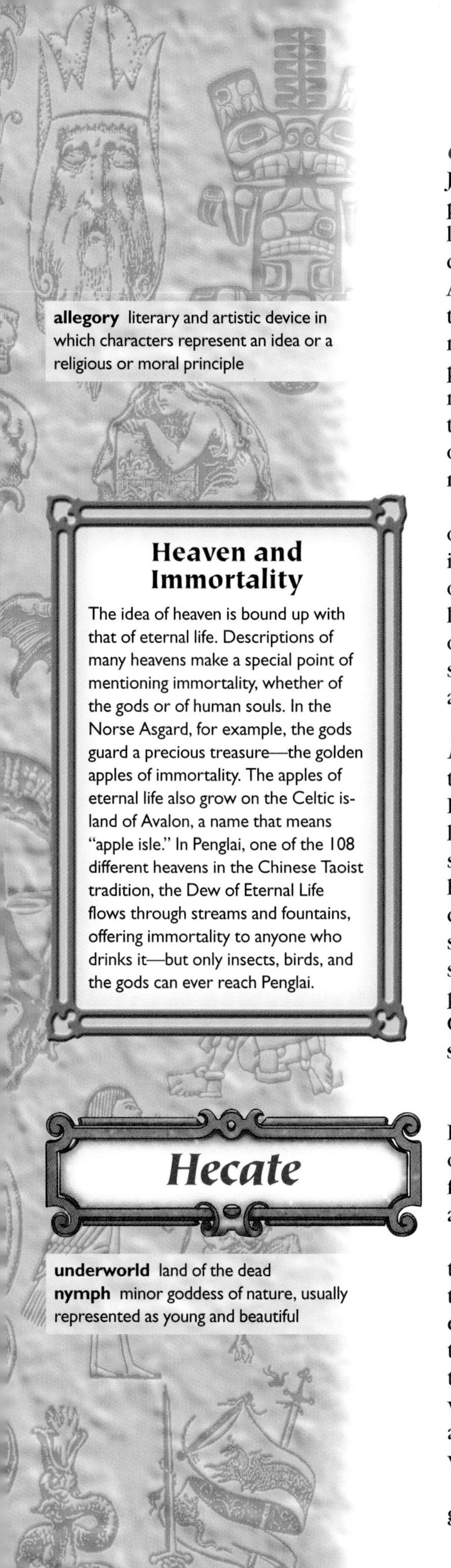

Christian View. The Christian idea of heaven is based on the Jewish one. Although modern Christians are more likely to interpret heaven as spiritual union with God, earlier generations of believers placed that union in a physical setting that was often described in great detail. In the early 1300s, Italian poet Dante Alighieri created a vision of heaven in the *Paradiso,* the last section of *The Divine Comedy,* a long **allegory** about the soul's journey. Drawing on both Christian and pagan traditions, Dante portrayed paradise as high above the earthly world. It consisted of nine heavens, one inside the other, rotating around the earth. The tenth heaven, which included all the others, was the destination of blessed souls who were ranked in order of their virtue, the more virtuous being closer to God.

allegory literary and artistic device in which characters represent an idea or a religious or moral principle

Artists and writers of the Renaissance developed three visions of heaven. The first, the realm beyond the skies, was the source of images of heaven as a place of clouds and winged angels. The second, the garden of paradise, was the natural world raised to the level of divine perfection—an image associated with the Garden of Eden, the lost paradise that once existed on earth. The third vision was that of the heavenly city, a symbol of perfect organization and harmony.

Heaven and Immortality

The idea of heaven is bound up with that of eternal life. Descriptions of many heavens make a special point of mentioning immortality, whether of the gods or of human souls. In the Norse Asgard, for example, the gods guard a precious treasure—the golden apples of immortality. The apples of eternal life also grow on the Celtic island of Avalon, a name that means "apple isle." In Penglai, one of the 108 different heavens in the Chinese Taoist tradition, the Dew of Eternal Life flows through streams and fountains, offering immortality to anyone who drinks it—but only insects, birds, and the gods can ever reach Penglai.

Islamic View. Building on earlier Jewish and Christian traditions, Islamic mythology also envisioned a multilayered paradise. Heaven was a pyramid, cone, or mountain rising from the lowest level to the highest. Some interpretations include eight levels, some seven. The phrase "seventh heaven," meaning the highest happiness, comes from this image. The Muslim heavens are garden paradises of shade trees, flowing streams, and abundant pleasure. The various levels are associated with precious substances such as gold, silver, and pearls, but the highest level is made of pure, divine light and is devoted to the ceaseless, joyous praise of God. ***See also*** **AFTERLIFE; ANGELS; AVALON; EDEN, GARDEN OF; ELYSIUM; HELL; VALHALLA.**

Hecate

Hecate was a complex, ancient goddess known to the Greeks but originally worshiped by people of Asia Minor†. She held several different roles, including earth goddess, queen of the **underworld,** and goddess of magic and witchcraft.

underworld land of the dead
nymph minor goddess of nature, usually represented as young and beautiful

According to the Greek writer Hesiod†, Hecate was the daughter of the Titan† Perses and the **nymph** Asteria. Hesiod claimed that Hecate was a favorite of Zeus†, who made her goddess of the earth, sea, and sky. As a triple goddess, she was also identified with the three aspects of the moon and was represented by women of three different ages. In the sky, she took the form of the old woman Selene, the moon. On earth, she was linked to Artemis (Diana), goddess of the hunt. In the underworld, she was connected with the maiden Persephone, wife of Hades.

Because of her association with the moon, Hecate was seen as a goddess of the night, magic, and spells. Magic was often practiced

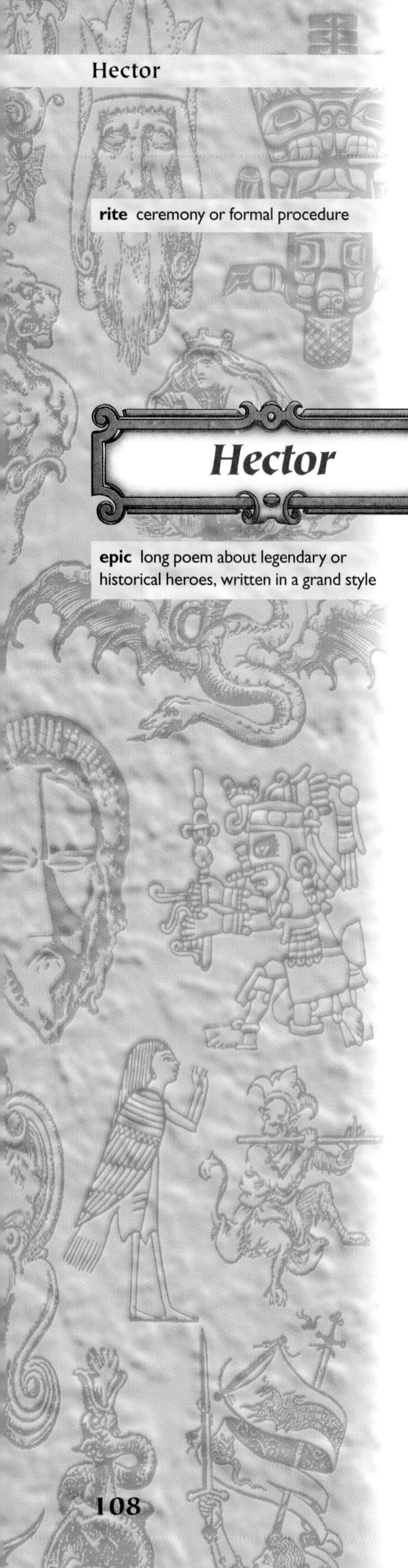

where roads met, and the Greeks established shrines to her at crossroads, especially where three roads came together. In her role as goddess of magic, Hecate is shown as a three-headed figure who keeps watch over the crossroads where her **rites** were performed. To her worshipers, she could bring good fortune and success, but she could also be a powerfully negative force. Later Christian tradition emphasized this side of her nature, portraying Hecate as an evil figure who was queen of the witches. ***See also*** **GREEK MYTHOLOGY; WITCHES AND WIZARDS; MOON.**

rite ceremony or formal procedure

Hector

In Greek mythology, Hector was the son of King Priam of Troy and his wife, Hecuba. A Trojan hero and warrior, he fought bravely against the Greeks in the Trojan War†. In the *Iliad,* Homer's **epic** about the war, Hector is portrayed as a noble and honorable leader. He was a good son, a loving husband to Andromache and father to Astyanax, and a trusted friend. Honest and forthright, he greatly disapproved of the conduct of his brother Paris, who carried off Helen, the wife of the Greek ruler Menelaus. These actions set the stage for the Trojan War.

epic long poem about legendary or historical heroes, written in a grand style

The Noble Warrior. Despite his feelings about Paris, Hector stood ready to defend Troy when the Greeks arrived to avenge the seduction of Helen. When the first Greek warrior set foot on Trojan land, it was Hector who killed him. In the long war that followed, Hector fought valiantly and with great vigor against the Greeks. He was the Trojans' greatest champion.

During the first nine years of the war, neither the Greeks nor the Trojans gained a clear advantage. The tide of war favored first one side and then the other. Then in the tenth year of the war, a dispute arose between Achilles†, the greatest of the Greek warriors, and Agamemnon, the leader of the Greek forces. As a result, Achilles left the field of battle and refused to fight. His absence provided Hector and the Trojans with an opportunity to march out from Troy and attack the Greeks.

With Achilles gone, Hector's most formidable opponents were the Greek champions Diomedes and Ajax. When Diomedes faced Hector in battle he saw that Ares, the god of war, accompanied the Trojans. The sight of Ares caused the Greeks to retreat. But then the goddesses Hera† and Athena†, who favored the Greeks, helped Diomedes wound Ares. When the wounded god left the field of battle, the Greeks attacked and forced the Trojans to turn back.

Faced with this crisis, Hector went back to Troy to consult with his father and to ask the Trojan women to pray to the gods for help. No longer confident of victory and certain that he would soon die, Hector bid a sad farewell to his wife and son.

The Death of Hector. Returning to battle, Hector met and fought the Greek champion Ajax in one-to-one combat. The duel continued until nightfall, with neither hero gaining victory. They finally stopped and exchanged gifts as a sign of respect for each other.

†*See **Names and Places** at the end of this volume for further information.*

The scene on this vase shows Achilles fastening Hector's body to a chariot. Achilles dragged the body around the city, preventing the Trojans from holding a proper funeral.

invincible too powerful to be conquered

When fighting between the Greeks and Trojans resumed, Hector and his forces seemed **invincible.** Hector killed many Greeks and succeeded in pushing them back to defenses they had built around their ships. Hector was about to burn the Greek ships when the god Poseidon† appeared, urging the Greeks to pull themselves together and fight back. At the same time, the Greek warrior Patroclus, the beloved friend of Achilles, entered the battle wearing Achilles' armor.

Believing that Achilles had returned, the Greeks rallied and caused the Trojans to retreat. But then Hector, under the protection of the god Apollo†, killed Patroclus and took the armor he was wearing. Hearing of his friend's death, Achilles reentered the battle and aimed his fury at Hector.

Achilles pursued Hector around the walls of Troy three times before catching him. Aware that Hector was fated to die at Achilles' hand, Apollo abandoned him and allowed Achilles to strike a mortal blow. As he lay dying, Hector pleaded with Achilles to return his body to his father, Priam. Achilles refused. Hector predicted that Achilles, too, would die very shortly.

After Hector died, Achilles tied the warrior's body to a chariot and dragged the body around Troy before the grief-stricken eyes of the Trojans. Then he dragged the body around the tomb of his friend Patroclus. When Achilles' fury and vengeance were finally satisfied, he left Hector's body on the ground to be devoured by dogs and birds of prey.

The abuse of the dead Hector angered Zeus†, who sent a messenger to order Achilles to release the corpse to Priam. He also sent word to Priam to offer a ransom for the body to Achilles. Priam did so and begged the Greek warrior for his son's body. Moved by Priam's grief, Achilles agreed.

Priam brought Hector's body back to Troy, and an 11-day truce allowed the Trojans to arrange an elaborate funeral to mourn their great warrior. Hector's funeral marks the conclusion of the *Iliad,* as well as the beginning of the end for the Trojans. They later suffered a devastating defeat at the hands of the Greeks. After the fall of Troy, the Greeks killed Hector's son Astyanax, fearing that he might try to avenge his father's death. Thereafter, the surviving Trojans honored Hector as one of their greatest heroes. ***See also*** **ACHILLES; AGAMEMNON; AJAX; ANDROMACHE; ASTYANAX; HECUBA; HEROES; ILIAD, THE; PRIAM.**

Hecuba

prophet one who claims to have received divine messages or insights
omen sign of future events

In Greek mythology, Hecuba was the second wife of Priam, king of the city of Troy†. She bore Priam many children, including Hector†, Paris†, Polydorus, and Cassandra†.

While pregnant with Paris, Hecuba had a dream in which she gave birth to a fiery torch that was covered with snakes. The **prophets** of Troy told her that this was a bad **omen** and predicted that if the child lived, he would be responsible for the fall of Troy. Therefore, upon Paris's birth, Hecuba ordered two servants to kill the child. Unable to perform such a terrible act, the servants

left Paris on a mountain to die, and he was found and raised by a shepherd.

Years later, Paris returned to Troy, and as predicted, he caused the city's destruction. He began the Trojan War† by taking away Helen, wife of King Menelaus of Sparta. All the rulers of Greece had sworn to defend Helen. To rescue her, they declared war on Troy, sacking and burning it after a long siege.

Hecuba became a slave to the Greek hero Odysseus†. On his way back to Greece, Odysseus journeyed through Thrace, which was ruled by King Polymestor. Before the war, Hecuba had asked Polymestor to protect her son Polydorus. However, upon reaching Thrace, she found that the king had killed the boy. The enraged Hecuba tore out Polymestor's eyes and murdered both of his sons. As Odysseus was trying to control her, she turned into a dog. Her tomb was placed on a rocky outcrop located on a narrow strip of water called the Hellespont between Greece and Turkey.

Hecuba is found in the *Iliad*† and the *Aeneid*†. She also appears in the plays *Hecuba* and *The Trojan Women* by Euripides† and is mentioned in Shakespeare's *Hamlet.* ***See also*** **Aeneid, The; Cassandra; Greek Mythology; Hector; Helen of Troy; Iliad, The; Odysseus; Odyssey, The; Paris; Trojan War.**

Heimdall

In Norse† mythology, the god Heimdall stood guard over Asgard, the home of the gods. He lived near Bifrost, the rainbow bridge that connected Asgard to the world of humans and from there kept watch for the approach of the giants, who were the enemies of the gods. Heimdall had incredibly sharp senses that allowed him to see great distances even at night and to hear sounds as soft as wool growing on sheep or grass growing. Furthermore, he needed little sleep.

According to legend, Heimdall would one day call the other gods to Ragnarok, the final battle that would result in the destruction of gods and humans. When the giants drew near to Asgard, Heimdall would summon the gods by blowing his horn, Gjallarhorn, which could be heard all over creation. During the battle, Heimdall would kill the evil **trickster** god Loki and then meet his own death.

trickster mischievous figure appearing in various forms in the folktales and mythology of many different peoples

Sometimes called Rig (meaning king), Heimdall was considered the father of all people on earth. According to legend, he traveled around the earth and stayed three nights with married couples from different social classes. First, he visited some **serfs,** then some peasants, and finally a noble couple. Nine months after each visit, a child was born to each couple. The first was an ugly but strong boy named Thrall, who became the ancestor of all serfs. The second, Karl, was skilled at farmwork and became the ancestor of all peasants. Jarl, the last of the children, was intelligent and quick to learn the skills of hunting and combat. He became the ancestor of all warriors and nobles. The words *thrall, karl,* and *jarl* mean serf, farmer, and nobleman in the Norse language. ***See also*** **Loki; Norse Mythology; Ragnarok.**

serf a peasant bound to a lord and required to work the lord's land

† *See* ***Names and Places*** *at the end of this volume for further information.*

Hel

trickster mischievous figure appearing in various forms in the folktales and mythology of many different peoples
underworld land of the dead

Hel was the Norse† goddess of the dead, daughter of the **trickster** god Loki and the giantess Angrboda. Shortly after her birth, Hel was cast out of Asgard, home of the gods, by Odin†. He sent her to Niflheim, the **underworld,** and made her queen of all who died from old age or sickness. Warriors who fell in combat did not become her subjects but went instead to the hall called Valhalla to live with Odin. In early Norse mythology, Hel was also the name of the world of the dead.

Sources describe the goddess as a half-flesh-colored and half-black monster. She lived in a castle called Eljudner and ate her meals with a dish named Hunger and a knife called Famine. She was attended by two servants, Ganglati and Ganglot, who moved so slowly that they appeared to be standing still. *Hell,* the English word for the underworld, comes from the Norse word *Hel.* ***See also*** **LOKI; NORSE MYTHOLOGY; ODIN; VALHALLA.**

Helen of Troy

In Greek mythology, Helen of Troy was the most beautiful woman in the world. A daughter of the god Zeus†, she is best known for the part she played in causing the Trojan War†, a story told by Homer in the *Iliad*† and the *Odyssey*†. Some scholars suggest that Helen was also a very ancient goddess associated with trees and birds.

Birth and Early Life. Some myths say that Helen's mother was Leda, the wife of King Tyndareus of Sparta†. Others name Nemesis, the goddess of revenge, as her mother. Helen had a sister Clytemnestra, who later became the wife of King Agamemnon† of Mycenae, and twin brothers Castor and Pollux, known as the Dioscuri.

Stories claiming Leda as Helen's mother tell how Zeus disguised himself as a swan and raped the Spartan queen. Leda then produced two eggs. From one came Helen and her brother Pollux. Clytemnestra and Castor emerged from the other. Other versions of the myth say that Zeus seduced Nemesis, and she laid the two eggs. A shepherd discovered them and gave them to Queen Leda, who tended the eggs until they hatched and raised the children as her own. In some variations of this legend, Helen and Pollux were the children of Zeus, but Clytemnestra and Castor were actually the children of Tyndareus.

When Helen was only 12 years old, the Greek hero Theseus† kidnapped her and planned to make her his wife. He took her to Attica in Greece and locked her away under the care of his mother. Helen's brothers Castor and Pollux rescued her while Theseus was away and brought her back to Sparta. According to some stories, before Helen left Attica, she had given birth to a daughter named Iphigenia.

Some time after Helen returned to Sparta, King Tyndareus decided that it was time for her to marry. Suitors came from all over Greece, hoping to win the famous beauty. Many were powerful leaders. Tyndareus worried that choosing one suitor might anger the others, who could cause trouble for his kingdom.

Related Entries
Other entries related to Helen of Troy are listed at the end of this article.

Among those seeking to marry Helen was Odysseus†, the king of Ithaca. Odysseus advised Tyndareus to have all the suitors take an oath to accept Helen's choice and promise to support that person whenever the need should arise. The suitors agreed, and Helen chose Menelaus, a prince of Mycenae, to be her husband. Helen's sister Clytemnestra was already married to Menelaus's older brother, Agamemnon.

The Trojan War. For a while, Helen and Menelaus lived happily together. They had a daughter and son, and Menelaus eventually became the king of Sparta. But their life together came to a sudden end.

Paris, a prince of Troy, traveled to Sparta on the advice of the goddess Aphrodite†. She had promised him the most beautiful woman in the world after he proclaimed her the "fairest" goddess. When Paris saw Helen, he knew that Aphrodite had kept her promise. While Menelaus was away in Crete, Paris took Helen back to Troy. Some stories say Helen went willingly, seduced by Paris's charms. Others claim that Paris kidnapped her and took her by force.

When Menelaus returned home and discovered Helen gone, he called on the leaders of Greece, who had sworn to support him if necessary. The Greeks organized a great expedition and set sail for Troy. Their arrival at Troy marked the beginning of the Trojan War. During the war, Helen's sympathies were divided. At times, she helped the Trojans by pointing out Greek leaders. At other times, however, she sympathized with the Greeks and did not betray them when opportunities to do so arose.

Helen had a number of children by Paris, but none survived infancy. Paris died in the Trojan War, and Helen married his brother Deiphobus. After the Greeks won the war, she was reunited with Menelaus, and she helped him kill Deiphobus. Then Helen and Menelaus set sail for Sparta.

Later Life. The couple arrived in Sparta after a journey of several years. Some stories say that the gods, angry at the trouble Helen had caused, sent storms to drive their ships off course to Egypt and other lands bordering the Mediterranean Sea. When they finally arrived in Sparta, the couple lived happily, although by some accounts, Menelaus remained suspicious of Helen's feelings and loyalty.

Many stories say that Helen remained in Sparta until her death. But others say that she went to the island of Rhodes after Menelaus died, perhaps driven from Sparta by their son Nicostratus. At first she was given refuge on Rhodes by Polyxo, the widow of Tlepolemus, one of the Greek leaders who had died in the Trojan War. Later, however, Polyxo had Helen hanged to avenge the death of her husband. One very different version of Helen's story claims that the gods sent an effigy, or dummy, of Helen to Troy but that she actually spent the war years in Egypt.

Helen and stories about her inspired many ancient writers, including the Greek playwright Euripides† and the Roman poets

*†See **Names and Places** at the end of this volume for further information.*

Virgil†, Ovid†, and Seneca. She also served as inspiration for later authors, including Italian poet Dante Alighieri and English playwrights William Shakespeare and Christopher Marlowe. It was Marlowe who wrote that Helen's was "the face which launched a thousand ships." ***See also*** **Agamemnon; Castor and Pollux; Clytemnestra; Greek Mythology; Iliad, The; Iphigenia; Menelaus; Odysseus; Odyssey, The; Paris; Theseus; Trojan War.**

Hell

Hell is a place of punishment after death or, in more abstract terms, a state of spiritual damnation. In religions and mythologies that separate the dead according to their conduct in life or the purity of their souls, the evil go to hell while the good go to heaven.

Hell is related to the concept of the underworld. In the myths of many ancient cultures, the underworld was the mysterious and often gloomy realm of the dead. Although usually imagined as a dark underground kingdom associated with caves and holes in the earth, hell was not always a place of punishment and suffering. Later belief systems introduced the idea of an afterlife in which the wicked received punishment, and hell was where that punishment occurred.

Although the word *hell* comes from Hel, the Norse† goddess of death, hells appear in the beliefs and mythologies of many cultures. Common features of hells include burning heat or freezing cold, darkness (symbolizing the soul's separation from light, goodness, and truth), physical agony that represents spiritual suffering, and devils or demons who torment the damned.

Hindu Version. Hinduism is based on the belief that each soul lives many, many lives. A soul may spend time in any of 21 hells to

In many myths, hell appears as a place of punishment and suffering after death. This section of Michelangelo's fresco *The Last Judgment* (1534–1541) depicts people asking for mercy.

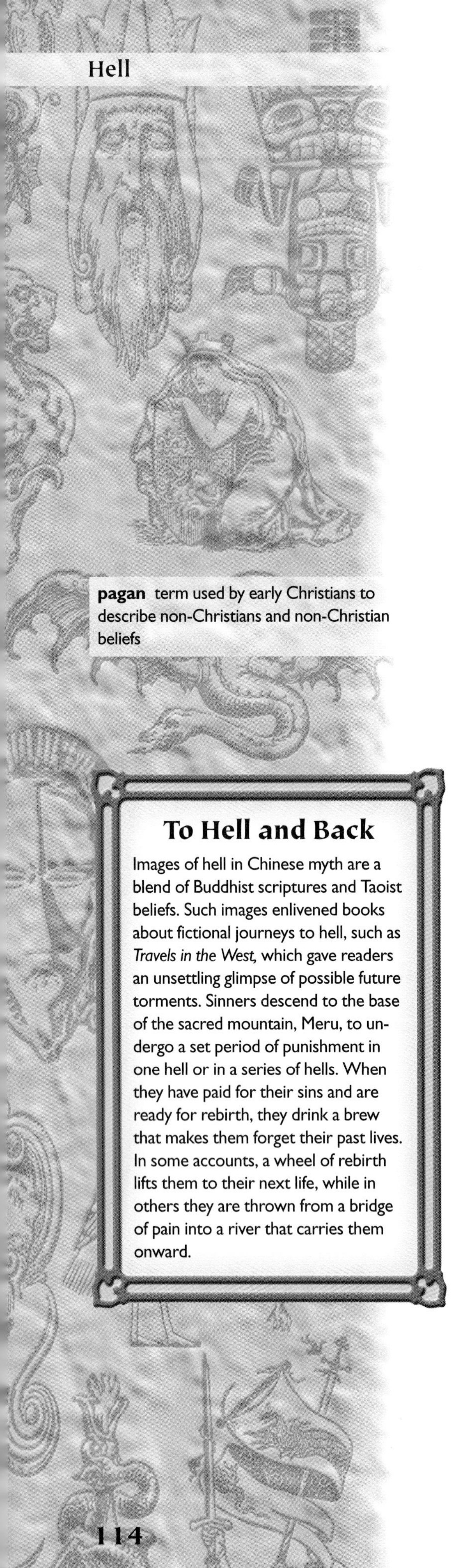

pay for wrong actions during a lifetime, but eventually that soul will be reborn in the world. In the Jain religion, which is related to Hinduism, sinners go to a hell called *bhumis,* where demons torment them until they have paid for whatever evil they committed in life.

Buddhist Version. There are numerous versions of Buddhism with various ideas of hell. The strictest form of Buddhism does not include a hell, but some Buddhists still follow the traditional belief of up to 136 hells. The hell to which a dead soul goes for punishment depends on the person's actions in the most recent life. Some Buddhist doctrines speak of the *karmavacara,* the realm of physical and sensory perceptions, as a series of hells. The Chinese belief that souls are punished after death to pay for sins or errors committed during life combines some Buddhist ideas with elements of traditional Taoist Chinese mythology.

Pre-Christian European Version. Before Christianity gave its own meanings to the concepts of heaven and hell, the **pagan** peoples of Europe imagined the dark side of the afterlife. The Norse pictured Hel, the corpselike goddess of death, as queen of a grim underground realm populated by those who had died of sickness and old age. This view of hell involves a dread of death and a horror of the cold, dark, decaying grave, but it does not suggest a place of punishment.

pagan term used by early Christians to describe non-Christians and non-Christian beliefs

The Greek underworld was divided into three regions: Hades, Tartarus, and Elysium. Most of the dead went to the kingdom of the god Hades. In the deepest part of the underworld, a terrible dark place known as Tartarus, the very wicked suffered eternal punishment at the hands of the Furies. The third region, Elysium or the Elysian Fields, was where exceptionally good and righteous people went after death.

To Hell and Back

Images of hell in Chinese myth are a blend of Buddhist scriptures and Taoist beliefs. Such images enlivened books about fictional journeys to hell, such as *Travels in the West,* which gave readers an unsettling glimpse of possible future torments. Sinners descend to the base of the sacred mountain, Meru, to undergo a set period of punishment in one hell or in a series of hells. When they have paid for their sins and are ready for rebirth, they drink a brew that makes them forget their past lives. In some accounts, a wheel of rebirth lifts them to their next life, while in others they are thrown from a bridge of pain into a river that carries them onward.

Persian Version. The image of hell as a place of torment for sinners emerged fully in the Persian mythology based on the faith founded in the 500s B.C. by Zoroaster. According to Zoroastrian belief, souls are judged after death at a bridge where their lives are weighed. If the outcome is good, the bridge widens and carries them to heaven. If they are judged to have been evil, the bridge narrows and pitches them down into a dreadful hell. Those whose lives were an equal mix of good and evil go to a realm called *hamestagan,* in which they experience both heat and cold.

Jewish Version. The early Hebrews called their afterworld Sheol and pictured it as a quiet, sad place where all the dead went. By around 200 B.C., under the influence of Zoroastrianism and other belief systems, the Jews had adopted the idea of judgment for the dead. The afterworld became a heaven for the good and a hell for the wicked.

A river of fire known as Gehenna ran through hell, and sometimes the whole region was called Gehenna. Scores of demons dwelled there and so did the gods and goddesses of the Greeks,

† *See **Names and Places** at the end of this volume for further information.*

Romans, Celts†, and other peoples who had also been turned into demons. Some interpretations described hell as a series of ever-smaller levels or rings, like a downward-pointing, seven-tiered mountain. Half the year the sinners being punished in hell endured the torments of fire. For the rest of the time they suffered the even worse misery of bitter cold.

Christian Version. Christian belief built upon the Jewish notion of hell as a place of punishment for the wicked and the home of Satan, the chief devil, and all of his evil demons, or fallen angels. Most often hell was pictured as an inferno, a place of flames and cruel heat. Many early Christian writings emphasized the agonies that sinners suffered in hell when demons boiled them in kettles or stabbed them with pitchforks. In such interpretations of hell the punishments were often tailored to fit specific sins.

During the Middle Ages, Christians sometimes pictured hell as a fiery dragon's mouth swallowing up sinners. In *The Divine Comedy,* an **allegory** of the soul's journey written in the early 1300s, Italian poet Dante Alighieri drew upon many mythological traditions. He portrayed hell as an inferno of punishment, descending through many levels where sinners of different categories received punishment. Dante also described the realm that Christians had come to call purgatory, a state between hell and heaven. Christian belief included the possibility that a soul could, after punishment in purgatory and true repentance, work its way toward heaven and salvation.

allegory literary and artistic device in which characters represent an idea or a religious or moral principle

Islamic Version. The Muslims inherited their vision of hell, like many other elements of their faith, from the Jews and the Christians. The Islamic hell is called Jahannam (or sometimes Gehenna). Jahannam can be portrayed as a devouring, fire-breathing monster or a multilayered, pitlike realm below the earth whose chief characteristic is fire. As in Persian mythology, the souls of the dead are required to cross a bridge of judgment, "sharper than a sword and finer than a hair," that stretches over Jahannam to paradise. Sinners and unbelievers slip and fall into hell. The kind of punishment that each sinner receives matches his or her sins.

Central American Version. According to the Maya, the souls of most of the dead went to an underworld known as Xibalba. Only individuals who died in violent circumstances went directly to one of the heavens. In the Mayan legend of the Hero Twins, told in the *Popol Vuh,* Xibalba is divided into houses filled with terrifying objects such as knives, jaguars, and bats. The twins undergo a series of trials in these houses and eventually defeat the lords of Xibalba. The Aztecs believed that the souls of ordinary people went to an underworld called Mictlan. Each soul wandered through the layers of Mictlan until it reached the deepest level. ***See also*** **Afterlife; Devils and Demons; Furies; Hades; Heaven; Hel; Satan; Sheol; Underworld; Xibalba.**

Hephaestus

See *Vulcan.*

Hera

patron special guardian, protector, or supporter

Titan one of a family of giants who ruled the earth until overthrown by the Greek gods of Olympus

nymph minor goddess of nature, usually represented as young and beautiful

prophecy foretelling of what is to come; also something that is predicted

The queen of heaven in Greek mythology, Hera was the sister and wife of Zeus, the king of the gods. The Greeks worshiped her as a mother goddess and considered her a protector of marriage and childbirth and a **patron** of women. Many of the myths and legends about Hera concern her terrible jealousy of and revenge against Zeus's numerous lovers and children. Hera's counterpart in Roman mythology was the goddess Juno.

Birth and Marriage. The daughter of the **Titans** Cronus† and Rhea, Hera was swallowed after birth by Cronus. Her siblings Demeter†, Hades†, Poseidon†, and Hestia suffered the same fate. However, Rhea managed to save Zeus, the youngest brother. Later Zeus rescued his brothers and sisters by giving Cronus a potion that caused him to vomit them up. Some stories say that Hera was raised by the Titans Oceanus and Tethys; others claim that she grew up under the care of Temenus, who ruled the region of Arcadia in Greece.

When Zeus and his brothers defeated the Titans and divided the universe among themselves, they gave nothing to their sisters. Hera was furious at being left out, and this anger persisted throughout her relationship with Zeus. According to some myths, Zeus seduced Hera while disguised as a cuckoo. Other tales say that he found her on an island and carried her away to a cave. Stories place their wedding at various sites: in the Garden of the Hesperides (the **nymphs** of the setting sun), at the top of Mount Ida in Anatolia (present-day Turkey), or on the island of Euboea in the Aegean Sea. Festivals commemorating the marriage took place throughout Greece.

As the wife of Zeus, Hera bore him four children: Hephaestus, the god of fire and crafts; Ares, the god of war; Ilithyia, the goddess of childbirth; and Hebe, the cupbearer of the gods. Zeus and Hera often quarreled, and their arguments sometimes became fierce enough to shake the halls of Olympus, the home of the gods. Most of their arguments concerned Zeus's seduction of other women, but they also argued about the nature of love itself.

In their most famous quarrel over love, Hera insisted that men received more sexual pleasure than women, while Zeus argued the opposite. In an attempt to end the dispute, Hera and Zeus agreed to consult Tiresias, a mortal who had been both male and female. Tiresias sided with Zeus, claiming that women had much greater pleasure than men. Enraged by his answer, Hera blinded Tiresias. Zeus compensated Tiresias for his loss of sight by giving him the gift of **prophecy.**

Anger and Revenge. Zeus wandered the world seducing beautiful women, goddesses, and nymphs—often while disguised as a mortal or an animal. His unfaithfulness made Hera insanely jealous.

†*See **Names and Places** at the end of this volume for further information.*

Most of her anger was directed at Zeus's lovers and their children, whom she persecuted and punished mercilessly. Many of the stories about Hera concern her revenge against these individuals.

One of the greatest victims of Hera's anger was Hercules†, the son of Zeus and a mortal women named Alcmena. Hera hounded and punished Hercules throughout his life. Soon after his birth, she sent two snakes to kill him, but the infant Hercules, who would become known for his tremendous strength, strangled the snakes instead. Another time, Hera drove Hercules temporarily insane, causing him to kill his own wife and children. Once, when she raised a storm against Hercules' ship, Zeus retaliated by hanging Hera from Mount Olympus by her wrists, with anvils attached to her feet.

Another of Hera's victims was Io, a Greek princess with whom Zeus had an affair. Hera suspected that Zeus had a new lover and went searching for him. To save Io from his wife's jealousy, Zeus turned the girl into a white calf. When Hera found Zeus, she asked to have the calf as a gift. Not daring to refuse, he agreed. Io roamed the meadows as a calf for a long time, constantly pestered by a horsefly sent by Hera to torment her. Feeling pity for Io, Zeus often visited her in the shape of a bull. Finally, he promised Hera that he would pay no more attention to Io, and Hera agreed to transform her back into a woman.

Semele, a mortal woman who gave birth to Zeus's son Dionysus†, was another of Hera's victims. Hera suggested to Semele that she ask her lover to appear in his full glory. Zeus, who had promised to grant Semele any wish, sadly did so and appeared with his thunderbolts, causing Semele to burn to death immediately. Athamas, the king of Thebes, and his wife Ino, who later became a sea goddess, raised Dionysus after his mother's death. Hera punished them as well by making them go mad.

Hera's vengeful nature was directed mainly at her husband's unfaithfulness, but there were other victims too. One famous story tells of a beauty contest between Hera and the goddesses Athena† and Aphrodite†. The judge of the contest, the Trojan prince Paris, chose Aphrodite as the most beautiful of the three. The angry Hera punished Paris by siding with the Greeks against the Trojans in the Trojan War and by acting as protector of the Greek hero Achilles†.

The Roman Juno. The Romans identified Hera with the goddess Juno. In many ways, Juno had greater authority than Hera. For the Greeks, Hera's long-lasting bond with Zeus—despite its many problems—symbolized the strength and importance of marriage. Marriage, home, and family were even more important to the Romans, so the **cult** of Juno was significant throughout ancient Rome.

cult group bound together by devotion to a particular person, belief, or god

Juno closely resembled Hera, and myths about her were basically the same. However, there were some differences. In Roman mythology, for example, Juno's origin is sometimes associated with an Italian mother goddess closely connected to fertility. She is often linked with the moon, and the month that the Romans

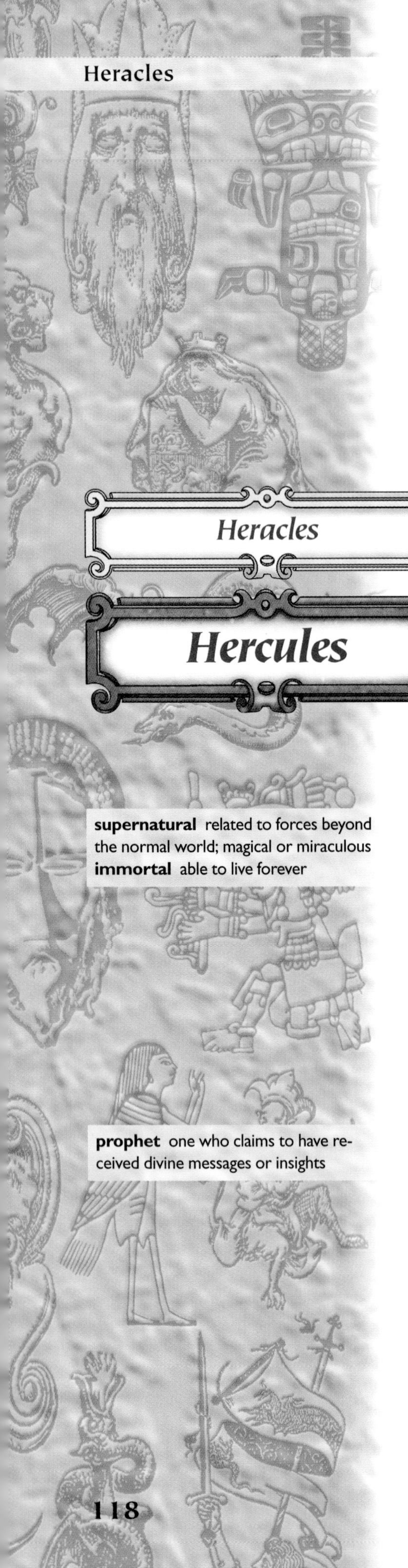

named in her honor—June—was considered the most favorable time of the year for weddings.

One of the principal Roman myths of Juno concerns Minerva, the Roman counterpart of the Greek goddess Athena. According to this story, Minerva was born from the head of Jupiter, which angered Juno. She complained to Flora, the goddess of flowers and gardens, who touched Juno with a magic herb that caused her to give birth to the god Mars†. A similar myth exists in Greek mythology, but in some versions of that story, Hera gives birth to the monster Typhon, who tries to defeat Zeus and take his power. While the Greek myth illustrates Hera's vengeful nature, the Roman story emphasizes fertility and motherhood. ***See also*** **Greek Mythology; Hercules; Io; Paris; Roman Mythology; Zeus.**

Heracles

See ***Hercules.***

Hercules

The greatest of all heroes in Greek mythology, Hercules was the strongest man on earth. Besides tremendous physical strength, he had great self-confidence and considered himself equal to the gods. Hercules (called Heracles by the Greeks) was not blessed with great intelligence, but his bravery made up for any lack of cunning. Easily angered, his sudden outbursts of rage often harmed innocent bystanders. When the fury passed, though, Hercules was full of sorrow and guilt for what he had done and ready to accept any punishment for his misdeeds. Only **supernatural** forces could defeat him, and it was magic that ended his mortal life. In Greek mythology, only two figures with half-mortal, half-**immortal** parentage—Hercules and Dionysus—became fully immortal and were worshiped as gods.

supernatural related to forces beyond the normal world; magical or miraculous
immortal able to live forever

Birth and Early Life. Hercules was the son of Zeus† and Alcmena, the wife of Amphitryon, a distinguished Greek warrior and heir to the throne of Tiryns. One night while Amphitryon was away, Zeus came to Alcmena disguised as her husband. The next day, the real Amphitryon returned and slept with his wife. Concerned that Amphitryon did not remember being with Alcmena on both nights, the couple consulted the blind **prophet** Tiresias, who told them that Zeus had slept with Alcmena the first night and predicted that she would bear a child who would become a great hero.

prophet one who claims to have received divine messages or insights

Alcmena bore twin boys—Hercules, the son of Zeus, and Iphicles, the son of Amphitryon. When the goddess Hera† discovered that Zeus had seduced Alcmena and fathered Hercules, she was furious. Hera was fiercely jealous of Zeus's lovers and children and pursued them mercilessly. She tried to kill the infant Hercules by having two poisonous snakes placed in his crib one night. However, the infant grabbed the snakes and strangled them. Though Hera failed to kill Hercules, she persecuted him throughout his life, causing many of the events that led to his great suffering and punishments.

†*See* ***Names and Places*** *at the end of this volume for further information.*

tribute payment made by a smaller or weaker party to a more powerful one, often under the threat of force

oracle priest or priestess or other creature through whom a god is believed to speak; also the location (such as a shrine) where such words are spoken

invulnerable incapable of being hurt

Hercules' Lesson

As a young boy, Hercules became aware of his extraordinary strength—and his temper. Like most Greek youths, he took music lessons. One day Linus, his music master, was teaching Hercules to play the lyre. Hercules became frustrated, flew into a rage, and banged the lyre down on Linus's head. The blow killed Linus instantly. Hercules was shocked and very sorry. He had not meant to kill his teacher. He just did not know his own strength.

While still a young man, Hercules went to fight the Minyans, a people who had been forcing Thebes† to pay **tribute.** As a reward for conquering the Minyans, the king of Thebes gave Hercules the hand of his daughter, Megara. Hercules was devoted to Megara and the three children she bore him.

One day after Hercules returned home from a journey, Hera struck him with a fit of madness during which he killed his wife and children. When he came to his senses, Hercules was horrified by what he had done. Devastated with sorrow and guilt, the hero went to the **oracle** at Delphi† to ask how he could atone for his misdeed. The oracle told him to go to King Eurystheus of Tiryns and submit to any punishment asked of him. The oracle also announced that if Hercules completed the tasks set before him, he would become immortal.

The Twelve Labors of Hercules. King Eurystheus gave Hercules a series of 12 difficult and dangerous tasks. Known as the Twelve Labors of Hercules, these were his most famous feats. The hero's first task was to kill the Nemean Lion, a monstrous beast that terrorized the countryside and could not be killed by any weapon. Hercules strangled the beast with his bare hands and made its skin into a cloak that made him **invulnerable.**

For his second labor, the hero had to kill the Lernaean Hydra, a creature with nine heads that lived in a swamp. One of the beast's heads was immortal, and the others grew back when cut off. With the help of his friend Iolaus, Hercules cut off the Hydra's eight heads and burned each wound, which prevented new heads from growing back. Because he could not cut off the ninth head, he buried the creature under a great rock.

The next task was to capture the Cerynean Hind, a golden-horned deer that was sacred to the goddess Artemis†. After hunting the animal for a year, Hercules finally managed to capture it. As he was taking it to Tiryns, Artemis stopped him and demanded that he return the deer. The hero promised that the sacred animal would not be harmed, and she allowed him to continue on his journey.

The fourth labor of Hercules was to seize the Erymanthian Boar, a monstrous animal that ravaged the lands around Mount Erymanthus. After forcing the animal from its lair, Hercules chased it until it became so exhausted that he could catch it easily.

The hero's fifth task was to clean the Augean Stables in one day. King Augeas, the son of the sun god Helios, had great herds of cattle whose stables had not been cleaned for many years. Hercules accomplished the task by diverting rivers through the filthy stables.

The sixth task involved driving away the Stymphalian Birds, a flock of birds with claws, beaks, and wings of iron that ate humans and that were terrorizing the countryside. Helped by the goddess Athena†, Hercules forced the birds from their nests and shot them with his bow and arrow.

Eurystheus next ordered Hercules to seize the Cretan Bull and bring it back to Tiryns alive. This savage bull had been a gift from

The first task of Hercules' Twelve Labors was to kill the Nemean Lion, a dangerous animal that terrorized the country. Hercules strangled the lion with his bare hands and made its skin into a cloak.

nymph minor goddess of nature, usually represented as young and beautiful

underworld land of the dead

centaur half-human, half-animal creature with the body of a horse and the head, chest, and arms of a human

Poseidon† to King Minos of Crete. The king gave Hercules permission to catch it and take it away.

For his eighth task, Hercules was ordered to capture the Mares of Diomedes, a herd of horses that belonged to King Diomedes of Thrace and that ate human flesh. Hercules killed Diomedes and fed him to the mares. Then the hero tamed the horses and brought them back to Eurystheus.

The ninth labor consisted of obtaining the Girdle of Hippolyte, the queen of the Amazons†. Hippolyte greeted Hercules warmly and agreed to give him the girdle. But then Hera caused trouble, making the Amazons think that Hercules planned to kidnap their queen. They attacked, and Hercules killed Hippolyte and took the girdle.

For his tenth labor, Hercules had to capture the Cattle of Geryon, a monster with three bodies that lived in the far west on the island of Erythia. After a difficult journey by sea and across the desert, Hercules killed Geryon, a herdsman, and an enormous guard dog. He then took the cattle and returned with them to Tiryns.

The eleventh labor involved bringing back the golden Apples of the Hesperides, a group of **nymphs** who lived in the far west. According to one account, Hercules requested help from the Hesperides' father, the giant Atlas, who held up the sky. Hercules offered to take Atlas's place under the sky if he would fetch the apples from his daughters. Atlas agreed and obtained the apples, but then he refused to take back the sky. Hercules asked Atlas to hold the sky for a just moment while he got a pad to ease the burden on his shoulders. Atlas agreed. But as soon as Atlas took back the sky, Hercules grabbed the apples and fled. In another version of this story, Hercules obtained the apples by himself after killing a dragon that stood guard over the tree on which they grew.

Hercules' final task was one of the most difficult and dangerous. He had to descend to the kingdom of Hades and capture Cerberus, the fierce three-headed dog that guarded the gates to the **underworld.** Hades said Hercules could take Cerberus if he used no weapons to overcome the beast. Hercules wrestled Cerberus into submission or gave him drugged food and carried him to Eurystheus.

Other Adventures and Later Life. Hercules had many other adventures during his lifetime. He killed other beasts and monsters, engaged in numerous battles against his enemies, joined the expedition of Jason† and the Argonauts, and even fought the god Apollo†. Throughout, he faced the hatred of Hera, who continued to persecute him because he was the son of Zeus.

Later in his life, Hercules married Deianeira, a princess whose hand he had won by fighting the river god Achelous. Hercules also saved Deianeira from a **centaur** named Nessus, who tried to harm her. As Nessus lay dying from Hercules' arrows, he urged Deianeira to take some of his blood, telling her it would act as a magic potion that could secure her husband's love forever.

Some years later, fearing that Hercules had fallen in love with another woman, Deianeira took the potion and smeared it on a

†*See **Names and Places** at the end of this volume for further information.*

robe for her husband. The potion was really a terrible poison, and when Hercules put on the poisoned garment, it burned his skin, causing an agonizing pain that could not be stopped. When Deianeira discovered what had happened, she killed herself.

pyre pile of wood on which a dead body is burned in a funeral ceremony

The dying Hercules ordered his son to build a funeral **pyre,** and the hero lay down upon it. As the flames of the pyre grew, a great cloud appeared, a bolt of lightning struck, and the body of Hercules disappeared. Hercules, now an immortal god, had been taken to Mount Olympus to be with his father, Zeus, and the other gods. Even Hera welcomed him and allowed him to marry her daughter Hebe. ***See also*** **AMPHITRYON; ARGONAUTS; ATLAS; CENTAURS; CERBERUS; GREEK MYTHOLOGY; HERA; HEROES; NEMEAN LION; ZEUS.**

Hermaphroditus

nymph minor goddess of nature, usually represented as young and beautiful

In Greek mythology, Hermaphroditus was the son of Hermes, messenger of the gods, and Aphrodite, goddess of love. The boy was so beautiful that a **nymph** named Salmacis fell in love with him and prayed that they would be united forever. The gods granted her the wish one day when Hermaphroditus came to the fountain where she lived. As he was bathing, Salmacis embraced him and pulled him underneath the water, and their bodies merged into one. The result was a person with the figure and breasts of a woman but with the sex organs of a man.

Other versions of the story claim that any man who bathed in the fountain was transformed into a half man, half woman just like Hermaphroditus. It was also said that the waters of the fountain caused anyone who drank from it to grow weak. The original story appears in the *Metamorphoses* by the Roman poet Ovid†. The English writer Edmund Spenser includes the notion of such a pool, which weakened those who drank from it, in the *Faerie Queene.* ***See also*** **GREEK MYTHOLOGY; NYMPHS.**

Hermes

patron special guardian, protector, or supporter

In Greek mythology, Hermes was the fleet-footed messenger of the gods. His parents were Zeus, king of the gods, and Maia, one of the seven sisters known as the Pleiades. The Romans identified Hermes with Mercury, the god of merchants and trade, and they placed his main temple near the merchants' quarter in ancient Rome.

The Greeks looked upon Hermes as a **patron** of travelers, merchants, and thieves and as a bringer of good luck. Because of his reputation as a speedy messenger, the god became popular among athletes. Many ancient sports arenas had statues of the god. In later art, Hermes was usually depicted as a young man wearing winged sandals and a wide-brimmed hat with wings. He also carried a staff with two snakes known as a caduceus.

While still an infant, Hermes killed a tortoise and used its shell to make a stringed instrument called a lyre. Soon afterward, he stole some cattle belonging to Apollo† and then returned to his cradle. When Apollo came looking for the animals, Hermes pretended to know nothing and told a cunning tale to prove his innocence. In the course of telling his tale, he stole Apollo's bow and arrows.

Zeus insisted that the cattle be returned, so Hermes brought Apollo to the place where they were hidden. There he took up his lyre and played so impressively that Apollo agreed to overlook the theft of the cattle if Hermes would give him the instrument. Hermes also handed back the bow and arrows he had stolen. Amused by the young god's antics, Apollo became his good friend and made Hermes the protector of herdsmen.

When Hermes grew up, he often came to the aid of other gods and mortals. He accompanied Zeus on many journeys and once helped him during a struggle with the monster Typhon. Another time, Hermes rescued Ares† when the god was imprisoned in a jar. He also played a role in arranging the return of Persephone† from the **underworld.** As a protector of travelers, Hermes escorted the spirits of dead mortals to the river Styx. Among the living mortals he assisted were King Priam of Troy†, Aeneas†, and Odysseus†.

underworld land of the dead

Hermes had love affairs with a number of goddesses and mortal women. The goddess he loved the most was Aphrodite†, with whom he had two children, Hermaphroditus and Priapus. Hermes was also the father of Pan, the god of shepherds and flocks who was half man and half goat. ***See also*** **Apollo; Caduceus; Hermaphroditus; Pan; Persephone; Pleiades; Priam; Styx; Underworld; Zeus.**

Hero and Leander

Hero and Leander were famous lovers in Greek mythology. Hero, who lived in the town of Sestos, served as a priestess of the goddess Aphrodite† (Venus). Leander was a youth from the nearby town of Abydos, located across a narrow strip of water called the Hellespont.

Hero and Leander met at a festival and fell in love. However, because she was a priestess of Aphrodite, Hero had to remain a virgin and was forbidden to marry. The two lovers decided to see each other secretly. Each night Hero would leave a lamp burning in a window of the tower in which she lived, and Leander would swim across the Hellespont, using the light to guide his way. One winter night, the wind blew out the flame in the lamp, causing Leander to lose his way and drown. The next morning, when Hero saw his lifeless body washed up on the shore, she killed herself by jumping out of the tower.

Several ancient poets, including Ovid† and Virgil†, told the tale of Hero and Leander. In 1598 the English author Christopher Marlowe used the story as the basis of his poem *Hero and Leander.* Lord Byron, John Keats, and Lord Tennyson were other well-known poets who wrote of the lovers. The tale also inspired paintings by Rubens, Turner, and Rossetti. ***See also*** **Greek Mythology; Venus.**

Heroes

At the heart of many of the world's most enduring myths and legends is a hero, a man or woman who triumphs over obstacles. Heroes are not all-powerful and **immortal** beings. Instead they represent the best of what it means to be human, demonstrating great strength, courage, wisdom, cleverness, or devotion.

immortal able to live forever

Not all heroes possess all these qualities. Through the ages cultures have produced various kinds of heroes who represent a wide

†*See* ***Names and Places*** *at the end of this volume for further information.*

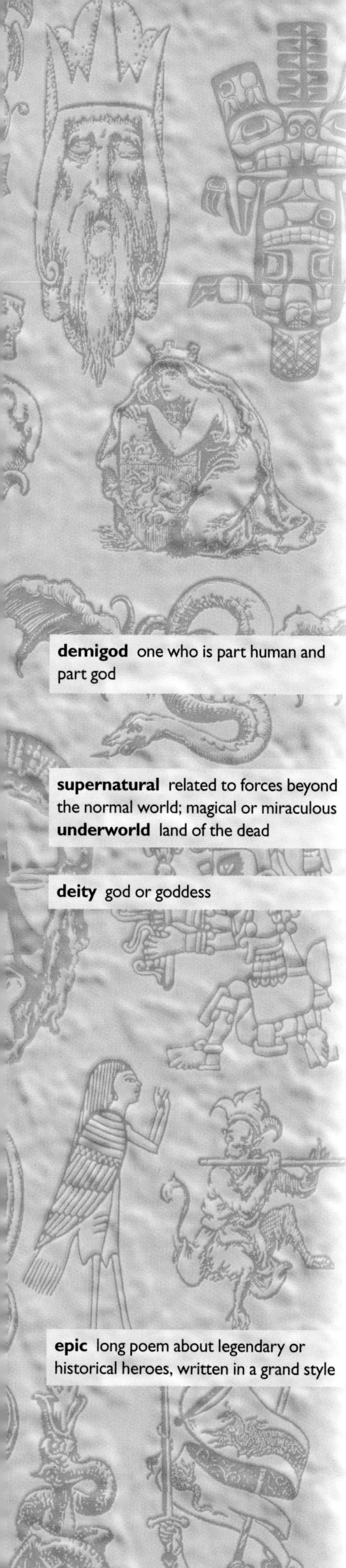

range of virtues. The male-dominated civilization of ancient Greece, for example, admired strong warrior heroes. By contrast, in the mythology of ancient Egypt, where religion played a central role at all levels of society, the heroes were often priest-magicians. In many cultures women became heroes by using their intelligence or forceful personalities to outwit a foe.

Some heroes of myth and legend are wholly fictional. Others are historical figures who have risen to the level of legendary heroes or who have been given such status by writers or by the public.

The Universal Myth

In studying myths and legends from around the world, scholars have identified a pattern that appears over and over again—the story of the universal hero. The writer Joseph Campbell has shown that these stories generally end with the hero gaining new knowledge or abilities. Often an element of miracle or mystery surrounds the birth of such heroes. Their true identity may be unknown; they may be the child of a virgin; or they may possess special powers or be **demigods.**

demigod one who is part human and part god

Many hero myths focus on a quest—a difficult task or journey that must be undertaken to achieve a goal or earn a reward such as the hand of a loved one. Leaving the everyday world, the hero follows a path filled with challenges and adventures, perhaps involving magic or the **supernatural.** A hero may even enter the **underworld** and confront death itself.

supernatural related to forces beyond the normal world; magical or miraculous
underworld land of the dead

Heroes must use strength, wits, or both to defeat enemies, monsters, or demons, although some are aided by luck or by a protective **deity** or magician. Sometimes heroes have to give up something precious to move forward in the quest. In the end the hero returns home enriched with powers, wisdom, treasure, or perhaps a mate won in the course of the quest.

deity god or goddess

The hero's quest may be seen as a symbol of the journey of self-discovery that anyone can make, the quest to overcome inner monsters and achieve self-understanding. But though quests form the basis of many myths and legends, not all heroes follow the quest pattern entirely or even in part.

Kinds of Heroes

There are almost as many kinds of heroes as there are human qualities and experiences. A great number of them fall into two or more categories.

Questing or Journeying Heroes. The hero on a quest or journey appears in dozens of myths, **epics,** legends, and fairy tales. Greek mythology has many questing heroes, including Odysseus†, Orpheus†, Jason†, and Hercules†. Odysseus just wants to return home after the Trojan War, but his adventure-filled voyage takes ten years. The musician Orpheus descends into the underworld in his quest to bring his beloved Eurydice back from death. Jason sails to

epic long poem about legendary or historical heroes, written in a grand style

distant lands in search of the Golden Fleece. The trials of the mighty Hercules are organized into Twelve Labors or quests.

Questing heroes appear in the mythology of many other cultures. Gilgamesh, the hero of an epic from ancient Mesopotamia†, travels in search of immortality. The Polynesian hero Rupe changes into a bird to search for his lost sister and bring her home. In Britain's Arthurian legends the knight Lancelot and his son Galahad seek the **Holy Grail,** and in a myth of the Tewa of North America, Water Jar Boy searches for his father—a symbol of the search for identity.

Holy Grail sacred cup said to have been used by Jesus Christ at the Last Supper

Warriors and Kings. A number of individuals rise to the level of heroes with their outstanding skills in combat. In myths about the Trojan War†, the warriors Ajax† and Achilles† fight valiantly, and the Amazon† queen Penthesilea leads a troop of her soldiers against the Greek forces. Beowulf is the monster-slaying hero of an early English epic. Chinese myths tell of Yi, an archer so skilled that he was able to shoot down extra suns in the sky. Rama, hero of the Hindu epic the *Ramayana,* defeats fearsome demons called Rakshasas in a series of duels. The Celtic† hero Finn leads a band of warriors against animal, human, and supernatural foes. Various Native American legends feature pairs of warriors—such as the Navajo warrior twins and the Zuni Ahayuuta brothers—who perform heroic tasks to help their people.

Shaka, a hero of the Zulu people of southern Africa, gathered a huge army and established a great empire in the early 1800s.

Some figures in mythology earned their hero status as legendary rulers. Britain's King Arthur, for example, may have begun as a historical figure but was transformed into a hero of great stature. Africa has a strong tradition of kingly heroes. Shaka, a leader of the Zulu people of southern Africa, gathered a huge army and established a great empire in the early 1800s. Osai Tutu, a ruler of the Ashanti people in the 1700s, succeeded in freeing the Ashanti from domination by a neighboring people with the help of a magical golden stool. Tibetans and Mongolians tell tales about the warrior-king Gesar (Gesar Khan), a god who reluctantly agreed to be born as a human in order to fight demons on earth.

National and Culture Heroes. A national hero is a mythological—or even historical—hero who is considered to be the founder of a city or nation or the source of identity for a people. In ancient Greece, heroes became the object of

† *See* ***Names and Places*** *at the end of this volume for further information.*

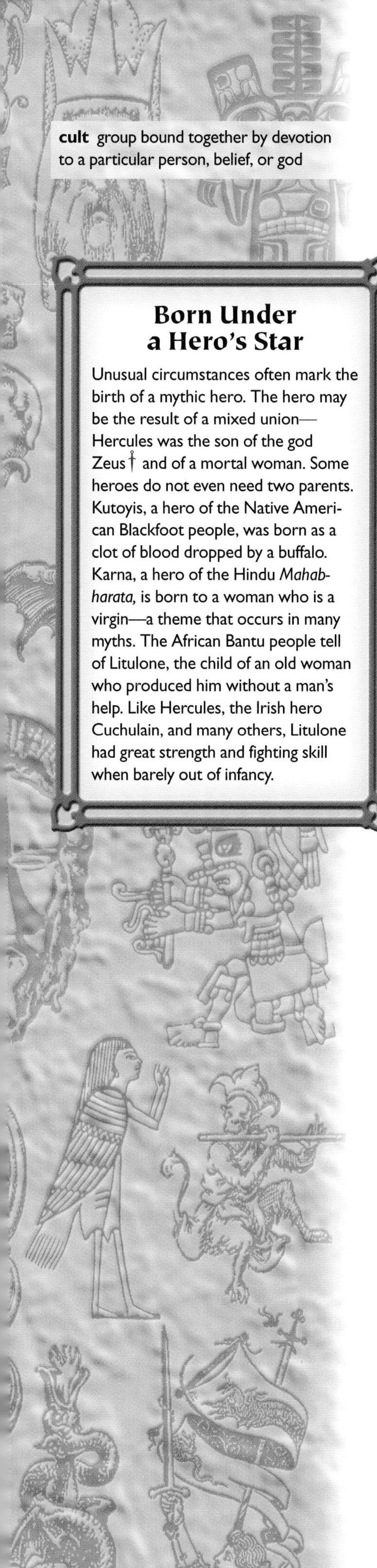

cult group bound together by devotion to a particular person, belief, or god

religious worship, and local **cults** developed to show devotion to particular local heroes. The Romans made Aeneas† their national hero. In North America, Iroquois legends say that the hero Hiawatha persuaded five tribes to come together as one group, thus giving the Iroquois greater power and a stronger identity.

Another type of ancestral hero is the culture hero who brings the gifts of civilization to a people. The Kayapo Indians of Brazil have a myth about a boy named Botoque, who stole fire from a jaguar and brought it to his people so they could cook food for the first time. In Greek mythology it is the Titan† Prometheus who steals fire for the benefit of humankind. The Daribi people of Papua New Guinea, a large island in the eastern Pacific, have myths about Souw, a wandering culture hero. Souw brought death, warfare, and black magic, but he also gave humans the first livestock and crops, allowing them to shift from hunting to agriculture.

Born Under a Hero's Star

Unusual circumstances often mark the birth of a mythic hero. The hero may be the result of a mixed union—Hercules was the son of the god Zeus† and of a mortal woman. Some heroes do not even need two parents. Kutoyis, a hero of the Native American Blackfoot people, was born as a clot of blood dropped by a buffalo. Karna, a hero of the Hindu *Mahabharata,* is born to a woman who is a virgin—a theme that occurs in many myths. The African Bantu people tell of Litulone, the child of an old woman who produced him without a man's help. Like Hercules, the Irish hero Cuchulain, and many others, Litulone had great strength and fighting skill when barely out of infancy.

Clever Heroes and Tricksters. In many myths heroes accomplish great tasks by outwitting evil or more powerful enemies. In the West African legend of Sunjata, the female character Nana Triban tricks the evil king Sumanguru Kante into telling her the source of his great strength. Nana Triban uses this knowledge to help her brother Sunjata triumph over Sumanguru. In Greek mythology, Penelope, the wife of Odysseus, outwits the many suitors pressing to marry her during her husband's long absence. Claiming that she must weave a shroud for her father-in-law before she can remarry, she weaves by day and unravels the cloth by night. In the Persian tale *Thousand and One Nights,* Sheherazade prevents the sultan from carrying out a plan to kill her. Capturing his attention with fascinating stories, she withholds the endings, promising to continue the following evening.

Some culture heroes are tricksters—human or animal characters whose mischievous pranks and tricks can benefit humans. Raven and Coyote fill the trickster role in many Native American myths. The Polynesians of the Pacific islands have myths about Maui, a trickster whose actions have bad results as often as good ones. He loses immortality for humans, for example, but acquires fire for them. Tricksters in African myth are generally small and weak creatures, such as the hare and the spider, who outwit the strong, rich, and powerful. The African trickster hare is the distant ancestor of Brer Rabbit, a clever hero in African American mythology.

Folk Heroes. Some heroes are ordinary individuals who have special skills. They may take up the causes of common people against tyrants and bullies or may be blessed with remarkable good fortune. Such heroes often become known through popular songs or folk tales, but they may also appear in various forms of literature.

Folk heroes include Robin Hood, an English adventurer who fought and robbed the rich in order to help the poor, and John Henry, an African American laborer who performed a humble job with exceptional—and fatal—strength and determination. With

its democratic traditions that recognize the worth of ordinary people, the United States has produced a number of folk heroes, including Daniel Boone, Davy Crockett, and Wyatt Earp.

Defiant and Doomed Heroes. The hero's story does not always have a happy ending. Some heroes knowingly defy the limits placed on them by society or the gods. Even if they face destruction, they are determined to be true to their beliefs—or perhaps to perish in a blaze of glory. Others are simply the victims of their own failings or of bad luck.

medieval relating to the Middle Ages in Europe, a period from about A.D. 500 to 1500

Yamato-takeru, a legendary warrior hero of Japan, brings about his own end when he kills two gods who have taken the form of a white deer and a white boar. Roland, a warrior hero of **medieval** European legends, falls in battle because he is too proud to summon help. Antigone, a Greek princess, defies the law in order to bury her brother, knowing that the penalty will be death. The most gruesomely doomed of all heroes may be Antigone's father, Oedipus, who outrages the gods by unwittingly killing his father

Yamato-takeru, a legendary warrior hero of Japan, fought battles against people and gods. Stories about his adventures appear in the *Kojiki* and the *Nihongi,* two books of Japanese myths and legends.

Heroes

Entries on individual heroes include

Achilles	Brer Rabbit	Galahad	Jason	Penelope	Sigurd
Aeneas	Bruce, Robert	George, St.	John Henry	Perseus	Sinbad the Sailor
Ajax	Bunyan, Paul	Gilgamesh	Kokopelli	Prometheus	Sunjata
Aladdin	Cid, El	Hector	Lancelot	Quetzalcoatl	Tell, William
Antigone	Coriolanus	Hercules	Maui	Rama	Theseus
Arthur, King	Crockett, Davy	Hiawatha	Odysseus	Robin Hood	Ulysses
Beowulf	Cuchulain	Hunahpú and Xbalanqúe	Oedipus	Roland	Yu
Boone, Daniel	Finn		Orpheus	Samson	

and marrying his mother. His heroism lies not in quests, adventures, or triumphs but in facing his tragic fate.

In Aztec myths, the culture hero Quetzalcoatl was tricked by his enemy Tezcatlipoca into leaving his kingdom. After getting Quetzalcoatl drunk, Tezcatlipoca showed him a mirror with Tezcatlipoca's frightening image. Believing that the mirror reflected his own face, Quetzalcoatl went away to purify himself, promising to return to his people at the end of a 52-year cycle. ***See also*** **Tricksters.**

Hestia

See *Vesta.*

Hiawatha

prophet one who claims to have received divine messages or insights

Hiawatha was a Native American leader of the 1500s who became a legend for his role in bringing the people of the five Iroquois nations together. According to the stories, he helped persuade the tribes to live in peace and join forces against their enemies.

Hiawatha (whose name means "he makes rivers") was a member of the Mohawk tribe of present-day New York. After becoming a chief, he met the **prophet** Dekanawida, who had a plan to unite the people of the Mohawk, Oneida, Onondaga, Cayuga, and Seneca nations. Hiawatha embraced Dekanawida's plan and set out to explain it to the individual tribes. However, he soon encountered opposition from the powerful Onondaga chief Atotarho, who refused to cooperate with Hiawatha. Iroquois tales say that Atotarho sent an enormous white bird to seize Hiawatha's daughter and kill her.

Despite this staggering loss, Hiawatha continued to work with the five nations, advising them to resolve their differences and live at peace with one another. The myths describe the magical white canoe he traveled in. For a time, the tribes lived in harmony. Then suddenly, the peace was shattered by the invasion of other Native Americans intent on war. Hiawatha called the leaders of the five nations together and declared that no tribe could withstand these

Hiawatha helped Dekanawida unite the people of the five Iroquois nations—the Mohawk, the Oneida, the Onondaga, the Cayuga, and the Seneca.

attacks alone. He assigned each tribe a task to carry out to protect and defend their new nation, which he named the Iroquois. Then he sailed into the air in his sacred canoe.

Another character named Hiawatha appears in *The Song of Hiawatha,* a poem written by Henry Wadsworth Longfellow in 1855. Longfellow's work has no connection with the Iroquois leader. It is based on an Algonquian hero who brought many of the gifts of civilization to his people. The poem's haunting rhythms and vivid images of woodland life have made a lasting impression on generations of readers. ***See also*** **DEKANAWIDA; NATIVE AMERICAN MYTHOLOGY.**

Hinduism and Mythology

epic long poem about legendary or historical heroes, written in a grand style

Hinduism, which has millions of followers in India and around the world today, is one of the world's oldest religions. For well over 3,000 years, it has been accumulating the sacred stories and heroic **epics** that make up the mythology of Hinduism. Nothing in this complex and colorful mythology is fixed and firm. Pulsing with creation, destruction, love, and war, it shifts and changes. Most myths occur in several different versions, and many characters have multiple roles, identities, and histories. This seeming confusion reflects the richness of a mythology that has expanded and taken on new meanings over the centuries.

Background and Themes

Around 1700 B.C., peoples from the area to the northwest of India began migrating to India. Called Aryans or Indo-Europeans, they brought a mythic tradition that became the basis of an early form of Hinduism. Over the years, as the Aryans mingled with the peoples and cultures of the Indian subcontinent, the mythology grew increasingly complex.

Stages and Sources. Hinduism has gone through various stages, which can be linked to the most important texts surviving from each period. The earliest stage is associated with the Vedas, the oldest Indian documents. One of them, the *Rig-Veda,* is a collection of 1,028 hymns of praise and prayers to the gods with references to myths. The Vedas are based on ancient Aryan traditions that were long communicated only in oral form.

The next group of texts, the *Brahmanas,* date from 900 to 700 B.C. Though concerned mainly with the rituals of Hinduism, the *Brahmanas* contain many myths. The *Upanishads,* written around 700 B.C. and after, focus on ideas but often communicate them through myths. The two great Hindu epics, the *Mahabharata* and

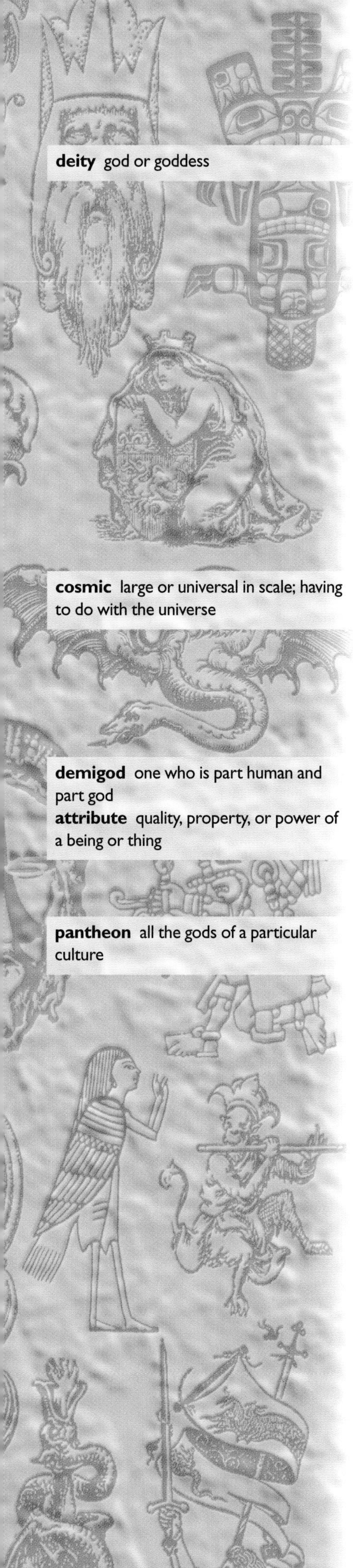

deity god or goddess

cosmic large or universal in scale; having to do with the universe

demigod one who is part human and part god
attribute quality, property, or power of a being or thing

pantheon all the gods of a particular culture

the *Ramayana,* written down sometime between 300 B.C. and A.D. 300, contain stories about a number of major **deities.** After that time, the chief expression of Hindu mythology and religion was in texts called *Puranas,* "stories of the old days." Most of the stories are devoted to one god or another. The *Puranas* often retell earlier myths, sometimes in the voices of the gods themselves.

Themes. Certain key beliefs in Hinduism form the background against which the myths unfold. One of these is the idea of reincarnation, sometimes called the transmigration of souls. In Hindu belief, each soul experiences many, many lives. After the death of one body, or incarnation, the soul is born again into a new living body. Even the gods can be reincarnated in human form.

Just as the individual soul is continually reborn, the universe is continually created and destroyed. Time moves in cycles of millions of years, endlessly building up and tearing down with no beginning or end. All change and decay are part of a divinely directed **cosmic** dance that will eventually result in renewal. Faced with this immense pattern, each individual has the duty to follow his or her own pattern of right behavior, called the dharma.

Major Figures

Hindu mythology is populated by an enormous cast of deities, demons, **demigods,** humans, and animals. Some had a central role in one era but remain in the background in later periods, while others have risen from obscurity to prominence. The **attributes** and histories of many mythological characters have changed considerably over the many centuries that Hinduism has existed.

Brahma, the creator of life on earth, is one of the Trimurti, the three gods at the center of the Hindu **pantheon** (along with Shiva and Vishnu). In the early Vedic texts, the creator god was Prajapati, but over time Brahma took the older god's place in many myths about the creation of the universe.

Hindu Deities

Deity	Role
Brahma	creator god
Devi	wife of Shiva, goddess who takes many forms—both kind and fierce
Ganesha	god of good fortune and wisdom
Indra	god of storms and rain
Shiva	avenging and destroying god
Varuna	originally a creator god and ruler of the sky, later became god of water
Vishnu	preserver god and protector of life

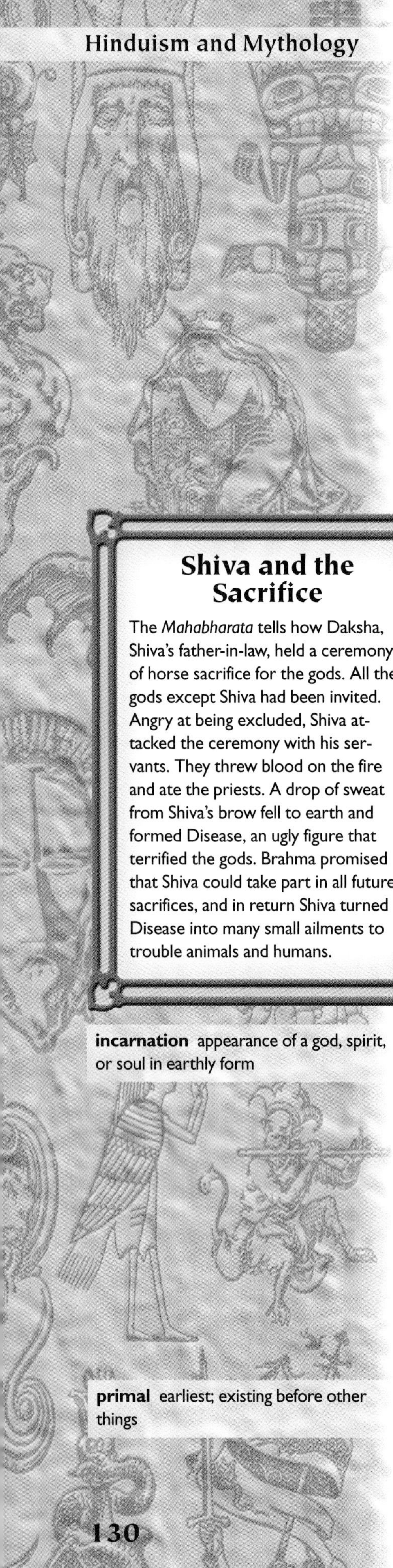

Vishnu, the second member of the Trimurti, is the preserver or protector of life. His attributes are mercy and goodness. Some Hindus regard Vishnu as the supreme being and Brahma and Shiva as aspects of him. Shiva, descended from the old Vedic storm god Rudra, is the third member of the Trimurti. He is the avenging and destroying god, but his destruction allows new creation to begin. Sometimes Shiva is portrayed as a dancer who directs the movements of the universe.

Devi, "the goddess," is one of the most ancient deities of the pantheon. Under her name are grouped various female deities, who represent different aspects of Devi. Among them are Parvati, the wife of Shiva; Durga, the warrior goddess and fighter of demons; and the even more ferocious Kali, "the dark one," who also fights demons but sometimes becomes intoxicated with blood and destruction.

The popular elephant-headed, four-handed god Ganesha is Parvati's son. One of the most popular gods in Hinduism today, he is associated with good luck and wisdom. Indra, god of storm and rain, was one of the most important deities of the *Rig-Veda* and may have represented the warrior chieftains of the ancestral Aryan peoples. Vedic hymns suggest that Indra replaced Varuna, the guardian of justice and order, as the king of the gods. As the mythology of Hinduism developed, however, Indra in turn moved to secondary status below the Trimurti. Krishna is one of the **incarnations,** or avatars, of Vishnu. He appears in the *Mahabharata* and the *Puranas.* Many stories about him focus on his prankish, playful nature and on his many love affairs.

Manu, sometimes described as a son of Brahma, is both a god and the first man, ancestor of the human race. According to one myth, a small fish warns Manu that the earth will soon be destroyed by a great flood. Manu takes care of the fish, which is really an incarnation of Vishnu, and when it is grown, it saves him from the flood so that he can repopulate the earth. The heroine Savitri, whose story is told in the *Mahabharata,* symbolizes love that defeats even death. She persuades Yama, the lord of death, to release her husband from death.

Shiva and the Sacrifice

The *Mahabharata* tells how Daksha, Shiva's father-in-law, held a ceremony of horse sacrifice for the gods. All the gods except Shiva had been invited. Angry at being excluded, Shiva attacked the ceremony with his servants. They threw blood on the fire and ate the priests. A drop of sweat from Shiva's brow fell to earth and formed Disease, an ugly figure that terrified the gods. Brahma promised that Shiva could take part in all future sacrifices, and in return Shiva turned Disease into many small ailments to trouble animals and humans.

incarnation appearance of a god, spirit, or soul in earthly form

Core Myths

Hindu mythology includes a huge number of stories. Some have proved to be especially enduring and central to an understanding of Hinduism. Among these are the tales told in the *Mahabharata* and the *Ramayana* and those described below.

Creation. Hindu mythology includes several different accounts of the beginning of things, but in each version, the act of creation is really an act of arranging, producing order from chaos. Vedic texts tell of the sacrifice of a **primal** being called Purusha, whose cut-up body becomes all the elements of the universe. Another image of creation, that of fertilization and pregnancy, occurs in myths about Prajapati, the father of all humans and animals. Sometimes

primal earliest; existing before other things

This illustration shows the three major Hindu gods—Brahma, the creator of life; Vishnu, the protector of life; and Shiva, the god of destruction.

heaven and earth are described as parents whose mating produces the gods. Myths of Tvashtar, a minor Vedic god of carpentry or architecture, explain creation as an act of building.

As Hinduism developed and the Trimurti gained importance, a complex vision of the creation, destruction, and recreation of the universe emerged. Brahma brings the universe into being through his thoughts. The world then passes through a Maha Yuga, or great age, that lasts 4,320,000 years. The Maha Yuga contains four yugas, or ages. Each is shorter and more immoral than the one before, from the Krita Yuga—Brahma's golden age—through two intermediate ages under Vishnu's protection to the Kali Yuga—Shiva's dark age.

Each dark age in turn gives way to a new golden age, and the cycle of the Maha Yuga repeats a thousand times. Then Shiva destroys all life with scorching heat and drowning flood, and the earth remains empty while Vishnu sleeps. After a thousand Maha Yugas, a lotus flower emerges from Vishnu's navel, and it becomes Brahma, ready to perform his creative act anew.

The Avatars of Vishnu. Many myths deal with Vishnu's avatars, the incarnations of the god on earth. The most common list of the ten avatars begins with Matsya, the fish that protects Manu from the flood. The second avatar is Kurma, a tortoise that holds Mount Mandara on his back so that the gods can use it as a paddle to churn the ocean and produce a drink of eternal life.

Varaha, a boar who appears after a demon giant pulls the earth to the bottom of the ocean, is the third incarnation. Varaha defeats the demon and raises the earth on his tusks. Narasinha, the fourth avatar, is half man and half lion. He defeats a demon who cannot be killed by man or beast. The dwarf Vamana, the fifth incarnation, triumphs over Bali, a being who had gained control of the world. When Bali grants Vamana as much land as he can cover in three strides, the dwarf becomes a giant and strides over heaven and

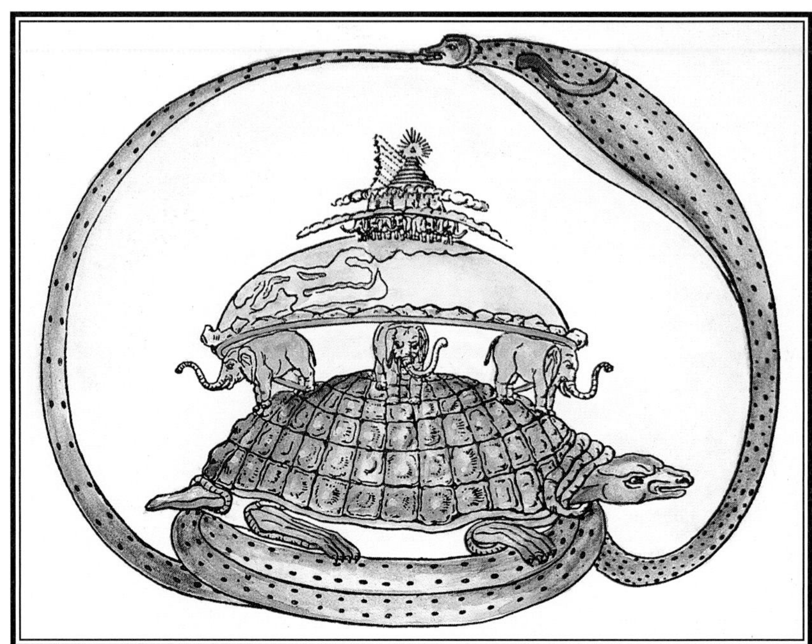

This drawing illustrates a Hindu creation myth. The tortoise supports elephants that hold up the world, and everything is encircled by the world serpent.

earth. The sixth avatar, ax-wielding Parashurama, frees the priests from the domination of the warriors.

The seventh incarnation, Rama, is the hero of the *Ramayana.* The eighth is the god Krishna; and the ninth is Buddha. Hindus believe that Buddha came to earth to draw people away from the proper worship of the Vedas so that the world would decline and be destroyed, as the cosmic cycle demands. The tenth avatar, Kalki, will appear at the end of the world to preside over its destruction and the creation of a new, pure world.

The Birth of Ganesha. Shiva's wife, Parvati, produced Ganesha—and did so without any help from Shiva, according to many accounts. Some say that Shiva, being **immortal,** had no desire for a son, but Parvati wanted a child and produced the boy from her own body. In other versions, Shiva gave Parvati a doll that at her touch magically came to life as a baby.

immortal able to live forever

According to one story, Shiva struck off the boy's head, either because Ganesha prevented him from approaching Parvati or because Shiva believed that his son was doomed to die. Parvati's grief, however, moved him to try to replace the head, and he finally succeeded in attaching an elephant's head to the boy's body.

Indra and the Serpent. Legends of the slaying of a serpent or dragon appear in many cultures. In Hindu mythology, one such story centers on the god Indra and the "footless and handless" demon Vritra, described as both snake and dragon. The tale is told in the Vedas and dates from the time when Indra was king of the gods.

Using a divine thunderbolt, Indra struck Vritra between the shoulders, slicing open the mountain on which Vritra lay. The

blow separated heaven from earth and land from water. The waters that Vritra had contained flowed forth to bring life. Indra's heroic victory made him the champion of all who struggled to overcome obstacles or resistance.

Modern Legacy

Hindu belief and mythology color every aspect of life and culture in India. They are the basis of countless works of art, from plays about Rama written in the 700s to modern Indian movies based on mythic stories. Temples and images of the deities are everywhere. Festivals—such as the ten-day autumn celebration of Rama and his wife, Sita—keep the traditional gods, heroes, and myths alive. Even place names have sacred associations. The city of Calcutta, for example, comes from Kalighat, the place where sacrifices to the goddess Kali once took place.

Besides inspiring generations of Indian artists and thinkers, Hindu mythology has appealed to many in the West as well. Ralph Waldo Emerson, an American writer of the 1800s, wrote *Brahma,* a poem celebrating the creator god. In the same era, English-speaking readers became familiar with the legends of Savitri through Edwin Arnold's poem *Savitri, or Love and Death.* A poem by the German writer Goethe called *The God and the Bayadere* (dancing girl) deals with an appearance on earth of the god Shiva.

English composer Gustav Holst wrote a chamber opera—one meant to be sung, not acted, with a small orchestra—called *Savitri.* Holst also translated many hymns from the *Rig-Veda* into English and wrote music to accompany them. These four sets of songs are grouped together under the title *Choral Hymns.* Bertram Shapleigh, an American composer, wrote *Vedic Hymn,* also based on a text from the *Rig-Veda,* and a piece of orchestral music called *Ramayana.* A 1989 film of the *Mahabharata* written by Jean-Claude Carrière and directed by Peter Brook has brought the ancient epic to modern movie audiences. ***See also*** **Bhagavad Gita; Brahma; Buddhism and Mythology; Devi; Ganesha; Indra; Krishna; Mahabharata, The; Manu; Nagas; Rama; Ramayana, The; Reincarnation; Rig-Veda; Savitri; Shiva; Upanishads; Varuna; Vedas; Vishnu.**

Holy Grail

medieval relating to the Middle Ages in Europe, a period from about A.D. 500 to 1500

According to **medieval** legend, the Holy Grail was the vessel from which Jesus Christ drank at the Last Supper, his final meal with his followers. Many works of literature describe the search for the Grail, which was believed to have sacred and mysterious powers. However, this quest, or search, did not always involve a physical object. For some, the Holy Grail represented a religious state of grace or union with God. In some accounts, the Grail held blood from Christ's wounds and was known as the Sangreal, meaning "royal blood."

The Legend of the Grail. Although many versions of the Grail legend exist, certain elements appear over and over again. Some

The highest and most noble goal of the Knights of the Round Table was to find the Holy Grail. Lancelot and Perceval searched for it, but only Galahad, seen here on horseback, achieved the goal.

stories of the Grail begin with Lucifer, originally an angel in heaven who wore a crown adorned with a magnificent emerald. Lucifer rebelled against God and was thrown out of heaven. His emerald fell to earth, where someone made it into a **chalice.** In other stories, images of the Grail have ranged from a humble clay or wooden bowl to a golden goblet studded with gems or an object bathed in a blinding light.

After the Last Supper, the Grail came into the possession of Joseph of Arimathea, who caught Christ's blood in it at the crucifixion. Joseph went to prison, but the Grail kept him alive by supplying daily nourishment. Released from prison, Joseph traveled to France and then to Glastonbury, England, carrying the Holy Grail. Soon, however, the Grail disappeared from the world because people were sinful. Hidden away in a mysterious castle, it was guarded by the descendants of Joseph's sister.

One of the best-known versions of the Grail's later history is connected with Arthur, the legendary king of Britain. This account says that the Grail lay somewhere in a wild and desolate part of Britain in the castle of the Fisher King, a wounded monarch who lay between life and death. Only if the purest of knights found his way to the castle and caught a glimpse of the Grail would the Fisher King's torment end and life be restored to his wasteland.

chalice drinking vessel or goblet

To the knights who sat around King Arthur's Round Table, seeing the Holy Grail was the highest and most noble goal. They roamed the nation in search of it. Lancelot nearly achieved the quest, but the sin of his love for Guinevere, Arthur's queen, kept him from seeing the Grail. A knight named Perceval (or Parsifal) saw the Grail but did not understand what it was. Only Galahad, Lancelot's son, was pure enough to see it with full understanding of its meaning. He had to travel to a distant land called Sarras to do so, for the Grail had left Britain at some point. The vision of the Grail brought such profound ecstasy that Galahad died moments later.

Development of the Legend. The Holy Grail legend fuses Christian elements with much older Celtic† mythology and appears to be the product of storytelling over hundreds of years. The Grail itself is related to various vessels in Celtic lore, such as the drinking horn of the god Bran, which produced any food or drink the user desired. It was also associated with a magic **cauldron** that could restore life to any dead body placed in it.

cauldron large kettle

†*See **Names and Places** at the end of this volume for further information.*

romance in medieval literature, a tale based on legend, love, and adventure, often set in a distant place or time

The earliest known work to give a Christian significance to the magical vessel was *Perceval,* **a romance** of the late 1100s by the French poet Chrétien de Troyes. A few decades later, Robert de Borron wrote *Joseph of Arimathea,* which established the connection between the Grail of Perceval and the cup used by Christ and later owned by Joseph. *Parzival,* by Wolfram von Eschenbach, expanded on the mystical story of the innocent knight and the Fisher King and also introduced an order of knights charged with guarding the Grail. This version of the story became the basis for the opera *Parsifal* by the modern German composer Richard Wagner.

Over time, versions of the Grail story began to link the Holy Grail with the popular legend of King Arthur. One account made Sir Galahad the virtuous hero and the Grail a symbol of a rare and mystical union with the divine. Late in the 1400s, Sir Thomas Malory wrote *Morte D'Arthur* (The Death of Arthur), the version of the Arthurian legend that was to become the best known. With it he established the story of the Grail quest by the knights of Arthur's Round Table and of Galahad's ultimate success. ***See also*** **ARTHUR, KING; ARTHURIAN LEGENDS; GALAHAD; LANCELOT.**

Homer

epic long poem about legendary or historical heroes, written in a grand style

lyre stringed instrument similar to a small harp

Two of the greatest works of ancient literature—the *Iliad* and the *Odyssey*—are credited to a Greek poet named Homer. However, Homer is a shadowy figure, and some scholars doubt that he ever existed. They suggest that the two **epics,** which tell of the Trojan War† and the events surrounding it, were woven together by generations of storytellers. Others, however, believe that one poet—perhaps Homer—could have gathered traditional legends and stories told for centuries and created the two great works of literature.

In any case, the ancient Greeks named Homer as the author of the *Iliad* and the *Odyssey.* Stories about the poet suggest that he lived in Ionia, a region on the west coast of Anatolia (present-day Turkey). The dates of his life are uncertain, possibly in the 800s or 700s B.C.

Homer is considered to be the author of the *Iliad* and the *Odyssey,* two epics of ancient Greek literature.

According to tradition, Homer was a blind poet who wandered from place to place telling tales of legendary heroes, gods, and goddesses. It was customary in that period for performers to sing or chant such tales while playing a **lyre** or other musical instrument. If Homer was, indeed, a wandering performer, he would have relied on voluntary contributions of food, money, and other goods for his support.

Whether or not Homer wrote the *Iliad* and the *Odyssey,* the two works had a profound influence on Western culture and education. To the ancient Greeks, they were a source of moral lessons as well as a symbol of Greek unity and achievement. The philosopher Aristotle, author of the *Poetics,* praised Homer highly. A number of later writers, such as the Roman poet Virgil†, modeled their own works on the style and patterns of Homer's epics. ***See also*** **GREEK MYTHOLOGY; ILIAD, THE; ODYSSEY, THE.**

Horatii

According to Roman legend, the Horatii were triplets who defended Rome against Alba Longa. To avoid a costly battle, the two cities decided to settle their dispute with a duel between champions from each side.

The Horatii brothers fought against triplets from Alba Longa called the Curiatii. After two of the Horatii were killed, the third, Publius Horatius, pretended to flee. The Curiatii pursued him but could not stay together because of their wounds. Horatius turned and attacked them one at a time and killed all three. Although Horatius won the contest, his sister was overcome with grief. She had been engaged to one of the Curiatii, and she wept when she realized her brother had killed her husband-to-be. Seeing her tears, Horatius stabbed her, saying, "So perish any Roman woman who mourns the enemy."

Horatius was sentenced to die for his act, but he successfully appealed to the people to spare his life. Some scholars believe that the story was created to explain the origin of the Roman tradition by which condemned prisoners could appeal to the public to avoid a death sentence. ***See also*** **ROMAN MYTHOLOGY.**

Horatius

Horatius, also called Horatius Cocles (meaning "one-eyed"), was a mythical Roman hero credited with saving Rome from Etruscan invaders in the 500s B.C. According to the legend, Horatius led a group of warriors who were defending the Sublician Bridge, which led across the Tiber River into Rome. He ordered his troops to take down the bridge, while he and two companions fought off the Etruscans. Horatius sent these men back over the bridge just before it collapsed. As the bridge fell, he jumped into the Tiber while still wearing his armor and swam to safety. Because Horatius's bravery saved Rome from invasion, the city erected a statue of him and gave him a large amount of land as a reward.

A statue of a figure with one eye stood near the famous bridge of ancient Rome. Early Romans said it was Horatius because of its location and because the figure had only one eye. The sculpture, however, almost certainly represented the god Vulcan†, who is typically shown in works of art as having one eye and being crippled. ***See also*** **ROMAN MYTHOLOGY; VULCAN.**

Horus

Horus was one of the earliest and most important Egyptian gods. He was originally portrayed as a hawk or falcon and worshiped as a sun god and creator of the sky. His right eye represented the sun, and his left eye represented the moon. Later images show him as a man with the head of a bird.

The early rulers of southern Egypt were followers of Horus. When they conquered northern Egypt and reunited the two lands (around 2200 B.C.), Horus became the symbol of the newly unified country, and the **pharaoh** was considered the **incarnation** of Horus. In time, the worship of Horus—under his various names—spread to many places.

pharaoh ruler of ancient Egypt
incarnation appearance of a god, spirit, or soul in earthly form

†*See* ***Names and Places*** *at the end of this volume for further information.*

Horus, worshiped as a sun god and creator god by the ancient Egyptians, was often shown with the head of a bird.

Horus became a major figure in Egyptian mythology. Before he was born, his father Osiris† died at the hand of his own brother Set†. When Horus grew up, he swore to avenge his father's death and fought Set many times.

In one version of this story, Set blinded Horus in his left eye, but the god Thoth healed it. Horus ended up killing Set, however, and the gods named Horus ruler of Egypt. The restored eye, called the *udjat* or *wedjat,* became a powerful magical symbol of protection in ancient Egypt. The Egyptians used the story of Horus's wounded eye to explain the changing phases of the moon.

In another account of the conflict between Horus and Set, the two came before a council of the gods to decide who would inherit Osiris's throne. Most of the council accepted Horus's claim, but the sun god Ra favored Set because he was older and more capable. As a result, Horus and Set undertook a series of contests to determine who would become the ruler.

On one occasion, both gods turned themselves into hippopotamuses to see who could stay under water longer. During the contest, Horus's mother Isis† had the chance to kill Set but chose not to do so. Horus was angry at his mother and fled into the desert. Set found him and put out his eyes, but the goddess Hathor repaired them with the milk of a small antelope. In the end, the gods agreed that Horus should be the ruler. Horus then invited Set to join him and live in the sky as the god of storms. ***See also*** **Birds in Mythology; Egyptian Mythology; Hathor; Isis; Osiris; Ra (Re); Set; Thoth.**

Hsien

See *Xian.*

Huehueteotl

pantheon all the gods of a particular culture

Huehueteotl was the Aztec god of fire and also the oldest god in the Aztec **pantheon.** He is typically shown as an aged man with a hunched back who carries a brazier—a pan for holding burning coals—on his head. He was loved by the Aztecs because he brought heat to the kitchen, bath, and laundry basin, where old clothes were made new. The image of Huehueteotl is sometimes combined with that of Xiuhtecuhtli, a young fire god associated with warriors and kingship. In this form, the god is shown wearing garments covered with turquoise and carrying a fire serpent on his back.

Aztec priests kept a fire at all times to honor Huehueteotl. To mark the completion of a full 52-year cycle in the Aztec calendar, the fire was carried between temples and into the homes of the

people. The Aztecs celebrated two festivals dedicated to Huehueteotl, one in August (the hottest part of the year) and the other in January (the coldest part of the year). ***See also*** **Aztec Mythology; Fire; Serpents and Snakes.**

Huitzilopochtli

Huitzilopochtli, the Aztec god of war, was associated with the sun. His name, which means "hummingbird of the south," came from the Aztec belief that the spirits of warriors killed in battle followed the sun through the sky for four years. After that, they were transformed into hummingbirds. In some myths, the warlike Huitzilopochtli appears in contrast to his brother the god Quetzalcoatl†, who represented life and the gifts of civilization.

According to legend, Huitzilopochtli's mother was the goddess Coatlicue. One day she found a bunch of hummingbird feathers and stuffed them into her breast. She immediately became pregnant with Huitzilopochtli. However, some of her other children—a daughter named Coyolxauhqui and 400 sons—were jealous of the unborn child. They plotted to kill Coatlicue, but when they attacked her, Huitzilopochtli emerged from his mother's womb fully grown. He cut off the head of his sister and killed most of his brothers as well.

The Aztecs believed that to nourish Huitzilopochtli and keep the world in motion, they needed to feed the god human blood every day. For this reason, Aztec priests conducted daily human sacrifices at the Great Temple in their capital city of Tenochtitlán. During these **rituals,** victims were led up the steps of a pyramid, and while they were still alive, their hearts were cut out of their chests. The victims' bodies were then thrown down the steps of the pyramid onto a stone that featured a carved image of Coyolxauhqui. In this way, the sacrifices reenacted the story about the young god killing his sister.

ritual ceremony that follows a set pattern

Another tale about Huitzilopochtli tells how he led the Aztecs to settle on the island where they built the great city of Tenochtitlán. Originally from the north of Mexico, the Aztecs followed Huitzilopochtli on

One legend about Huitzilopochtli, the Aztec god of war, concerns the origin of the city of Tenochtitlán. The god told the Aztecs to settle at a place where they found an eagle perched on a cactus.

†*See **Names and Places** at the end of this volume for further information.*

a long journey south in search of a new home. The god told them to settle at a place where they saw an eagle perched on a cactus growing out of a rock. As predicted, they saw the sign described by the god and ended their journey. This story echoes some events in Aztec history. In 1345 the Aztecs were driven onto an island in the middle of a lake by a tribe called the Culhua. There they founded Tenochtitlán, which would later become the capital of the Aztec empire. ***See also*** **Animals in Mythology; Aztec Mythology; Coatlicue; Quetzalcoatl; Serpents and Snakes.**

Hunahpú and Xbalanqúe

underworld land of the dead

The twin gods Hunahpú and Xbalanqúe were heroes in the mythology of the Maya, a people of central America. Through bravery and quick thinking, they outwitted the lords of Xibalba, the **underworld,** and destroyed them. Their story is told in the sacred Mayan text, the *Popol Vuh.*

According to legend, the twins' father, Hun-Hunahpú, had also struggled with the gods of the underworld. The gods challenged him and his own twin brother to play a game of ball. Then they killed him and hung his head on a tree. A young woman passing by reached up to pick some fruit from the tree, and the head spat into her hand, saying "In my saliva and spittle I have given you my descendants." She soon gave birth to twin boys, Hunahpú and Xbalanqúe.

When the two brothers met the lords of Xibalba, the gods sent them through a series of frightening places in the underworld. They began in the House of Gloom and then passed into the House of Knives, where they managed to avoid being stabbed. They built a fire in the House of Cold to avoid freezing and then faced the House of Jaguars, where they fed bones to the animals to escape being eaten themselves. After the next trial, the House of Fire, they entered the House of Bats, where disaster struck. One of the bats cut off Hunahpú's head. The gods hung the head up in a ball court and challenged the twins to play ball with them.

Xbalanqúe found a turtle to sit on Hunahpú's shoulders in place of his head, and they strode onto the ball court. During the game, the gods became distracted by a rabbit near the court. Xbalanqúe seized this opportunity to steal his brother's head from the wall and put it back in place. Much to the annoyance of the gods, the twins were now strong enough to tie the game.

Hunahpú and Xbalanqúe performed a series of tricks, during which they appeared to die in a stone oven and then transform themselves into traveling actors. When the lords of Xibalba asked the twins to perform for them, the two brothers refused at first. Eventually, they presented several acts, such as burning down and restoring a house and sacrificing Hunahpú and bringing him back to life. Impressed, the gods asked the twins to do the same for them. The brothers agreed, but after sacrificing the gods, they did not revive them. Having eliminated the gods of the underworld and avenged the murder of their father, Hunahpú and Xbalanqúe went into the heavens, where in some versions they became the sun and the moon. ***See also*** **Mayan Mythology; Popol Vuh; Xibalba.**

Hydra

immortal able to live forever

In Greek mythology, the Hydra was a giant water snake with many heads that lived in a swamp near Lerna in the land of Argos. The number of heads is variously reported from as few as 5 to more than 100.

The second of the 12 labors of Hercules† was to kill the Hydra. However, when one of the Hydra's heads was cut off, two more grew in its place. The monster also had one **immortal** head. To defeat the Hydra, Hercules called on his friend Iolaus for help. As soon as Hercules cut off one head, Iolaus would seal the wound with a hot iron or a torch so that nothing could grow to replace it. After removing the Hydra's immortal head, Hercules buried it under a large rock. He then collected the monster's poisonous blood. In later adventures, he dipped his arrows in the blood so that they would instantly kill whomever they struck. ***See also*** **Animals in Mythology; Greek Mythology; Hercules; Serpents and Snakes.**

Hypnos

underworld land of the dead

The ancient Greeks said that Hypnos, the god of sleep, visited people during the dark of night to ease them into a state of rest. Hypnos hid from the sunlight during the day. According to Greek myth, he was the son of Nyx, the goddess of night, and his brother was Thanatos, the god of death.

Some writers claimed that Hypnos lived in the **underworld,** but others said that he dwelled in a cave on the Greek island of Lemnos. Lethe, the river of forgetfulness, rippled through his dim, foggy cave. The Dreams, some of his many sons, lived with him. The most important ones were Morpheus, who caused sleepers to dream about people; Icelus (or Phobetor), who delivered dreams about animals or monsters; and Phantasus, who brought dreams about lifeless objects.

In the *Iliad,* Homer† tells a story about the goddess Hera† requesting help from Hypnos during the Trojan War†. She asked him to put Zeus† to sleep to prevent him from interfering on behalf of Troy. At first, Hypnos hesitated, fearful of Zeus's anger. However, Hera convinced him to help by promising him Pasithea, one of the Graces, as his bride. ***See also*** **Graces; Hera; Lethe; Thanatos; Trojan War; Zeus.**

Icarus

See *Daedalus.*

Idun

immortal able to live forever

trickster mischievous figure appearing in various forms in the folktales and mythology of many different peoples

In Norse† mythology, Idun (Iduna) was the goddess of spring and rebirth. She and her husband, Bragi, the god of music and poetry, lived in Asgard, the home of the gods. Idun took care of the magic apples the gods ate to remain **immortal.**

The *Prose Edda,* a book of Norse legends written in the 1220s, contains a story about Idun and the magic apples. One day Loki, the **trickster** god, was captured by a giant named Thiassi. The giant refused to free Loki until he agreed to bring Idun and the apples to Thiassi's home. Loki gave his word and sped off to Asgard.

†*See **Names and Places** at the end of this volume for further information.*

He invited Idun to bring her apples and walk into the forest, where he knew of some even more precious apples. Eager to compare her special fruit with that mentioned by Loki, Idun joined the trickster. But as soon as they reached the forest, Thiassi, in the form of an eagle, dove from the sky and seized the goddess and her apples.

Without Idun's apples, the gods in Asgard began to age. They became bent and feeble and demanded that Loki rescue Idun from Thiassi. Loki flew to the giant's home disguised as a falcon. He changed Idun into a nut and hid her in his claws. As he flew back to Asgard, Thiassi became an eagle again and followed him. However, as soon as Loki and Idun were inside Asgard, the gods lit a fire on the walls of Asgard. Thiassi's wings caught fire as he crossed the flames, and he dropped to the ground, where the gods killed him. ***See also*** **Birds in Mythology; Bragi; Fruit in Mythology; Loki; Norse Mythology.**

Igaluk

Igaluk is one of the names the Inuit people of North America use to refer to the god of the moon. According to Inuit legend, Igaluk was once a man who lived on earth. He and his sister were both attending a dance in the village when a wind blew the lights out. In the dark, Igaluk forced himself on a woman in the dance hall. However, when the lamps were lit again, he found that the woman was his sister.

Horrified at this discovery, Igaluk's sister cut off her breasts and threw them at her brother. Then she snatched a burning torch and ran outside into the dark. Her brother followed, carrying his own torch to search for her, but he tripped and fell in the snow. His torch went out, leaving only a glowing ember. The wind carried both siblings up into the sky, where the woman turned into the sun—with her bright torch still shining—and her brother—with his weakly flickering beam—became the moon. The moon still chases his sister across the sky while she races ahead to avoid him. ***See also*** **Moon; Native American Mythology; Sun.**

Ile-Ife

Ile-Ife, also known as Ife or Ife-Lodun, is the holy city of the Yoruba people who live in Nigeria in West Africa. Ile-Ife appears in myths as the birthplace of creation and the location where the first humans took form.

According to Yoruba mythology, the world was originally a marshy, watery wasteland. In the sky above lived many gods, including the supreme god Olorun, the Owner of the Sky. These gods sometimes descended from the sky on spiderwebs and played in the marshy waters, but there was no land or human being there.

One day Olorun called Orisha Nla, the Great God, and told him to create solid land in the marshy waters below. He gave Orisha a pigeon, a hen, and the shell of a snail containing some loose earth. Orisha descended to the waters and threw the loose earth into a

Ile-Ife, a holy city in Nigeria, appears in African mythology as the birthplace of creation. It is the home of the *Oni*, the spiritual leader of the Yoruba people, who is shown here.

small space. He then set loose the pigeon and hen, which began to scratch the earth and move it around. Soon the birds had covered a large area of the marshy waters and created solid ground.

chameleon lizard that can change color

Orisha reported back to Olorun, who sent a **chameleon** to see what had been accomplished. The chameleon found that the earth was wide but not very dry. After a while, Olorun sent the creature to inspect the work again. This time the chameleon discovered a wide, dry land, which was called Ife (meaning "wide") and Ile (meaning "house"). All other earthly dwellings later sprang from Ile-Ife, and it was revered forever after as a sacred spot. It remains the home of the *Oni,* the spiritual leader of the Yoruba. ***See also*** **AFRICAN MYTHOLOGY; ANIMALS IN MYTHOLOGY; CREATION STORIES; OLORUN.**

† *See* ***Names and Places*** *at the end of this volume for further information.*

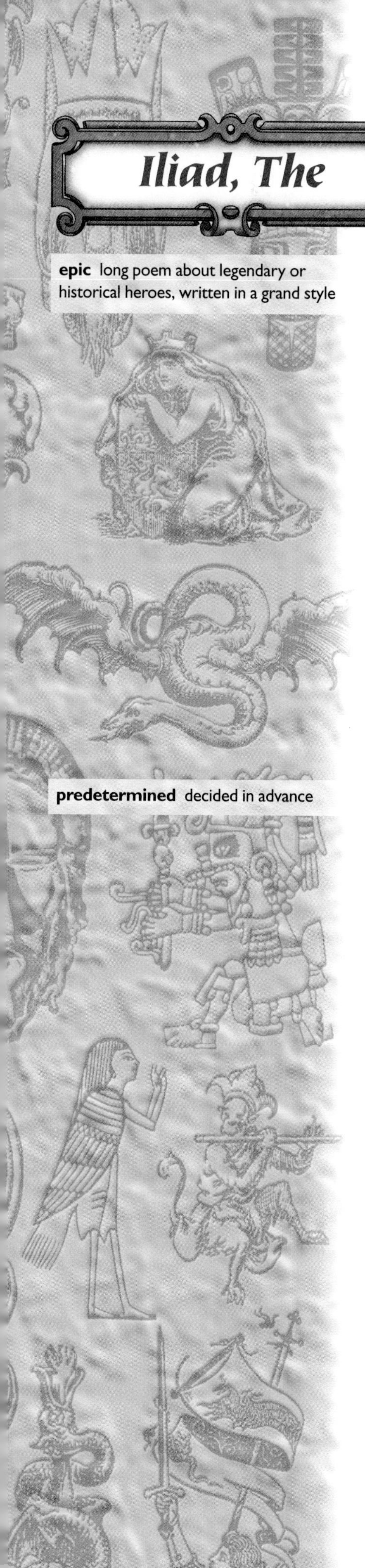

Iliad, The

epic long poem about legendary or historical heroes, written in a grand style

One of the greatest **epics** of ancient Greece, the *Iliad* tells of events during the final year of the Trojan War†. *Iliad* means "poem of Ilios," one of the names of the city of Troy in Asia Minor†.

The Greek poet Homer is credited with creating the *Iliad.* Some scholars, however, doubt that Homer ever existed and suggest that the poem was woven together by generations of storytellers. In any case, the *Iliad* had a tremendous impact on Greek culture and holds an important place in world literature.

Background of the Trojan War. Long before the events described in the *Iliad,* the Greeks had been drawn into a war with Troy because of the beautiful Helen of Troy. Helen was actually Greek, the wife of King Menelaus of Sparta†. She lived happily with Menelaus until Prince Paris of Troy—promised the most beautiful woman in the world by the goddess Aphrodite†—came to Greece in search of the famous beauty. Paris took Helen back to Troy. Honoring a pledge to Menelaus, the kings and princes of Greece joined together to rescue Helen and set sail for Troy with their armies to wage war.

The war between the Greeks and the Trojans dragged on for nine years, with neither side gaining a decisive advantage. Involved in the background were the major Greek gods and goddesses, who supported or opposed certain of the humans in the struggle. In the tenth year of the war, events came to a head, leading ultimately to victory for the Greeks and the destruction of Troy, outcomes **predetermined** by the gods.

predetermined decided in advance

The Story of the Iliad. As the *Iliad* opens, a dispute between two Greek leaders—the hero Achilles† and King Agamemnon† of Mycenae, commander of the Greek armies—sets in motion events that shape the course of the war. The trouble begins when Agamemnon receives a young woman, the daughter of a priest of Apollo†, as a prize of war. The priest appeals to Apollo, who sends a plague to the Greek camp. When the Greeks learn the cause of the sickness, they force Agamemnon to give up his prize.

To make up for his loss, Agamemnon demands the woman who was awarded to Achilles. Furious, Achilles puts down his weapons and refuses to fight any longer, thus depriving the Greeks of their most formidable warrior. Meanwhile, the sea goddess Thetis, Achilles' mother, persuades Zeus† to let the Greeks suffer losses in combat to show how crucial her son is to their victory.

Without Achilles, the Greeks begin to lose ground to the Trojans. During the course of battle, Paris and Menelaus fight each other, but neither can claim victory. At one point, Hector, leader of the Trojan forces, leaves the battlefield and enters Troy. Telling the Trojan women to pray for help from the gods, he bids farewell to his wife, Andromache, and his young son. He knows that he will die soon and that the Greeks will destroy the city and its people.

After suffering significant losses, several Greek leaders, including Odysseus†, go to Achilles and ask him to rejoin them. Even Agamemnon sends a number of gifts and promises to reward

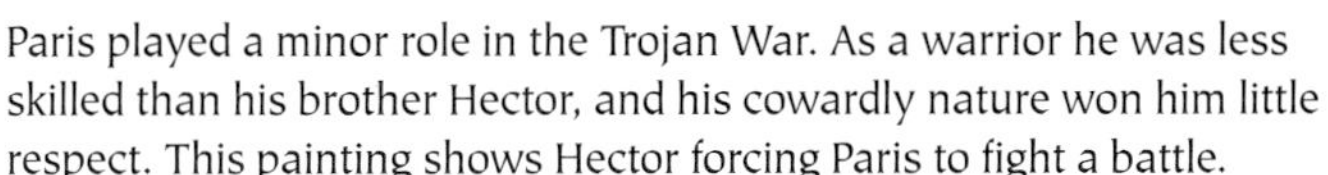

Paris played a minor role in the Trojan War. As a warrior he was less skilled than his brother Hector, and his cowardly nature won him little respect. This painting shows Hector forcing Paris to fight a battle.

Achilles when the war is over. But Achilles refuses to reconsider his decision.

Soon after, Achilles' beloved friend Patroclus convinces the hero to let him wear his armor so that the Trojans will think that Achilles is fighting again. The sight of the warrior in Achilles' armor worries the Trojans, and the Greeks are able to push them back. But the god Apollo lets Hector see that another warrior is wearing Achilles' armor, and Hector kills Patroclus and takes the armor.

When Achilles learns that his beloved friend has been killed, he is overwhelmed with grief and determined to avenge his friend's death. Wearing new armor from his mother, Achilles reenters the battle and slaughters many Trojans while searching for Hector. When the two warriors finally meet, Hector flees and Achilles chases him around the walls of Troy.

The goddess Athena† tricks Hector by appearing as his younger brother and telling him to stand and fight. When Hector does so, Achilles kills him. Achilles removes his old armor from Hector's body and then drags the corpse behind his chariot.

Meanwhile the Trojans, angry because Achilles will not return Hector's corpse for proper funeral ceremonies, mourn the death of their hero. Again the gods intervene, forcing Achilles to accept a ransom of gifts from Hector's father, King Priam, and return the body of his son.

† *See **Names and Places** at the end of this volume for further information.*

The story in the *Iliad* ends as the Trojans hold a funeral for their fallen hero. But the Trojan War continues. Tales of the deaths of Paris and Achilles, the Greek's cunning use of the Trojan horse to get inside the city walls, and the defeat and destruction of Troy are told in other works.

Significance of the Iliad. The *Iliad* is more than just a story about ancient heroes, gods, and goddesses. For the Greeks of later centuries, the poem was a history of their ancestors that also revealed moral lessons about heroism, pride, revenge, and honor. As such, it also had great value as a symbol of Greek unity and culture.

Modern scholars believe that certain elements of the story in the *Iliad* may be based on historical events from more than 3,000 years ago. Almost certainly, the poem reflects the values and ideals of Greek society at that time. Perhaps more importantly, as a work of literature, the *Iliad* illustrates various universal themes and provides a realistic view of the human condition. Its major characters, though shrouded in the distant past, exhibit personality flaws and strengths that are as real for people today as when the work first appeared. ***See also*** **ACHILLES; AGAMEMNON; AJAX; ANDROMACHE; GREEK MYTHOLOGY; HECTOR; HELEN OF TROY; HOMER; MENELAUS; ODYSSEUS; ODYSSEY, THE; PARIS; PRIAM; THETIS; TROJAN WAR.**

Inanna

underworld land of the dead

cult group bound together by devotion to a particular person, belief, or god

An important goddess of the ancient Near East, Inanna was worshiped primarily as the goddess of love and fertility. The daughter of either the sky god Anu or the storm god Enlil, she was also associated with forces of nature such as rain and thunderstorms. Inanna is the Sumerian counterpart of the Semitic goddess Ishtar.

A well-known myth about Inanna tells of her descent to the "land of no return," the **underworld** ruled by her sister Ereshkigal. Condemned to death there, Inanna is later brought back to life with help from Enki, the god of wisdom. To remain in the world of the living, however, Inanna must provide a substitute for her position in the dark realm. She chooses her husband, Dumuzi (known as Tammuz in Semitic mythology). This myth, as well as others about Inanna, was subsequently adopted by the **cult** of Ishtar.

In later versions of the story, Dumuzi stays in the underworld during the winter and returns to the world of the living for the summer, when his sister Geshtinanna takes his place among the dead. Dumuzi's annual death and rebirth are sometimes associated with the seasons, similar to the story of Persephone in Greek mythology. ***See also*** **ANU; ENLIL; ISHTAR; PERSEPHONE; SEMITIC MYTHOLOGY; UNDERWORLD.**

Inari

In the mythology of Japan, the god Inari is associated mainly with the growing of rice. Because of the importance of this crop as a staple food in Japan, Inari is thought to bring prosperity not only to farmers but also to other groups of people, including merchants and traders. Many Japanese villages have a shrine to Inari, and people pray to him

for good harvests. Many Japanese families used to worship Inari inside their homes, and he is sometimes associated with Uke-mochi, the goddess of food.

Portrayals of Inari in art vary considerably. He is generally shown either as a bearded old man or as a woman with long flowing hair. Whatever form Inari takes, the god appears with bags of rice. He is usually accompanied by two foxes, which act as his messengers. Shrines to Inari often contain statues of foxes. The most famous shrine to Inari is the Fushimi Shrine near the ancient city of Kyoto in Japan. ***See also*** **Animals in Mythology; Japanese Mythology.**

Inca Mythology

The Inca civilization flourished in the Andes mountains of South America during the A.D. 1400s and early 1500s. At the center of Inca religion and mythology was the worship of the sun, believed to be the ancestral father of the Inca people. For this reason, sun worship was closely linked to ancestor worship, and many of the myths of the Incas focus on their origins. The Incas tailored their mythology to glorify their own culture and to reinforce the idea that they were a superior people destined to rule others.

Origins and Influences

Based in the city of Cuzco in what is now Peru, the Incas were one of many small groups who lived in the Andes mountains in the 1300s. Gradually, the Incas expanded and absorbed the surrounding peoples, peacefully at first and later by conquest. In 1438 a strong leader named Pachacuti became their king. He and his descendants made the Inca state into a vast empire that stretched from southern Colombia south into Chile and covered much of modern Bolivia and part of Argentina. Throughout this great empire the Incas built a network of roads as well as temples, fortresses, and other public buildings.

As the empire grew, the Incas absorbed the myths and legends of the cultures they conquered. They often reworked the old stories of others to give them a new, pro-Inca twist. Although they allowed their subjects to continue to worship their own gods, they expected everyone in the empire to participate in the state religion and to worship the Inca **deities.** The Incas had no written language so they did not record their myths in writing. Instead, a class of professional storytellers and performers recited the official state history, which contained both fact and myth.

In 1531 the Incas came under attack by Spanish **conquistadors.** The following year their empire fell. The Spanish began converting the Indians to Christianity and wiping out **pagan** traditions and practices. However, some Spanish military and religious personnel recorded what they learned about Inca mythology, as did a few of the newly Christianized and educated Incas. Though somewhat colored by European and Christian views and values, these accounts offer a glimpse into the mythology of the Incas' mountain empire.

deity god or goddess
conquistador Spanish military explorer and conqueror
pagan term used by early Christians to describe non-Christians and non-Christian beliefs

Born into Two Worlds

Much of what we know about Inca mythology comes from the writings of Inca Garcilaso de la Vega (1539–1616), the son of a Spanish conquistador and an Inca princess. He learned the Inca legends from his uncles, who were members of the nobility. Moving to Spain as an adult, Garcilaso turned his early notes on Inca history and culture into *The Royal Commentaries of the Inca.* Although European and Christian influences may have affected his accounts, they provide a window into the Inca world in which Garcilaso was raised.

Major Deities and Sacred Ceremonies

Most of the principal deities of the Inca **pantheon** represented forces of nature that operate in the sky. The state religion focused on the worship of a few major figures.

The figure in this Inca textile wears a decorative headdress with a sky dragon. Worship of the sun and sky played a central role in the mythology and religion of the Inca people.

pantheon all the gods of a particular culture
mummify to preserve a body by removing its organs and allowing it to dry

Gods and Goddesses. The creator god, Viracocha, had many titles, such as Old Man of the Sky and Lord Instructor of the World. Viracocha was believed to have had a special bond with the Inca king Pachacuti, who dreamed that the god helped his people gain victory in a war they were fighting. After winning the war, Pachacuti built a great temple to Viracocha at Cuzco. The temple contained a large solid gold statue of the god as a bearded man. According to Inca tradition, Viracocha had white skin, which explains why some of the Indians at first thought that the bearded, pale-skinned Spanish soldiers were representatives of their creator god.

Viracocha, a rather remote and impersonal god, figured less prominently in the daily life of the Incas than did some other deities. Most important of all was Inti, the sun god, regarded as the ancestor of the Incas. He was associated with gold, called "the sweat of the sun," and the Incas honored him with magnificent golden artworks. The Coricancha, or Sun Temple, at Cuzco housed a golden image of Inti that looked like the sun. Facing the image stood the **mummified** remains of dead emperors, and the walls of the chamber were covered with gold.

Inti's wife, the mother of the Incas, was the moon goddess, Mama Kilya. Her shrine in the Coricancha had walls of silver, a metal that was sacred to her because it was believed to be her tears. The Incas marked the passage of time with the phases of the moon. Mama Kilya was thus the driving force of the calendar the Incas used to schedule their **rituals** and festivals.

ritual ceremony that follows a set pattern

Illapu, the god of weather who gave the rain, had an important place in a culture that depended on agriculture. The Incas saw the Milky Way, the band of stars that arc across the sky, as a heavenly river. Illapu's sister stored the river's water in a jug until it was needed on the earth. When Illapu struck the jug with a bolt of lightning from his slingshot, making the sound of thunder, he broke the jug and released the rain. Other deities included Cuichu, the rainbow; Paca Mama, the earth mother; and Mama Qoca, the sea mother.

Sacred Ceremonies. Inca religious life was administered by a large organized priesthood and centered on honoring ancestors—especially royal ones—as well as the gods. The bodies of dead kings and queens were mummified, dressed and cared for, and thought to have special powers. Young women called Acllas, "chosen women" or Virgins of the Sun, served both Inti and the king, tending the god's sacred fires and serving as the king's sexual partners.

Priests relied on **divination** to resolve all sorts of matters, from identifying illnesses to determining guilt or innocence to deciding what kind of sacrifice to make to which god. They had many ways

divination act or practice of foretelling the future

Machu Picchu, located high in the Andes mountains in Peru, was a holy city of the Incas. The site contains the ruins of a temple where the Incas worshiped their sun god.

of asking for **supernatural** guidance, including studying the movements of spiders or the patterns made by leaves. The chief method of divination, though, was the use of **oracles,** which involved making frequent sacrifices to the gods. Inti, for example, received sacrifices of corn every day. Besides offering food and drink to the gods, the Incas also made animal and human sacrifices. White llamas were often used for animal sacrifices, and young children were particularly prized as human sacrifices. Often they were left to die on high mountaintops, sacred places remote from human life but close to the sky gods.

Major Myths

Many Inca myths dealt with the origin of the Inca people. These myths helped support the idea that the gods intended the Incas to be rulers. Other myths dealt with the creation of the world and the arrival of a great flood.

supernatural related to forces beyond the normal world; magical or miraculous

oracle priest or priestess or other creature through whom a god is believed to speak; also the location (such as a shrine) where such words are spoken

Creation. According to one myth, Viracocha's first creation was a dark world inhabited by giants that he had fashioned from stone. These creatures proved disobedient, however, and Viracocha destroyed them. He may have turned them back to stone, or he may have swept them away in a great flood. Once they were gone, Viracocha made a second race, this time forming people from clay. He equipped them with the clothes, languages, songs, skills, and crops of different nations. Before the people spread out and populated the world, Viracocha ordered them to sink into the earth and to reappear on the surface again from lakes, caves, and hilltops. They did so, and each group of people built a shrine at the spot where they emerged.

Inca Civilization. According to a legend recorded by Inca Garcilaso de la Vega, long ago people were ignorant and brutal, living like wild animals, without clothes or houses. The god Inti, known as Our Father the Sun, felt sorry for them and sent one of his sons and one of his daughters to earth to teach them how to live properly. The son was Manco Capac, whom Inti made the ruler of all the races of people around Lake Titicaca in Bolivia. "I want you to rule these peoples as a father rules his children," Inti told Manco Capac.

The god gave his son and daughter instructions about how to find the best place for their court. Starting at Lake Titicaca, they were to visit the villages and look for a place where they could drive a gold stake into the ground with one blow. The site became the location of Cuzco, the capital of the Inca empire.

Related Entries
Other entries related to Inca mythology are listed at the end of this article.

On reaching the earth, Manco Capac and his sister-wife, Mama Ocllo, taught the people the arts of farming and weaving. Manco Capac also showed his people how to make and use weapons so that they could enlarge their kingdom. In this way, the sun god himself set the Inca empire on its road to glory. Later generations honored Manco Capac as the legendary first Inca.

The myth establishes some of the rights and customs of the Inca royal class, such as the practice of brothers marrying sisters. It also paints a picture of the ancestral Incas as superior to other people and firmly identifies them as descendants of the sun god.

Great Flood. Like many peoples, the Incas had a story about a great flood that wiped out a race of wicked and unruly people. The flood myth says that during ancient times people were cruel and greedy and failed to pay proper attention to the gods. Only in the highlands of the Andes mountains were the people not given over to evil. One day two worthy shepherd brothers there noticed that their llamas were sad and acting strange. The llamas told the brothers that a great flood was coming. The brothers took their families and herds to high caves, and then rain fell for months, drowning the world below. Finally, the sun god Inti appeared again, and the warmth of his smile dried the waters. The families descended to repopulate the world. Legend says that although people now live everywhere on earth, llamas remember the flood and live only in the highlands.

Inca Legacy

Although the Spanish destroyed the Inca empire, they did not wipe out the Inca people. Their descendants live in the Andean highlands today. Many of them speak Quechua, the Inca language.

Andean peoples still believe, as the Incas did, that high mountain peaks are sacred places and make pilgrimages to them to ensure good crops and productive herds. In the same way, people have continued the Inca practice of making offerings to local gods at shrines and holy places scattered across the land that once made up the Inca empire.

Inca Deities

Deity	Role
Cuichu	god of the rainbow
Illapu	god of weather
Inti	sun god and supreme god
Mama Kilya	moon goddess
Mama Qoca	sea mother
Paca Mama	earth mother
Viracocha	creator god

The Incas left larger monuments in stone as well. Walls from their temples can still be seen in the city of Cuzco. Elsewhere in the former empire stand forts and temples. One of the best-known Inca monuments is the mountaintop complex called Machu Picchu, where the Incas once worshiped their sun god. American explorer Hiram Bingham discovered the ruins of this vast temple and brought them to the notice of the outside world in 1912. Today Machu Picchu is one of Peru's main tourist attractions. ***See also*** **INTI; MANCO CAPAC.**

Indian Mythology

See ***Buddhism and Mythology; Hinduism and Mythology; Native American Mythology.***

Indra

deity god or goddess

Indra was the ruler of the gods in early Hinduism. The son of the sky and the earth, he is a warrior god who protects people and animals and provides rain to water the land. In later Hindu texts Indra loses some of his power and his warrior characteristics. Other **deities,** such as Vishnu†, take his place as defender of gods and humans, while Indra continues to serve as the god of rain.

Indra appears as a central figure in the *Rig-Veda,* an ancient Indian religious text, and its many stories involve Indra's fights with demons. In a famous myth, he faces a demon named Vritra, sometimes described as a dragon or serpent. Vritra had taken all the waters of the earth and placed them in a mountain where he remained on guard. In the devastating drought that followed, the people suffered greatly from thirst and famine.

Indra, a warrior god and the ruler of the gods in early Hindu myths, later became known as the god of rain.

Indra decided to fight Vritra and rescue the waters from captivity. To prepare for battle, Indra drank a large quantity of an intoxicating beverage called soma that gave him enormous strength. Then he stormed the mountain and delivered a deadly wound to the demon with his thunderbolt. Vritra's death released the waters, which flowed down from the mountain to revive the people and the countryside. Some sources suggest that Indra's defeat of Vritra takes place again whenever strong winds and rains, such as those associated with a monsoon, arrive after a seasonal drought.

Legends about Indra describe him as riding either in a golden chariot pulled by two horses or mounted on a white elephant named Airavata. In addition to rainfall, a rainbow or the sound of a gathering storm indicates that he is present. ***See also*** **HINDUISM AND MYTHOLOGY; RIG-VEDA; VISHNU.**

†*See* ***Names and Places*** *at the end of this volume for further information.*

Inti

pantheon all the gods of a particular culture

deity god or goddess

In Inca mythology, Inti was the sun god and the supreme god of the Inca **pantheon.** The Incas believed that Inti was the ancestor of their people, linking him with the Inca emperor who was known as the "Son of the Sun." From the early 1400s to the mid-1500s, the Inca empire included much of western South America.

The Incas generally portrayed Inti as a golden disk with a human face surrounded by rays and flames. Images of the god were often of gold, which was called "the sweat of the sun." His wife, Mama Kilya, was the goddess of the moon. Both **deities** were thought of as kind and generous.

Every June the Incas honored Inti in a *raymi,* or festival, that included dancing and the sacrifice of animals. Throughout the Inca empire stood stone posts or columns called *intihuatanas,* "hitching posts of the sun." These structures were probably solar calendars, like sundials, used for observing and predicting the sun god's motion through the heavens. ***See also*** **INCA MYTHOLOGY.**

Io

deity god or goddess

In Greek mythology, Io was a young woman who was loved by Zeus, king of the gods. His attentions toward her aroused the jealousy of his wife, Hera†, and both **deities** used their powers in various ways to try to gain control over Io.

The daughter of the river god Inachus, Io was a priestess at one of Hera's temples. Zeus fell in love with her and seduced her. When Hera learned about Zeus's behavior, she turned the girl into a white cow. In some versions of the myth, it was Zeus who transformed Io into the cow, to conceal her from Hera.

After tying Io the cow to an olive tree, Hera sent Argus, a giant with 100 eyes, to watch over her. Zeus responded by sending the messenger god Hermes to rescue Io. Hermes put Argus to sleep by singing and telling stories, and then he killed the giant.

Angry that Io was released, Hera sent a gadfly—a type of insect that bites animals—to torment her. Io wandered distractedly until she reached Egypt. There, after Zeus turned her back into a woman, Io gave birth to a son named Epaphus. Many of Io's descendants returned to Greece. Among them were Cadmus, Perseus, and Hercules. ***See also*** **ARGUS; CADMUS; HERA; HERCULES; HERMES; PERSEUS; ZEUS.**

Names and Places

Achilles foremost warrior in Greek mythology; hero in the war between the Greeks and the Trojans

Aeneas Trojan hero who founded Rome; son of Aphrodite (Venus) and the Trojan Anchises

Aeneid epic by the Roman poet Virgil about the legendary hero Aeneas and the founding of Rome

Agamemnon Greek king and commander of Greek forces in the Trojan War; later killed by his wife, Clytemnestra

Ajax Greek hero of the Trojan War

Amazons female warriors in Greek mythology

Aphrodite Greek goddess of love and beauty (identified with the Roman goddess Venus)

Apollo Greek god of the sun, the arts, medicine, and herdsmen; son of Zeus and Leto and twin brother of Artemis

Ares Greek god of war; son of Zeus and Hera (identified with the Roman god Mars)

Artemis in Greek mythology, virgin goddess of the hunt; daughter of Zeus and Leto and twin sister of Apollo (identified with the Roman goddess Diana)

Arthurian legends stories about the life and court of King Arthur of Britain

Asia Minor ancient term for modern-day Turkey, the part of Asia closest to Greece

Assyria kingdom of the ancient Near East located between the Tigris and Euphrates Rivers

Athena in Greek mythology, goddess of wisdom and war; the daughter of Zeus (Roman goddess Minerva)

Atlas Titan in Greek mythology who held the world on his shoulders

Baal god of the ancient Near East associated with fertility and rain

Babylonia ancient kingdom of Mesopotamia; **Babylon** city in Babylonia; **Babylonians** (noun) people of Babylonia; **Babylonian** (adj) referring to kingdom or people

Brahma Hindu creator god

Canaan name given to Palestine and Syria in ancient times; **Canaanites** people of Canaan

Celtic referring to the **Celts,** early inhabitants of Britain whose culture survived in Ireland, Scotland, Wales, Cornwall, and Brittany

Ceres Roman goddess of vegetation and fertility; mother of Proserpina (Greek goddess Demeter)

Cronus Greek deity, king of the Titans; son of Uranus and Gaia

Cyclopes one-eyed giants in Greek mythology

Delphi town on the slopes of Mount Parnassus in Greece that was the site of Apollo's temple and the Delphic oracle

Demeter Greek goddess of vegetation; sister of Zeus and mother of Persephone (Roman goddess Ceres)

Devi Hindu goddess; wife of the god Shiva

Diana Roman goddess of hunting and childbirth (Greek goddess Artemis)

Dionysus Greek god of wine and fertility; son of Zeus by Theban princess Semele (Roman god Bacchus)

Druids priests and political leaders of an ancient Celtic religious order

Euripides (ca. 480–406 B.C.) Greek playwright who wrote many tragedies

Franks early Germanic people who invaded and eventually ruled Gaul (present-day France) between the A.D. 200s and the mid-800s

Golden Fleece hide of a magic ram that hung in a sacred grove guarded by a serpent

Hades Greek god of the underworld; brother of Zeus and husband of Persephone (Roman god Pluto)

Hector in Greek mythology, a Trojan prince and hero in the Trojan War

Helen of Troy in Greek mythology, a beautiful woman and the wife of the king of Sparta; her kidnapping by a Trojan prince led to the Trojan War

Hephaestus Greek god of fire and crafts; son of Zeus and Hera and husband of Aphrodite (Roman god Vulcan)

Hera Greek goddess, wife and sister of Zeus; queen of heaven (Roman goddess Juno)

Hercules (Heracles) Greek hero who had 12 labors to perform; Roman god of strength

Hermes in Greek mythology, the messenger of the gods; escorted the dead to the underworld (Roman god Mercury)

Hesiod (ca. 700 B.C.) Greek poet who wrote the *Theogony*

Homer (ca. 700s B.C.) Greek poet thought to be the author of the great epics the *Iliad* and the *Odyssey*

Iliad Greek epic poem about the Trojan War composed by Homer

Indo-Iranian having to do with the peoples and cultures of northern India, Pakistan, Afghanistan, and Iran

Isis Egyptian goddess of rebirth and resurrection; mother of Horus

Jason Greek hero and leader of the Argonauts who went on a quest for the Golden Fleece

Jupiter Roman god of the sky and ruler of the other gods (Greek god Zeus)

Mars Roman god of war (Greek god Ares)

Medusa in Greek mythology, a monster whose hair was made of snakes and whose face turned humans to stone

Mercury Roman messenger god (Greek god Hermes)

Mesopotamia area between the Tigris and Euphrates Rivers, most of present-day Iraq

Metamorphoses narrative poem by the Roman author Ovid

Mongol referring to an empire in southeastern Asia that existed from about 1200 to the 1700s

Neptune in Roman mythology, god of the sea (the Greeks called him Poseidon)

Norse referring to the people and culture of Scandinavia: Norway, Sweden, Denmark, and Iceland

Odin in Norse mythology, one-eyed deity and ruler of the gods

Odysseus Greek hero who journeyed for ten years to return home after the Trojan War

Odyssey epic by the Greek poet Homer that tells the story of the journey of the hero Odysseus

Oedipus in Greek mythology, king of Thebes

Olympus in Greek mythology, home of the gods

Orpheus Greek hero known for his musical skills; son of Apollo and Calliope

Osiris in Egyptian mythology, the chief god of death

Ovid (ca. 43 B.C.–A.D. 17) Roman poet who wrote the *Metamorphoses*

Palestine ancient land located on the site of modern Israel and part of Jordan

Pegasus in Greek mythology, a winged horse

Perseus Greek hero, son of Danaë and Zeus, who cut off the head of Medusa

Persia ancient land in southwestern Asia, including much of present-day Iran and Afghanistan

Philistines ancient people who lived along the coast of Canaan (present-day Palestine and Syria)

Phoenicia ancient maritime country located in an area that is now part of Lebanon

Phrygia ancient country located in present-day Turkey

Pindar (ca. 522–438 B.C.) Greek poet

Plutarch (ca. A.D. 46–120) Greek author who wrote biographies of important Greeks and Romans

Poseidon Greek god, ruler of the sea, and brother of Zeus (Roman god Neptune)

Prometheus in Greek mythology, Titan said to have created the human race

Pueblos Native American groups of the southwestern United States, including the Hopi, Keresan, Tewa, Tiwa, and Zuni

Quetzalcoatl Feathered Serpent god of Central America; Aztec god of learning and creation

Ra (Re) in Egyptian mythology, the sun god

Saturn Roman god of the harvest

Semitic relating to people of the ancient Near East, including Jews, Arabs, Babylonians, Assyrians, and Phoenicians

Set in Egyptian mythology, god of the sun and sky; brother of Osiris

Sophocles (ca. 496–406 B.C.) Greek playwright who wrote many tragedies

Sparta ancient Greek city-state

Sumer part of ancient Babylonia in southern Mesopotamia; **Sumerians** people of Sumer

Thebes ancient Egyptian city on the Nile River

Theogony epic written by the Greek poet Hesiod explaining the creation of the world and the birth of the gods

Theseus Greek hero who killed the Minotaur of Crete with Ariadne, the daughter of King Minos of Crete

Thor in Norse mythology, the thunder god

Titan one of a family of giants who ruled the earth until overthrown by the Greek gods of Olympus

Trojan War legendary war between the Greeks and the people of Troy that was set off by the kidnapping of Helen, wife of the king of Sparta; inspiration for Homer's epics the *Iliad* and the *Odyssey*

Troy ancient city that was the site of the Trojan War; present-day Turkey near the Dardanelles

Valhalla in Norse mythology, the home of the dead heroes

Valkyrie in Norse mythology, one of the handmaidens to the god Odin

Virgil (ca. 70–19 B.C.) Roman poet who wrote the *Aeneid* explaining the founding of Rome

Vishnu Hindu god, preserver and restorer

Vulcan Roman god of fire (Greek god Hephaestus)

Zeus in Greek mythology, king of the gods and husband of Hera (Roman god Jupiter)

Index

Italicized page numbers refer to illustrations or charts.

Aborigines, 32. *See also* Australian mythology
Achilles, 98, 108, 109
 in *Iliad,* 143–45
 as hero, 124
Acis, 80
Acoetes, 31
Acrisius, 18
Adam and Eve
 forbidden fruit eaten by, 76, 77
 in Garden of Eden, 40–41
Admetus, 55
Adonis, death of, 70
Aeëtes, 91
Aegisthus, 49
Aello, 105
Aeneas
 Dido and, 29
 Golden Bough and, 89–90
 Harpies and, 105
 as national hero, 125
Aeolus, 104
Aeschylus, 79
Aesir, 74
African mythology
 creation story in, 6
 devils and demons in, 27
 Eshu in, 52–53, *53*
 fire in, 63
 Gauna in, 82
 genies in, 82
 hero kings in, 124
 Ile-Ife in, 141–42, *142*
 trickster heroes in, 125
Afterlife
 in Egyptian mythology, 47
 Elysium and, 50
 heaven and, 105–7
 hell for the wicked in, 113–15
Agamemnon, 49, 108
 in *Iliad,* 143–44
Agni, 63
Ahriman, 7, 25–26
Ahura Mazda, 7, 25
Aife, 13
Aino, 58, 59, 60
Ajax, 108
 as warrior hero, 124
Akhenaten, 11
Alcmena, 117, 118
Alexander the Great, 41
 Gordian knot and, 92
Allecto, 78
Altsé hastiin and Altsé asdzaá. *See* First Man and First Woman
Amalthaea, 77
Amida, heaven and, 106
Amphitryon, 118
Amun, in Egyptian mythology, 43, 44, 45–46
Amun-Ra, 43, 44
Anat, El and, 48
Ancestral giants, 85–86
Andromache, 108, 143
Anemones in mythology, 70
Angels, 26, 107
Angrboda, 57, 111
Animals in mythology
 in Egyptian mythology, 43
 Fenrir, 57
 firebird, 64
 foxes, 146
 Gluskap and, 88–89
 griffins, 101
 Halcyone and, 104
 in Ile-Ife, 141–42
 Twelve Labors of Hercules and, 119–20
Ankh, *11,* 11
Antigone, as doomed hero, 126
Anu, 50, 87, 145
Anubis, in Egyptian mythology, 44, 45–46
Aonghus, 17
Apep, 47
Aphrodite, 52, 79, 95, 96, 121
 Hathor identified with, 105
Apocalypse, fire in, 61
Apollo, 95, 96
 Clytie and, 73
 Dionysus and, 32
 Fates and, 55
 Hermes and, 121–22
 Hyacinthus and, 70–71
 oracle at Delphi, 20, *21*
Apophis, 34
Apples in mythology
 apples of eternal life, 107
 golden Apples of the Hesperides, 120
 symbolic meanings of, 75–76
Apuleius, Lucius, 47
Aqhat, 48
Arachne, in Greek mythology, 99
Ares, 52, 95, 96, 116–18
Argonauts
 Golden Fleece, search for, 91
 Harpies and, 105
 Hercules and, 120
Argus, Io and, 151
Ariadne, 16, 31
Aristaeus, 53
Artemis, 28, 95, 96
Arthur, King
 Excalibur, sword of, 54
 Guinevere, wife of, 101–2
 as hero king, 124
 Holy Grail and, 134
Arthurian legends, 54, 124
 Galahad in, 80
 Guinevere in, 101–2
 Holy Grail and, 134, 135
Aryans (Indo-Europeans), 128
Asclepius, Cyclopes and, 15
Asgard, 106, 107, 110
Ashurbanipal, 87
Asteria, 107
Astyanax, 108, 109
Asuras, 27
Aten, in Egyptian mythology, 44, 45–46
Athamas, 90–91, 117
Athena, in Greek mythology, 95, 96
Atlas, 49
Atropos, 55
Attis, Cybele and, 14, 73
Atum, in Egyptian mythology, 45–46
Augean Stables, 119
Australian mythology
 creation story in, 8
 Djang'kawu in, 32–33
 Dreamtime in, 35–36
 fire rituals, *62*
 flood myth in, 68–69
Avalon, heaven and, 107
Awakkule, 39–40
Aztec mythology
 ankh as symbol in, 11
 corn in, 1, 2–3
 creation story in, 5, 7
 fire in, 62
 flood myth of, 68
 flowers in, 69–70
 hell in, 115
 heroes in, 127
 Huehueteotl in, 137–38
 Huitzilopochtli in, *138,* 138–39

Babylonian mythology
 Enuma Elish in, 51
 floods in, 67
Bacchus. *See* Dionysus
Bagadjimbiri brothers, 86
Balder, 75
Baucis and Philemon, in Greek mythology, 98, 99
Be' al, 36
Bedivere, Sir, 54
Belus (Mutto), 29
Beowulf, 35, 124
Bible, Old Testament of
 creation story, 4
 Delilah in, 19
 dragons in, 34
 El in, 48
 Garden of Eden in, 40–41
Birds in mythology
 firebird, 63, 64
 Halcyone and, 104
 Horus and, 136–37
 Huitzilopochtli and, 138
 Idun and, 141
Book of the Dead, 47
Bragi, 140–41
Brahma, 7, 129, *131*
Brahmanas, 128
Bralbral, 32
Brutus, 86, 89
Buddha, as avatar of Vishnu, 132
Buddhism and mythology
 creation story in, 7
 devils and demons in, 27
 fruits in, 77
 heaven in, 106
 hell in, 114
 Hinduism and, 132
 lotus in, *71,* 72
Bumba, 6
Bushongo people of the Congo, myths of, 6
Bushpeople of southern Africa, myths of
 devils and demons in, 27
 dwarfs in, 39
 Gauna in, 82
Buyan, 106

Caesar, Julius, 36
Cagn, Gauna and, 82
Cagn-Cagn, 39
Campbell, Joseph, 123
Canaanite mythology, 48. *See also* Semitic mythology
Carnation in mythology, 70
Carthage, Dido as founder of, 29
Castor and Pollux, 111
Catholicism. *See* Christianity; Saints
Celaeno, 105
Celeus, 22
Celtic mythology, 17, 18, 34, 54, 56, 76, 106
 Cuchulain in, 12–14
 Druids in, 36–38, *37*
 Finn in, 57–58
 Hamlet in, *104,* 104
 Holy Grail in, 134–35
Centaurs, Hercules and, 120
Central American mythology, 39. *See also* Aztec mythology; Mayan mythology
Centzon Totochtin, 1
Cerberus, 102, 120
Cerynean Hind, 119
Ceto, 92
Ceyx, 104
Changing Woman, First Man and First Woman and, 65
Chaos, 4, 79, 97
Charities. *See* Graces
Charon, Hades and, 102
Charu, 26
Cherries in mythology, 77
Chicomecoatl, 1
Chinese mythology, 75, 86, 106, 114
 creation story in, 7
 devils and demons in, 27
 dragons in, *34,* 35
 fire in, 63
 floods in, 67–68
 fruits in, 77
Chiricahua Apache, flood myth of, 68
Chloe. *See* Daphnis and Chloe
Chloris, 70
Chrétien de Troyes, 135
Christianity, 35, 70, 71, 72–73, 101
 cross as symbol of, 10, 12
 devils and demons in, 26–27
 heaven in, 107
 hell in, 115
Cleta, 93
Clotho, 55
Clytemnestra, 49, 111, 112
Clytie, Apollo and, 73
Coatlicue, 138
Coconuts in mythology, 77

Conchobhar
  Cuchulain and, 12, 13
  Druids and, 38
Connla, 13
Con Tiqui Viracocha, 6
Coricancha (Sun Temple), 147
Cormac MacArt, 58
Corn, 1-3, *2*
  First Man and First Woman and, 64
Corn Mother, 1, 3
Cornucopia, 77
Cosmogonies. *See* Creation stories
Creation stories, 3-9, *7, 8*
  Djang'kawu, 32-33
  Egyptian, 44-45
  Enuma Elish, 51
  First Man and First Woman, 64-65
  floods in, 4, 8, 65-66
  in Greek mythology, 97
  in Hindu mythology, 130-31, *132*
  in Ile-Ife, 141-42, *142*
  in Inca mythology, 148
Cremation, 62
Cretan Bull, 119-20
Crispin, St., 9
Crispinian, 9
Crockett, Davy, 9-10
Croesus of Lydia, King, 20
Cronus, 10, 97
  Demeter, daughter of, 21-22
  Gaia, mother of, 79
  Hades, son of, 102-3
  Hera, daughter of, 116-18
Cross, 10-12, *11, 12*
Crucifixion, 12, 70
Cuchulain, 12-14
Culture hero, 125
Cupid. *See* Eros
Curiatii, 136
Cybele, 14, 97
  Attis and, 14, 73
  Dionysus and, 30
  Gordian knot and, 92
Cyclopes, 15
  Cronus and, 10
  Gaia, mother of, 79
  giants, 85
Cyrus the Great of Persia, 20

Daedalus, 15-16, *16*
Dagda, 17
Dagon, 17
Damocles, sword of, 17
Dana. *See* Danu
Danaë, 18
Dante Alighieri, 107, 115
Danu, 18
Daoist mythology. *See* Taoist mythology
Daphne, 98
Daphnis and Chloe, 18-19
Dardanus, 49
Dechtire, 12-13
Decuma, 55
Deianeira, 120
Deiphobus, 112
Dekanawida, 19
  Hiawatha and, 127, *128*
Delilah, 19
Delphi, 19-21, *21*
  Gaia worshiped at, 79
Demeter, 21-22, 78, 95-96
  Dionysus, son of, 32
  Hades and, 103
Demons. *See* Devils and demons
Demophon, 22
Deucalion, 67, 97
Devi, *23,* 23-24, 129, 130
Devils and demons, 24-28, *26*
  Faust and, 56-57
  in hell, 113, 114-15
Dharma, 129
Diana, 28-29
  Golden Bough and, 90
Dictys, 18
Dido, 29
Dike, 56
Diomedes, 120
  Hector and, 108
Dionysius, sword of Damocles and, 17
Dionysus, 30-32, *31*
  in Greek mythology, 95, 96-97
Divination, in Inca religion, 147-48
Divine Comedy, The (Dante Alighieri), 107, 115
Djang'kawu, 32-33
Djinni. *See* Genies
Dogon of West Africa, myths of, 5
Dökkalfar, 38-39
Don. *See* Danu
Dracula, 33
Dragons, *34,* 34-35
  St. George and, 83
Dreamtime, 35-36
  creation during, 8
Druids, 36-38, *37*
  Dagda, patron of, 17
  Finn as pupil of, 57-58
Dryads. *See* Nymphs
Dualism, in creation stories, 5, 6
Dumuzi (Tammuz), 145
Durga, Devi in form of, 23-24, 130
Dwarfs and elves, 38-40, *39*
  Freyr and, 74
Dybbuk, 40

Ea, 50
Echo, 40
  Gaia, mother of, 79
Eden, Garden of, 40-41
  forbidden fruit in, 76, 77
  heaven and image of, 107
Egg, in creation, 4, 9
Egyptian mythology, 41-47, *42, 46*
  creation story in, 4, 6-7, *8,* 44-45
  devils and demons in, 25
  dragons in, 34
  floods in, 67
  Hathor in, 105
  Horus in, 136-37, *137*
El, 48
El Dorado, 48-49
Electra, 49
Elegba. *See* Eshu
Eleusinian Mysteries, 22
Elijah of Chelm, 91
Elves. *See* Dwarfs and elves
Elysium, 50, 114
  Hades and, 102
  as heaven, 106
Emer, 13
Enceladus, 85
Endymion. *See* Moon
Enki, 67, 145
Enkidu, 50
  Gilgamesh and, 87-88
Enlil, 50-51
  flood and, 67
  Inanna, daughter of, 145
Ennead, 43
Enuma Elish, 51
  creation story of, 3-4, 5
Epaphus, 151
Ephesus, Diana as goddess of, 28
Epic of Gilgamesh, 86-88
  Enkidu in, 50
  flood myth in, 67
Ereshkigal, 145
Erinyes. *See* Furies
Eris, 75
Eros, 52, 98
Erymanthian Boar, 119
Eshu, 52-53, *53*
Eunomia, 56
Euphrosyne, 93
Euryale, 92
Eurydice, 53-54, 99
Eurynome, 93
Eurystheus, Twelve Labors of Hercules and, 119-20
Excalibur, 54

Fafnir, 34-35
Fas-ta-chee, 1
Fate, in Greek mythology, 99
Fates, 54-56, *55*
Fatima, 56
Faust, 27, 56-57
Fenrir, 57
Ferdiad, 13
Fianna, 57, 58
Figs in mythology, 77
Finn, 57-58
  Druids and, 38
  as warrior hero, 124
Finnish mythology, 58-61, *59*
Fionn (Fenian) Cycle, 57
Fire, 61-63, *62*
  Huehueteotl and, 137-38
Firebirds, 63, 64
First Man and First Woman, 64-65. *See also* Eden, Garden of
Fish, Vishnu in form of, 68. *See also* Animals in mythology
Fisher King. *See* Holy Grail
Floods, 65-69, *66*
  creation stories based on, 4, 8, 65-66
  Enlil and, 51
  in *Epic of Gilgamesh,* 87, 88
  First Man and First Woman and, 64
  in Inca mythology, 149
Flora, *70,* 70
Floral goddesses, 69-70
Flowers in mythology, 69-73, *70, 71*
  fruits and, 77-78
Flying Dutchman, 73
Folk heroes, 125-26
Fon of West Africa, myths of, 6
Fortuna, 56
Freyja, 74
  giants and, 85
Freyr, 74
Frigg, 74-75
Frija. *See* Frigg
Fruit in mythology, 75-78, *76*
  Idun and apples, 141
Furies, 78-79
  Hades and, 103
  Harpies and, 105

Gaia, 79, 97
  creation story and, 9
  Cronus, son of, 10
  Delphi, oracle at, 19-20
  giants, children of, 84-85
Galahad, 80
  Holy Grail and, *134,* 134, 135
Galatea, 80
Ganesha, 80-81, *81*
  birth of, 132
  in Hindu mythology, 129, 130
Ganymede, 82
Gauna, 82
  as devil in African mythology, 27
Gauri, 24
Gautama, Siddhartha, 77
Geb, *8,* 44, 45
Gehenna river, 114
Genesis, 4, 67
Genies, 82
  as devils and demons, 27
George, St., *83,* 83
  dragon slain by, 35
Gerda, 74
Germanic mythology, elves in, 39
Geryon, 120
Geshtinanna, 145
Giants, *84,* 84-86
  Cronus and, 10
  Gog and Magog, 89
Gigantes, 84
Gigantomachy, 84-85
Gilgamesh, 86-88, *87*
  Enkidu and, 50
  flood myth and, 67
  as hero, 124
Ginnungagap, 8
Gjallarhorn, 110
Gleipnir, 57
Gluskap, 5, 88-89
Godiva, Lady, 89
Gog and Magog, 89
  as giants, 86
Golden Bough, 89-90, *90*
Golden Fleece, 90-91
Golem, 91
Gordian knot, 92
Gorgons, *92,* 92
Graces, 93
  Furies linked with, 79
Graeae, 92
Grail. *See* Holy Grail
Great Ennead of Heliopolis, 43, 45

Greek mythology, 93–101, *96, 99*
apples in, 75
creation story in, 5, 9
Cronus in, 10
Cybele in, 14
Cyclopes in, 15
Daedalus in, 15–16, *16*
Danaë in, 18
Delphi in, 19–21, *21*
Demeter in, 21–22
Dido in, 29
Dionysus in, 30–32, *31*
dragons in, 34
Echo in, 40
Electra in, 49
Elysium in, 50
entries relating to, 100
Eros in, 52
Eurydice in, 53–54
Fates in, 54–56, *55*
fire in, 63
flood myth in, 67
flowers in, 70–71, 73
fruits in, 77, 78
Furies in, 78–79
Gaia in, 79
Galatea in, 80
Ganymede in, 82
giants in, 84–85
Golden Fleece in, 90–91
Gordian knot in, 92
Gorgons in, *92*, 92
Graces in, 93
griffins in, 101
Hades in, 102–3, *103*
Halcyone in, 103–4
Harpies in, 105
heaven in, 106
Hecate and, 107–8
Hector in, 108–9, *109*
Hecuba in, 109–10
Helen of Troy in, 111–13
hell in, 114
Hera in, 116–18
Hercules in, 118–21, *120*
Hermaphroditus in, 121
Hermes in, 121–22
Hero and Leander in, 122
heroes in, 123, 124–25
Homer and, *135*, 135
Hydra in, 140
Hypnos in, 140
Iliad in, 143–45, *144*
Io in, 151
Green Corn Dance, *2*, 2
Griffins, 101
Gui, 27
Guinevere, 101–2
Gun, 68

Hades, 102–3, *103*, 114
Eurydice and, 54
in Greek mythology, 95, 96, 99
Persephone and, 21, 22, 78
Halcyone, 103–4
Hamlet, *104*, 104
Hariti, 24
Harpies, 105
Hathor, 105
in Egyptian mythology, 43, 44, 45–46
flood myth and, 67
Horus and, 137
Hayagriva, 27
Heaven, 105–7, *106*
Hebe, 116
Hecate, 107–8
Diana and, 28
Hector, 108–9, *109*
in *Iliad*, 143, *144*
Hecuba, 109–10
Heh and Hehet, 44
Heimdall, 110
Hel, 57, 111, 113, 114
Helena, St., and the true cross, 12
Helen of Troy, 111–13
Hecuba and, 110
in *Iliad*, 144
Hell, *113*, 113–15
demons in, 26
fire in, 61
Helle, 91
Hellespont, 122
Hephaestus. *See* Vulcan
Hera, 116–18
apple trees of, 75
Dionysus and, 30
Echo and, 40
in Greek mythology, 94–95
Hercules and, 118–19, 121
Hypnos and, 140
Io and, 151
Roman Juno, 117–18
Heracles. *See* Hercules
Hercules, 118–21, *120*
apples obtained by, 75
giants defeated by, 84–85
in Greek mythology, 98
Hera's anger at, 117
Hydra and, 140
Hermaphroditus, 121
Hermes, father of, 122
Hermes, 121–22
Golden Fleece and, 91
in Greek mythology, 95, 96
Io and, 151
Hero and Leander, 122
Heroes, 122–27, *124, 126. See also specific heroes*
entries on individual, 127
in Greek mythology, 98–99
Hesiod, 15, 52, 54–55, 97–98
as source for Greek mythology, 94
Hestia. *See* Vesta
Hiawatha, 127–28, *128*
Dekanawida and, 19
Kalevala's influence on, 61
as hero, 125
Hinduism and mythology, 128–33
creation story in, 4, 5, 7
Devi in, *23*, 23–24
devils and demons in, *26*, 27
fire in, 63
Ganesha in, 80–81, *81*
hell in, 113–14
Indra in, *150*, 150
lotus in, *71*, 72
Hippolyte, Hercules and, 120
Holy Grail, 133–35, *134*
Galahad and, 80
heroes and, 124
Homer, *135*, 135
Fates portrayed by, 54
Iliad by, 143–45, *144*
as source for Greek mythology, 94
Hopi Indians, myths of, 6
Horae, 56
Horatii, 136
Horatius, 136
Horus, 136–37, *137*
in Egyptian mythology, 43, 44, 45–46, 47
Set and, 25
Hrungir, 85
Huehueteotl, *7*, 137–38
as fire god, 62
Hui Lu, 63
Huitzilopochtli, *138*, 138–39
Humbaba (Huwawa), 87
Hummingbirds, 138
Hunahpú and Xbalanqúe, 139
Hundred-Armed giants, 85
Hyacinthus, Apollo and, 70–71
Hydra, 140
Hypnos, 140
poppies associated with, 72

Iarbas, 29
Iblis, 27
Icarus, 15, 16, 99
Icelus, 140
Idun, 140–41
magical golden apples guarded by, 75–76
Ife (Ife-Lodun). *See* Ile-Ife
Igaluk, 141
Ile-Ife, 141–42, *142*
Iliad, 143–45, *144*
Dionysus in, 32
Hector in, 108–9
Hecuba in, 110
Homer and, 135
as source for Greek mythology, 94
Ilithyia, 116
Illapu, 147, 149
Ilmarinen, 58, 59, 60
Ilmatar, 59, 60
Inachus, 151
Inanna, 145
Inari, 145–46
Inca mythology, 146–50, *147, 148*
creation story in, 6
Inti in, 151
Indian mythology. *See* Buddhism and mythology; Hinduism and mythology; Native American mythology
Indra, *150*, 150
in Hindu mythology, 129, 130
serpent Vritra and, 132–33
Ino, 30, 91, 117
Inti, 151
in Inca mythology, 147, 148, 149
Inuit mythology. *See also* Native American mythology
Igaluk in, 141
Io, 151
Hera's torment of, 117
Iolaus, 119, 140
Iphicles, 118
Iphigenia, Helen of Troy and, 111
Irene, 56
Irish mythology, Druids in, 38
Ishtar, 71, 87, 145
Isis
in Egyptian mythology, 44, 45–46
Horus, son of, 137
lotus flower and, 71
Osiris, brother and husband of, 46, 47
Islamic mythology
devils and demons in, 27
Gog and Magog in, 89
heaven in, 107
hell in, 115
Shiite sect of Islam, 56
Iyatiku, 1, 3

Jaganmata, 24
Jahannam, 115
Japanese mythology
cherries in, 77
creation story in, 7
devils and demons in, 27
dragons in, 35
Inari in, 145–46
lotus in, 72
Jason, 90, 91, 98, 105
Jewish mythology. *See also* Semitic mythology
devils and demons in, 26–27
dybbuk in, 40
flood myth, 67
heaven in, 106
hell in, 114–15
Jewish tradition. *See* Judaic mythology; Semitic mythology
Jinni. *See* Genies
John Henry, as folk hero, 125
Jormungand, 57
Joseph of Arimathea, 134
Joukahainen, 58, 59, 60

Kajanus, Robert, 61
Kalevala, 58–61, *59*
Kali, Devi as, 24, 130
Kali Yuga, 131
Kalki, 132
Kayapo Indians of Brazil, myths of, 125
Kek and Ketet, 44
Keres, 54
Keresan people, myths of, 3
Kingu, 51
Kojiki, 7
Kothar, 48
Krishna, 129, 130, 132
Krita Yuga, 131
Kullervo, 58, 60
Kurma, 131
Kuura, 58, 59, 60
Kyllikki, 59

Lachesis, 55
Lady of the Lake, 54
Lakota Plains Indians, myths of, 3
Lancelot, 80, 134
Guinevere and, 101–2
Last Supper, Holy Grail and, 133, 134

Leander. *See* Hero and Leander
Legba. *See* Eshu
Lemminkainen, 58, 60
Leodegran of Scotland, King, 101
Lernaean Hydra, 119
Lethe, Hypnos and, 140
Lilith, as demon, 26
Lily in mythology, 71
Literature
  Dionysus in, 32
  El Dorado in, 49
  Electra in, 49
  Helen of Troy in, 112–13
  Hero and Leander in, 122
  Iliad, 143–45
  influence of Greek mythology on, 100
  legacy of Hindu mythology in, 133
Ljosalfar, 38–39
Lo Hsüan, 63
Loki, 57, 62, 76, 110, 111
  Freyja and, 74
  Frigg and, 75
  Idun and, 140–41
Lotus flower, *71,* 71–72
Louhi, 58, 59, 60
Low ben Bezulel, Judah, 91
Lucina. *See* Diana
Lug, Cuchulain and, 13
Lugalbanda, 86

Ma'at (idea of order), 42
Machu Picchu, *148,* 150
Maenads, 30, 31
Magic, 44, 107–8
Mahabharata, 81, 128, 130
Mahadevi. *See* Devi
Maha Yuga, 131
Mahisha, 23–24
Maia, 121–22
Maiden of Pohjola, 58, 59, 60
Malory, Thomas, 135
Malsum, 5, 88
Mama Kilya, 147, 149, 151
Mama Ocllo, 149
Manasa, 24
Manco Capac, 148–49
Manu, 68, 129, 130
Maori of New Zealand, myths of, 4
Mara, the Evil One, 27
Marduk, 5, 51
Mares of Diomedes, 120
Marjatta, 58, 60-61
Marlowe, Christopher, 113
Mars, 118
Matsya, 131
Mayan mythology, 1, 2–3, 5, 115
  flood myth of, 68
  Hunahpú and Xbalanqúe in, 139
Medb of Connacht, Queen, 13
Medea, Golden Fleece and, 91
Medusa, 18, 92
Megaera, 78
Megara, 119
Melanesian mythology, creation story in, 8
Mende people of Sierra Leone, myths of, 82
Menelaus, 112, 143
Mensa people of Ethiopia, myths of, 84
Mephistopheles, Faust and, 56–57
Merlin, Guinevere and, 101
Mesopotamian mythology. *See also* Semitic mythology
  Enlil in, 50–51
Metamorphoses, as source for Greek mythology, 94
Metanira, 22
Metis, 97
Micronesian mythology, creation story in, 8
Mictlan, 115
Midas, 32, 99
Mimas, 85
Minerva, Juno and, 118
Minos, 15–16
Minotaur, 15–16
Minyans, 119
Mistletoe, 37, 75
Moirai, 54
Monsters, 25
  dragons, *34,* 34–35
  giants, *84,* 84–86
  Gorgons, *92,* 92
Moon, 107–8, 141
Mordred, 54, 102
Morpheus, 72, 104, 140
Morrigan, 56
Morta, 55
Muhammad, 56
Muisca people, myths of, 48
Muses, Graces linked with, 93
Mwooka, 86

Nana Buluku, 6
Nana Triban, 125
Nanna, 51
Narasinha, 131
Narcissus, 72, 99
  Echo and, 40
Native American mythology, 39–40, 63, 68, 85, 125
  creation story in, 4, 6
  Dekanawida in, 19
  First Man and First Woman in, 64–65
  Gluskap in, 88–89
  Hiawatha in, 127–28, *128*
  Igaluk in, 141
Naunet, 44
Navajo of North America, myths of
  First Man and First Woman, 64–65
  flood myth, 68
Nehebkau, 25
Neith, 47
Nemean Lion, 119, *120*
Nemesis, 111
Nephele, 90–91
Nephthys, 47
Nero, 20
Nessus, 120
Nibelungenlied, 35
Nichirin, 72
Nicostratus, 112
Nietzsche, Friedrich, 32
Ninlil, 51
Ninsun, 86
Nirvana, 106
Njord, 74
Noah
  Epic of Gilgamesh as inspiration for story of, 87
  flood and, 65, 67
Nona, 55
Norse mythology, 34–35, 56, 75–76, 104, 106, 107, 114
  creation story in, 4, 8–9
  dwarfs and elves in, 38–39, *39*
  Fenrir in, 57
  Freyja in, 74
  Freyr in, 74
  Frigg in, 74–75
  giants in, 85–86
  Heimdall in, 110
  Hel in, 111
  Idun in, 140–41
Nun, 4, 44
Nut, *8,* 44, 45
Nymphs, 40, 80, 121
Nyx, 140

Ocypete, 105
Odin, 8, 74–75, 111
Odysseus, 98–99, 143
  Cyclopes and, 15
  Hecuba, slave to, 110
  Helen of Troy and, 112
Odyssey, 15, 94, 135
Oedipus, 99
  as doomed hero, 126–27
Og, 86
Old Testament. *See* Bible, Old Testament of
Olofat, 63
Olorun, Ile-Ife and, 141–42
Olympian gods, 94–97. *See also specific gods and goddesses*
Olympus, Mount, 106
Omphalos, 19
Oni, 27, *142,* 142
Oracle at Delphi, 19–20
Oracles, Inca, 148
Orestes, 49, 79
Orion, Halcyone and, 103–4
Orion (constellation), 104
Orisha Nla, 141–42
Orpheus, 53–54, 99
Osai Tutu, 124
Osiris, 44, 45–47, 137
Oure, 79
Ovid, 100

Paca Mama, 149
Pachachamac, 6
Pachacuti, 146, 147
Padma, 72
Paiyatemu, 1
Pan, 40, 122
Pandareos, 105
Pan Gu, 7, 86
Parashurama, 132
Parcae, 55. *See also* Fates
Paris, 109–10, 112, 117, *144,* 144
Parvati
  Devi as, 24, 130
  Ganesha, son of, 80–81, 132
Pasiphae, 16
Pasithea, 93, 140
Patroclus, 109, 144
Pears in mythology, 77
Peitho, 93
Penglai Shan, 106, 107
Penobscot Indians, myths of, 3
Penthesilea, as warrior hero, 124
Pentheus, 31
Perceval, 134
Persephone, 78, 95, 99, 122
  Demeter, mother of, 21–22
  Golden Bough and, 89–90
  Hades and, 21, 22, 78, 103
Perses, 107
Perseus, 98
  Danaë, mother of, 18
  Medusa and, 18, 92
Persian mythology, 25–26, 101, 114
Phantasus, 140
Pharaohs, 42–43
Phineus, 105
Phorcys, 92
Phrixus, 90–91
Plants in mythology, flowering, 69–73
Pleiades (constellation), 104
Pleiades (sisters), 49, 103–4
Pleione, 49
Plums in mythology, 77–78
Plutarch, 47
Podarge, 105
Polydectes, 18
Polydorus, 110
Polymestor, 110
Polynesian mythology
  breadfruit in, 76–77
  creation story in, 5, 8
  heroes in, 124, 125
Polyphemus, 15, 80
Polyxo, 112
Pomegranates in mythology, 78
Pontus, 79
Popol Vuh, 4, 115, 139
Poppy, 72
Poseidon, 95
Prajapati, 129, 130
Priam
  Hector, son of, 108–9
  Hecuba, wife of, 109–10
  in *Iliad,* 144
Priapus, 122
Prometheus, 95
  as culture hero, 125
  as fire bringer, 63
  flood myth and, 67
Prose Edda, 104, 140–41
Psyche, 52, 98
Ptah, 44, 45–46
Puranas, 129, 130
Purgatory, 115
Purusha, 7, 130
Pygmalion, 29, 80
Pylades, 49
Pyramids, Egyptian, *42*
Pyramus and Thisbe, in Greek mythology, 98
Pyrrha, 97
Pytho, 20

Quetzalcoatl, 127

Ra-Atum, 44, 45
Ragnarok, 57, 110
Rakshasas, *26,* 27
Raktabija, 24
Raktavira, 24
Raleigh, Walter, 49
Rama, 124, 132
Ramayana, 129, 132
Ra (Re), 43–44, 45–46
  flood myth and, 67
  Horus and, 137
Red Dwarf, 39
Reincarnation, in Hinduism, 129
Resurrection, Dionysus as symbol of death and, 32
Rhea. *See also* Cybele
  Cronus, sister and wife of, 10
  Demeter, daughter of, 21–22
  Hades, son of, 102–3
  Hera, daughter of, 116–18
Rig. *See* Heimdall
Rig-Veda, 128, 130, 133, 150
Robin Hood, as folk hero, 125
Roland, as hero, 126
Roman Catholic Church. *See* Christianity; Saints
Roman mythology, 9, 34, 77, 78, 82, 117–118
  Cybele in, 14
  Demeter in, 21–22
  Diana in, 28–29
  Elysium in, 50
  Furies in, 78–79
  Golden Bough in, 89–90, *90*
  Gordian knot in, 92
  Graces in, 93
  Horatii in, 136
  Horatius in, 136
Roses in mythology, 72–73
Round Table, 80, 101
Rupe, 124
Russian mythology, firebird in, 64

Sacrifice
  Aztec, 138
  in creation stories, 5
  by Druids, 37
  Inca, 148
St. Andrews cross, 11
Saints
  Crispin, 9
  George, *83,* 83
Salmacis, 121
Samson, Delilah and, 19
Sani, 81
Santa Claus, elves and, 38
Satan, 26–27, 115, 134
Sati, Devi as, 24
Saturn, Cronus and, 10
Satyrs, Dionysus and, 30
Savitri, 129, 130
Saxo Grammaticus, 104
Scatha, 13
Schliemann, Heinrich, 97
Sekhmet, 43, 47
Selu, 1
Semele, 30–32, 117
Semitic mythology, 7, 26, 27, 40, 82, 91, 101, 145
  Dagon in, 17
  El in, 48
  Enlil in, 50–51
Semnai Theai, 79
Seneca Indians, myths of, 2
Serpents and snakes
  in *Epic of Gilgamesh,* 88
  in Garden of Eden, 41
  Huehueteotl and, 137
  Hydra, 140
Set, 25, 43, 44, 45–47
  Horus and, 137
Setanta, 13
Shahrazad, 125
Shaitan, 27
Shaka, 124
Shakespeare, William, 100, 104
Shape-shifters, 38
Shen, 27
Sheol, 114
Shinto mythology, Inari in, 145–46
Shiva, 129, 130, 131
  Devi, wife of, 23–24
  Ganesha, son of, 80–81, 132
Shu, 45
Sibyl, Golden Bough and, 89–90
Silenus, 30, 32
Sisyphus, in Greek mythology, 99
Skadi, 74
Slavic mythology, 106
Solar myths, Egyptian, 45–46
Souw, as culture hero, 125
Spanish conquistadors, Inca mythology and, 146
Stheno, 92
Stoker, Bram, 33
Strawberries in mythology, 78
Stymphalian Birds, 119
Styx, 102, 122
Sublician Bridge, 136
Sulla, 20
Sumanguru Kante, 125
Sumerian myth of floods, 67
Sun, Inca worship of, 146
Sunflower, 73
Sunjata, 125
Swastika, 11

Tall Man, 85
Talus (Perdix), 15
Tammuz (Dumuzi), 145
Tangaloa, 8
Taoist mythology, *106,* 106
Tapio, 60
Tartarus, 102, 114
Tefnet, 45
Tenochtitlán, Huitzilopochtli and, *138,* 138–39
Tezcatlipoca, 127
Thalia, 93
Thanatos, 140
Themis, 55
Theseus, 98
  Daedalus and, 16
  Helen of Troy and, 111
Thetis, in *Iliad,* 143
Thiassi, Loki and, 140–41
Thor, conflict with giants, 85
Thoth, 45–46
Thousand and One Nights, heroes in, 125
Tiamat, 5, 34, 51
Tiresias, 116, 118
Tisiphone, 78
Titans
  Cronus, 10
  Dionysus and, 32
  Gaia, mother of, 79
  Hades, son of, 102–3
  Hera, daughter of, 116–18
Transylvania, 33
Trees in mythology, 67–73, 75–78
  in Garden of Eden, 40, 41
  Golden Bough, 89–90
Tricksters
  Eshu, 52–53
  as heroes, 125
Trimurti, 129–30, 131
Triptolemus, 22
Trojan War, 98, 143–45
  golden apple as cause of, 75, *76*
  Hector in, 108–9
  Hecuba and, 110
  Helen of Troy in, 111, 112
  Hypnos and, 140
Troy, search for, 97
Tsuillgoab, 105
Tuatha Dé Danaan, 17, 18
Twelve Labors of Hercules, 119–20
Tyndareus, 111–12
Typhon, 122
Tyr, Fenrir and, 57

Uke-mochi, 146
Ukko, 60
Ulster Cycle, 12
Uma, 24
Underworld, 47, 99
  Aeneas and Golden Bough in, 89–90
  Elysium in, 50
  Enlil in, 51
  Eurydice in, 53–54
  Gauna in, 82
  Hades, god of, 102–3
  Hathor and, 105
  Hel in, 111
  hell and, 113, 114
  Hunahpú and Xbalanqúe and lords of, 139
  Inanna in, 145
Upanishads, 4, 128
Uranus, 97
  creation story and, 9
  Cronus and, 10
  Furies, children of, 78–79
  Gaia, mother of, 79
Utnapishtim, 67, 88

Vainamoinen, 58, 59, 60–61
Valhalla, 106
Vamana, 131–32
Vampires, Dracula and, 33
Vanderdecken, 73
Vanir, the, 74
Varaha, 131
Varuna, in Hindu mythology, 129, 130
Vega, Garcilaso de la, 146, 148
Venus, Leander as priestess of, 122
Vesta, 95, 96
  sacred flame associated with, 62
Vestal Virgins, 62
Violet, 73
Viracocha, 147, 148, 149
Virbius, 28
Virgil, 55, 100
Vishnu, 129, 130, *131*
  avatars of, 131–32
  Devi and, 24
  in Hindu mythology, 129, 130, *131*
  Indra and, 150
Vlad the Impaler, 33
Vritra, 132–33, 150
Vulcan, 95, 96
  fire and, 62
  Hera, mother of, 116–18
  Horatius and, 136

Wanagemeswak, 40
Wandjina, flood myth of, 68–69
Water Jar Boy, 124
Waziya, 84
White Shell Woman, 65
Wine, Dionysus and, 31–32
Witches and wizards, 25, 63
  Hecate and, 107, 108

Xbalanqúe. *See* Hunahpú and Xbalanqúe
Xibalba, 115, 139
Xiuhtecuhtli, 137
Xi Wang Mu, 77
Xochiquetzal, 69

Yama, 130
Yamato-takeru, as doomed hero, *126,* 126
Yao people of southern China, myths of, 68
Yellow Woman, 1
Yi, as warrior hero, 124
Ymir, 8, 85–86
Yoruba people of Nigeria, myths of
  Eshu in, 52–53, *53*
  Ile-Ife in, 141–42, *142*
Yu, flood myth of, 68
Yurlunggur, 69

Zephyrus, 70
Zeus, 67, 94, 95, 97, 98
  Cronus, father of, 10
  Danaë and, 18
  Demeter, sister of, 21–22
  Dionysus, son of, 30–32
  Fates, children of, 55
  Ganymede and, 82
  Graces, children of, 93
  Hades and, 102, *103,* 103
  Helen, daughter of, 111
  Hera, wife of, 116–18
  Hercules, son of, 118, 121
  Hermes, son of, 121–22
  Hypnos and, 140
  Io and, 151